# AUSTRIAN WOMEN IN THE
# NINETEENTH AND TWENTIETH CENTURIES

AUSTRIAN STUDIES

General Editor: David F. Good, Department of History,
University of Minnesota

**Volume 1**

*Austrian Women in the Nineteenth and Twentieth Centuries:
Cross-Disciplinary Perspectives*
Edited by David F. Good, Margarete Grandner, and
Mary Jo Maynes
ISBN 1-57181-065-X (hardback)    1-57181-045-5 (paperback)

**Volume 2**

*From World War to Waldheim: Culture and Politics in Austria
and in the United States*
Edited by David F. Good and Ruth Wodak
ISBN 1-57181-103-6 (hardback)

# AUSTRIAN WOMEN IN THE NINETEENTH AND TWENTIETH CENTURIES
## Cross-Disciplinary Perspectives

Edited by

*David F. Good, Margarete Grandner, and Mary Jo Maynes*

*Berghahn Books*
Providence • Oxford

First published in 1996 by
**Berghahn Books**
Editorial offices:
165 Taber Avenue, Providence, RI 02906, USA
Bush House, Merewood Avenue, Oxford, OX3 8EF, UK

**Library of Congress Cataloging-in-Publication Data**

Austrian women in the nineteenth and twentieth centuries : cross
-disciplinary perspectives / edited by David F. Good, Margarete
Gradner, and Mary Jo Maynes.
        p.    cm.
    Includes bibliographical references.
    ISBN 1-57181-065-X (alk. paper)
    1. Women--Austria--History--19th century.   2. Women--Austria-
-History--20th century.    I. Good, David F.   II. Gradner, Margarete,
1953-    .  III. Maynes, Mary Jo.
HQ1603.A97   1996
305.4'09436--dc20
                                                                95-24905
                                                                     CIP


**British Library Cataloguing in Publication Data**
A catalogue record for this book is available from the British Library.


Printed in the USA on acid-free paper.


This publication was supported in part by the
Austrian Cultural Institute, New York.

# CONTENTS

..............................

# LIST OF TABLES AND FIGURES

............................

## Tables

# Figures

# PREFACE

The essays in this volume have their origins in a symposium on "Women in Austria" organized by the Center for Austrian Studies and held at the University of Minnesota in April 1991. Since 1977, the Center for Austrian Studies has served as an international focal point for the interdisciplinary study of Austria thanks to the generous gift of one million dollars from the Austrian people on the occasion of America's bicentennial. By placing Austria at the center of an important scholarly issue, the 1991 symposium typifies the strategy used by the Center for Austrian Studies to pursue its mission as an international, interdisciplinary institution.

The conference fostered a stimulating gathering of scholars from both sides of the Atlantic. Most of the participants are engaged in important research on some aspect of the female experience in Austria in the present or the past. They were joined by a number of scholars who, as specialists in other geographic areas, gave the discussions a significant comparative dimension. In the Austrian context, women's studies is a relatively undeveloped but fast-growing academic field; the conference encouraged lively exchanges among the scholars in Austrian studies, and between them and feminist scholars who were less familiar with Austria. The articles published here are the product of that encounter; they represent some of the most exciting work being done in this newly emerging field.

The volume is truly cross-disciplinary; it draws together the work of historians who trace the evolution of modern gender relations, and of scholars from other social science and humanities disciplines who address the issue from a variety of theoretical and methodological perspectives. The contributions embrace the period from the early nineteenth century to the present, an era that Eve Dvorak describes in her introduction as one of dramatic change and turmoil in Austrian history.

Taken together, these diverse studies provide a surprisingly complete and coherent picture of Austrian women over the last century and a half. We hope that the volume will provide valuable comparative material for feminist scholars in all fields and that it will stimulate research among the growing number of scholars who study Austrian women. More generally, by explicitly adopting gender as a category of analysis in the Austrian context, these contributions provide new perspectives on contemporary Austria in the context of its rich and complicated history.

We wish to thank several colleagues who are not represented directly in the volume but who contributed indirectly to its success as active participants in the conference: Sara Evans, Elizabeth Faue, Fritz Fellner, Harriet Freidenreich, Judith Kegan Gardiner, Jane Jenson, Helga Leitner, Elisabeth List, Brigitte Mazohl-Wallnig, Marsha Rozenblit, and Klaus Zeyringer. We are grateful for major funding supplied by the Austrian Cultural Institute of New York.

Carol Duling, Craig Anderson, and Tomislav Urban prepared the manuscript with exceptional care as Assistant Editors.

Both the Austrian Cultural Institute and the Center for Austrian Studies have generously subsidized the publication of the volume.

– David Good and Mary Jo Maynes, Minneapolis
– Margarete Grandner, Vienna
April, 1995

# INTRODUCTION

...........................

### *Eve Nyaradi Dvorak*

In the last two decades the field of women's studies has experienced exceptional growth. Both monographs and journal articles on women continue to multiply, while refinements in feminist theory and gender analysis offer valuable new insights into social and historical processes. As they train their disciplinary lenses on the female subject, scholars from a host of fields have illuminated the lives of women from a wide array of cultures and eras in all their psychological, sociological, and ethnographical dimensions. Even more promising has been the advance in interdisciplinary methodologies, characterized by historians' borrowings from both literary theory and the social sciences, and the reciprocal historicization of much social science research.

Little of this scholarly ferment has touched the study of Austrian women. This is as true of women living under the aegis of the Habsburg Empire, as it is of those inhabiting modern Austria. Such scholarly neglect appears to cut across disciplines, as evidenced by a cursory scan of reference materials in the field of women's studies, such as core bibliographies and dissertation indexes.[1] Within the

---

1. See, for instance, Loeb, Searing, and Stineman (1987) whose index reveals just two Austrian citations, one concerning the post-World War II writer Ilse Aichinger, and one a comparative study of European female parliamentary participation. See also Gilbert and Tatla (1985) whose index lists only three dissertations on Austrian subjects.

field of history the lack of attention toward Austrian women is readily demonstrated by examining syllabi for women's history courses and the standard texts on which they rely.[2]

In part this is a function of broader disciplinary realities. In general, Austrian studies in the United States stands as a productive but small sub-field of European studies. Austrian women suffer a double marginalization within this configuration: first, as inhabitants of a geographical area overshadowed in scholarly investigation and in academic departments by its larger neighbors, Germany and Russia; and, second, as subordinate subjects of interest among the majority of scholars who study this area. Thus, even where attention is paid to Austrian women, they are commonly marginalized both within their own national tradition and in a larger comparative context. Ironically, this is true even of Austria's imperial period, despite the prominent place in European affairs occupied by the Habsburg Empire, from its inception in the thirteenth century until its demise in the early twentieth. As a rule, what little attention Austria receives within more general treatments of European women's history revolves around Maria Theresa, the socialist women's movement (especially its leader, Adelheid Popp), the activities of peace movement founder Bertha von Suttner, and the relevant writings of Sigmund Freud.

Nor is such relative invisibility restricted to works produced in the United States and Western Europe. Standard Austrian historiography, for example, has traditionally been guilty of largely ignoring women altogether or, at best, dealing with them in outmoded ways.[3] The identification and, in many cases, subsequent valorization of "great women" was often the point of departure for focused studies of women within the Austrian context. This had its roots in traditional history, where women had always been a footnote, yet in some cases occupied a more central position on the basis of their own activities. Obviously no history of early modern Austria, political or otherwise, could be judged credible without some allusion to

---

2. See, for instance, Strobel and Miller (1987). Exemplary standard texts (by no means exhaustive) include: Bridenthal and Koonz (1987), Boxer and Quataert (1987), Tilly and Scott (1978), and, more recently, Duby and Perrot (1993).

3. Nor does the trend seem to be reversing itself. Even in the most recent general histories of Austria, such as the acclaimed work of Erich Zöllner (1990), gross deficits remain with respect to its coverage of women. As historian Edith Saurer (1994) is quick to point out, Zöllner saw no reason to even obliquely refer to, much less integrate, the crucial "Woman Question"(Frauenfrage) into his treatment of the "national" and "social" questions in the late nineteenth and early twentieth centuries.

Maria Theresa. Much of the interest that existed in the historical experience of women focused upon similar examples.[4]

This situation must be viewed within the context of Austrian academic and education institutions. Women's studies as an accredited academic program leading to a degree is still non-existent within Austria. Moreover, university courses and broad-based research activities dealing with women have only been underway since the 1980s.

The picture is not altogether grim, however. In response to this deficit in official institutional backing, an active community of interested scholars has established an alternative framework of annual conferences, a newsletter, and summer schools (Frauen-Sommer-Universität). The new Austrian journal *L'Homme: Zeitschrift für Feministische Geschichtswissenschaft* serves as the literary vehicle for feminist historical work. Begun in 1990, it was the first journal of its type in the German-speaking world. Taking up the banner of such feminist scholars as Joan Scott, *L'Homme* is dedicated to the proposition that gender-related studies do not merely expand the field of historical investigation but in fact rewrite it (Mazohl-Wallnig 1990; Scott 1988).

In a recent article in *L'Homme*, Austrian historian Edith Saurer provides a useful overview of Austrian historical scholarship on women. Saurer's 1994 survey of the field is a valuable source for scholars interested in assessing recent trends within the field. As she notes, considerable gaps remain despite much progress in the last decade.

The Austrian landscape thus remains fertile ground for historians of women, feminist theorists, and those involved in gender studies to explore. The particular fault lines of Habsburg and Austrian history offer these scholars a unique and important terrain upon which to focus their investigations. Without the incorporation of the Austrian case, our understanding of the contours of European women's experience must remain incomplete; without the application of feminist theoretical frameworks and an exhaustive unearthing of their past, our appreciation of the experience of Austrian women will remain similarly wanting.

## The Austrian Setting

Austria's history is rooted in the European tradition of dynastic bases that consolidated and, over time, emerged as modern nation-states. Little of Austria's history as a medieval duchy under the

4. See, for example, Hamann (1982), Schiel (1990), and Spiel (1962).

dukes of Babenberg (973-1246) and then as a rising early modern state under the powerful Habsburgs (from 1282) has been explored from a gendered standpoint.[5]

In the early eighteenth century, Austria was a conglomeration of Central European territories (plus the Austrian Netherlands, present-day Belgium) united only by Habsburg overlordship. During the reign of Maria Theresa (1740-80) and the subsequent reign of her son, Joseph II (1780-90), a broad-based regime of modernization was instituted and aimed chiefly at centralizing state power at the expense of feudal and Church privilege.

While scholars have mined the Theresian period for its insights on the dynamics of state formation, little is known about the impact of these reforms on women and gender relations. Just as an analysis of the gendered dimension of state-building has been integral to a more complete understanding of political development within other European countries, an examination of the Austrian case would generate a more balanced perspective while providing an important new comparative dimension to the general field.[6] The same holds true for changing work regimes in this period, marked by the advance of proto-industrialization and subsequent industrialization, and their effects on the sexual division of labor. Associated issues of male out-migration and agricultural modernization within Austria could also provide a rich new contextual field for economic, labor, and gender historians to explore these by-now standard preoccupations of the field.[7]

The Napoleonic Wars brought an end to the reform era in Austria, and, as in most of Europe, the defeat of Napoleonic France ushered in a period of conservative reaction. While much is known about women and gender in France in the revolutionary and war period (Hunt 1984; Levy, Applewhite, and Johnson 1979), the Austrian case remains virtual "terra incognita." Focusing on this period from the perspective of gender would engage feminist concerns with periods of disruption and their potential for influencing gender relations. It would also cast light on women's political fortunes in such politically fluid eras and their subsequent outcomes during phases of reaction.

---

5. Notable exceptions for the early modern period include work by Hermann Rebel (1983) and Michael Mitterauer (1979). Witches and witchcraft have also been a central topic of Austrian scholars studying this period (Saurer 1994). For a recent survey of how gender analysis is revising conceptions of early modern Europe (excluding Austria), see Wiesner (1994).
6. For an example of gender and state formation in France, see Hanley (1989). For gender negotiations in Reformation Germany, see Roper (1989).
7. For work already done in the Austrian sphere, see Mitterauer (1989), Eder (1990), Ehmer (1981), and Ehmer (1991).

The Biedermeier era, as this period of conservative retrenchment is sometimes referred to, was marked by a flowering of aesthetic sensibility and concern for economic matters at the expense of political participation on the part of the bourgeoisie. In Chapter 9, Marie-Luise Angerer provides a fascinating glimpse of at least one way in which the repressive milieu of this period impacted bourgeois women: internalizing the discourse of contemporary medical practitioners, female intellectuals and salonistes promoted an image of femininity based on the passive "virtues" of domesticity, self-effacement, and, especially, female sexlessness.

A crucible for social and ethnic unrest, the repressive regime of the Biedermeier era was swept away in the Revolution of 1848. Although historians have studied women in both periods, the position of peasant and urban women during the Biedermeier as well as their role during the upheaval of 1848 begs further investigation.[8]

The second half of the nineteenth century saw the rise of a second phase of monarchical retrenchment in response to the revolutionary challenge of 1848. This "neoabsolutist" period was suspended under the strains of failed military defeat and rising domestic tensions, ushering in a formal constitutional era in the 1860s and a period of intense economic expansion known in German as the *Gründerzeit*. Although little is known of the specific fortunes of women during these periods, what is certain is that in the last quarter of the nineteenth century, Austrian women began to emerge as political actors. Pieter Judson (Chapter 1) analyzes this process within the context of the rising German nationalist movement. Similarly, Birgitta Bader-Zaar (Chapter 4) examines the rise and rhetoric of the various women's movements in this era, while James Albisetti (Chapter 3) investigates women's efforts in securing wider access to advanced education. At the same time, as Karin Jušek relates in Chapter 2, female sexuality took on formal political overtones as feminists and conservatives debated its meaning in the fin-de-siècle discourse surrounding prostitution.

The late nineteenth century also saw the first of four major "shocks" to the Austrian socio-economic infrastructure that were part of the general pattern of European development and political strife during the past century and a half. While disruptive to all the economies and societies of Europe, these successive convulsions – the Industrial Revolution, World War I, World War II, and the Cold

---

8. On a female cultural icon of the Biedermeier era, see Bolognese-Leuchtenmüller (1983). For women's activism in the Revolution of 1848, see Hauch (1990).

War – had particularly dramatic effects within Central and Eastern Europe. In the Habsburg territories, uneven economic development resulted in social dislocation as agrarian and urban societies were put under severe pressure. The ensuing effect on family structure and work regimes has been under investigation for some time, yet only recently have women's contributions and experiences in this changed socio-economic climate come to light (Mitterauer 1989; Hahn 1992; Ehmer 1981).

World War I proved fatal for the Habsburg Empire, and led to its dismemberment into the "successor states" of the interwar period. The First Austrian Republic was the site of strident political infighting between the Catholic centrist regime, the socialist bastion of "Red Vienna," and the rapidly growing forces of National Socialism. On the eve of Hitler's entry into Austria in March 1938, democracy had already succumbed to dictatorial authoritarianism under the twin blows of the Great Depression and civil war in the 1930s. Summarily incorporated into the Third Reich, Austria's Anschluss with Germany heralded the triumph of National Socialism within the German ethnic core and was but the first step on Hitler's road to war.

Against this potent political backdrop, the collaborationist dimensions of Austria's Nazi past have only recently come to the fore as a subject of political and historiographical debate. Irene Bandhauer-Schöffmann and Ela Hornung (Chapter 11) contribute to this ongoing discussion by exposing the activities and reactions of women sympathetic to the fascist cause during the war. This is all the more intriguing because, as they point out, for Austrians, even this process of confronting the past has gendered overtones. The ostensibly "apolitical" position of women as wives and daughters on the homefront deterred scrutiny of their complicity in Nazi actions, and allowed them to avoid acknowledging their responsibility in a way different from men.

In the aftermath of World War II Austria stood at the frontier: it was the easternmost outpost of Western Europe poised on the edge of the Soviet Empire. Struggling to maintain its official neutrality within an increasingly polarized Cold War climate, the Second Austrian Republic successfully negotiated its release from four-power occupation with the State Treaty of 1955, and emerged in the 1960s and 1970s as a crucial meeting ground for diplomatic negotiations between the superpower blocs. While the stable neo-corporatist structure of Austria greatly contributed to its prodigious economic growth after the war, it also effectively excluded women from its higher echelons. As Gerda Neyer shows in Chapter 5, this was to have grave effects on women's exercise of power in the postwar era.

Beyond these confines of basic chronology, Austria offers rich paradigmatic soil. A significant feature of Austria's unique historical legacy is the relative economic backwardness of the Habsburg Empire and the First Republic vis-à-vis its neighbors to the west (Gerschenkron 1962 and 1977). Such relative underdevelopment dictated that a disproportionate share of the institutional infrastructure required for modernization was assumed by the state. How these structural features affected the fortunes and experience of Austrian women and rendered them different from women both inside and outside the Monarchy is a question that has yet to be posed in a systematic, synthetic way.[9] Erna Appelt (Chapter 6) pushes us in this direction in her examination of the Austrian civil service as a major employer of women in the late nineteenth century.

In addition, and as Judson's essay attests, scholars are just beginning to broach the vital question of how gender and ethnicity interacted within the unique socio-political constellation of the multinational Empire. The notion that bitter ethnic antagonism directly contributed to the Empire's demise is a hallmark of the field; the role of women in contributing to or mediating against such strife, or the effect of their participation in both the formal and informal operations of the many nationalist and separatist movements, is much less apparent.[10]

Vienna itself provides a microcosm for the study of such ethnic agitation. As the capital of the "ramshackle realm" it became a cauldron of social and ethnic tensions in the latter stages of the nineteenth century as waves of Jewish immigrants from remote regions of the Empire (especially from the east) generated a virulent anti-Semitic backlash, couched in the rise of mass politics from both the right and the left. Jewish ethnic identity in fin-de-siècle Vienna was largely determined by social class, yet we are left contemplating how class, gender, and Jewish ethnicity intersected in a wider sense. While ethnicity in the more traditional sense also played a significant role in the working and class experience of Viennese women (many of the new immigrants were not Jews but nationals from poorer parts of the Empire), its impact is ultimately left for a nuanced application of feminist methodology to determine.[11]

---

9. Although in terms of social policy Saurer (1994) cites the state as a locus of Austrian women's oppression.

10. This theme is gaining currency in the field. For the Czech case, in addition to the works cited by Albisetti in Chapter 3, see Nolte (1993).

11. A positive step in this direction is Wegs (1989), whose study of Viennese working class culture includes ethnicity and gender as key variables.

That Austria offers scholars a rich and varied legacy is perhaps best exemplified by the number of celebrated research traditions it has inspired. In many cases, these have extended beyond the region itself. Works by Alexander Gerschenkron (1962) on economic development, Hans Kohn (1944) and Robert Kann (1950) on nationalism, Michael Mitterauer and Reinhard Sieder (1982) on family history, and Carl Schorske (1980) on culture and politics in fin-de-siècle Vienna have reached a wide audience and continue to have a significant impact on contemporary scholarship.

In its many incarnations, then, Austria has offered and continues to offer scholars a prime field for academic inquiry. The experience of a formidable multinational empire that was an important part of the European political landscape for over six hundred years and whose frayed nationalist umbrella was hopelessly rent in the crucible of World War I; the "rump" First Republic, struggling throughout the interwar period to build democracy in an unstable region; the Nazi client state, and Austria's post-World War II resurrection as a prosperous nation-state founded on neutrality and neo-corporatist institutions, all provide fertile ground for scholarly investigation. Within these shifting institutional and political contours the experience of women remains largely obscured, awaiting the attention of scholars armed with gender-interested methodologies.

The essays that appear below provide significant evidence that the intellectual darkness surrounding the lives of Austrian women is beginning to be penetrated in conceptually innovative ways. They amply demonstrate the case argued above: they reflect the rich potential of training feminist methodologies on the Austrian case in order to inform wider notions of the history and experience of European women. The book is structured around three general areas, each of keen interest to contemporary feminist scholars: gender and politics, women and work, and female identity.

## Gender and Politics

Much contemporary debate within women's studies is driven by the relationship of women to the "public sphere," especially in the realm of formal and activist politics and public policy. The essays in this section explore several dimensions of this relationship, examining to what extent and in what ways the Austrian political terrain was gendered throughout the course of the nineteenth and twentieth centuries. The juxtaposition of contributions by Pieter Judson, Karin

Jušek, James Albisetti, Birgitta Bader-Zaar, and Gerda Neyer provide intriguing glimpses into a century of female political agency. The mixed outcomes of women's strategies point to the many ways gender solidarity among women was undercut by other social identities (ethnicity, class, etc.) as well as the hegemonic nature of the prevailing sex/gender system. The state's role in suppressing or advancing the interests of women is also implicitly weighed.

How gender mediates and is mediated by nationalist issues is most fully developed in the essay by Pieter Judson. Judson argues that, beginning in the 1880s, the bourgeois German nationalist movement created spaces for female agency by opening up avenues for political activism to women. At the same time, it restricted women's political and ideological freedom of movement by co-opting their more self-interested goals under the rubric of ethnic solidarity and by propagating a restrictive stereotype of bourgeois female behavior. Although women were encouraged to join nationalist associations and gained status as bearers of culture, they were largely quarantined from meaningful political participation by their relegation to the domestic sphere as the exponents of national motherhood. Judson thus demonstrates the double-edged sword that the nationalist (and liberal) cause implied for women.

Karin Jušek examines both the efforts and rhetoric of the primary Austrian women's movements vis-à-vis the political discussion of prostitution, a pressing social question in fin-de-siècle Vienna owing to a licensing system of registration and to escalating fears about the spread of syphilis.[12] Interestingly, this was one front on which social democratic and bourgeois women could work in tandem, although the former were principally interested in alleviating the deplorable working conditions of such women rather than calling for a radical reorientation of the relations between the sexes. Neither group, however, was prepared to tolerate the objectification of the female sex that prostitution implied.

Building upon the work of Austrian feminist historians (Heindl, 1987; Heindl and Tichy, 1990), James Albisetti charts the evolution of female education within constitutional Austria (1866-1914) in comparison with Switzerland and Germany. Albisetti provides a much needed corrective to both the scant research on Austria in this area, and the currently dominant interpretation that the Austrian experience was universally inferior and characterized by an arrested development when compared to other European nations. His more nuanced ap-

---

12. For expanded coverage on this subject, see Jušek (1994).

proach reveals evidence of subtle but telling flaws in this thesis, for he notes a number of "firsts" within the Austrian context that enabled Austria to outstrip developments in the commonly perceived more progressive German states. In nineteenth-century Austria, women gained admittance into the teaching profession, the salaries for female elementary teachers were equal to those of men beginning in the 1870s, and women were accepted as regular students in the philosophical faculties of the university in 1897.

While he does not elaborate in great detail, Albisetti also touches on an area rich in analytical potential. He notes that scholars generally ascribe the comparatively late evolution of female education in Austria to the economic context of Austrian "backwardness," but seem to ignore the fact that Russia, a country whose economic backwardness was substantially more profound than that of Austria, had a much more open and advanced system of female education early on. This is provocative ground for research because so much in both newer and traditional Austrian historiography centers either directly or indirectly around the issue of Austrian "backwardness."

In an essay that provides a comparative discussion of similar developments in the United States, Birgitta Bader-Zaar examines the vision and goals of the Austrian suffrage campaign (1890-1918) against the backdrop of disappointing political realities once the vote was gained.[13] Ironically, as notions of liberalism and individualism gained currency in Austria toward the end of the nineteenth century, eventually eclipsing earlier conceptions of suffrage based on property, the franchise was significantly expanded among males, but was simultaneously constricted for women. This was accomplished by the deliberate exclusion of those few women who had formerly been qualified to vote on the basis of their status as property holders. In this way, gender was institutionalized as a signal criterion for determining political status once the effects of class were vitiated through reform. This is consistent with the experience of women elsewhere in Europe and points out how a gendered perspective revises our understanding of liberalism.

Such exclusion stirred many Austrian women to launch a suffrage campaign in the 1890s (much later than their English or American counterparts). This was met with firm opposition on the part of the state and the entrenched political parties. Bader-Zaar contends that class divisions hampered initiatives between liberal and socialist women, further impeding overall progress. She also emphasizes that

13. For an elaboration, see Zaar (1994).

ethnicity was a divisive element as Czech, Slovenian, Polish, and Hungarian women all organized separately from German-speaking suffragists. The provocative permutation of the interplay between gender and nationalism clearly demonstrates how nationalist realities served to undermine gender solidarity. Bader-Zaar's essay also suggests how the various Austrian women's movements appropriated and only mildly refashioned prevailing gender ideology.[14]

Such inquiries into women's political participation are brought up to date by Gerda Neyer. She shows how gaining access to formal political structures within Austria has failed to accord women real power, owing to their persistent exclusion from the unofficial but all-powerful institutional mesh of the "social partnership," the basis of the contemporary Austrian neo-corporatist arrangement between business and labor. Although women have steadily gained seats in Parliament since the early 1980s, they are still blocked from participating in the promulgation and vetting of legislation carried on within the institutions of the social partnership, and are denied key positions on legislative committees. Thus, although gender equality is fixed by law and there have been modest changes in the behind-the-scenes distribution of power, the results have not been dramatic and remain far from satisfactory. Neyer's essay is a forceful testimony to the highly subtle machinations of both historical and contemporary gender discrimination.

All of these essays thus address issues currently in the forefront of feminist inquiry. Judson, Bader-Zaar, and Neyer each attest to the subtle ways in which formal political power and participation on the part of women was deflected and neutralized by prevailing gender ideology, institutional inertia, or "higher" political concerns. They all point to the elusive workings of power and how it can elude even formal players of the game. They also testify to what many have known from other cases: that, in entering the public sphere, women did not fully reconstruct it to their benefit. This was due as much to their own complicity in accepting prevailing gender, class, and ethnic norms as to the male-centered resistance that sought to deny them real power.

In historicizing female access to higher education, Albisetti provides a regional perspective on a staple of feminist scholarship and skillfully problematizes the relationship between economic and con-

---

14. See Gellott (1991) who stresses the evolutionary and progressive nature of female agency and thought within the Catholic Women's Movement in the 1920s and 1930s. See also Anderson (1990) for a fascinating discussion of the role of men in the primary Austrian women's movements.

stitutional contexts and gendered educational outcomes. Similarly, Judson and Bader-Zaar offer comparativists yet another example of how the rhetoric of motherhood and female moral authority became a central organizing theme for female political activism in the nineteenth century.[15]

Jušek brings Austria into the historical discussion of female sexuality.[16] She argues that the ideals of Austrian feminists parted from those of contemporary European and American discourse. The Austrian feminists she analyzes subscribed neither to the model of the lustful seductress perpetuated by the church (especially in Russia) nor to that of the passionless vessel underpinning Victorianism and most women's movements. Jušek's research thus complements both the extant literature on the female reform discourse surrounding prostitution and the emergent history of European female sexuality.[17]

## Women and Work

In examining the history of women and work, feminist scholars continue to debate how wage earning affected women's status in the family and society. The essays below suggest that theories that posit a linear relationship between increased female presence in the workforce and increased gains for women in other realms are reductive at best, and perhaps misleading. In addition to the many obvious factors involved in judging such relative advance and decline (e.g., the nature of work, relative pay scales, degree of control over wages and consumption) there is also the question of the gendered "meaning" of work. Ideological considerations play a huge part in the way work effects women. Such ideological assumptions are shaped both by and for women, and speak to the many ways gender relations inform the world of work and economic organization in general.[18] The historical examination of how work is valued, sex-typed, and allocated between the domestic and market spheres reveals much about the operations of gender. As such, the study of women and their work remains at the center of modern discourse and modern, especially feminist, concerns.

15. For discussion of the political use of notions of motherhood elsewhere in Europe, see Allen (1991) and Offen (1988).
16. See also several contributions in Nautz and Vahrenkamp (1993).
17. For literature on European prostitution, see Walkowitz (1980) and Harsin (1985). For historical studies focusing on sexuality see Gay (1987), Jeffries (1982), and McLaren (1983).
18. For a compelling discussion of these themes, see Boydston (1990).

Through her investigation of the gendering of the service sector in Austria toward the end of the nineteenth century, Erna Appelt provides a fascinating example of the ambiguous relationship between an expanded female presence in the labor force and female power. While women in this period made significant numerical inroads into the lower echelons of white collar work (as secretaries, bookkeepers, telegraph operators, etc.) their advancement was limited by stiff resistance on the part of male employees concerned with defending their higher-status positions against female encroachment. Such resistance translated into a segmented labor market within the government-dominated service sector and the denial to women of customary (male) employee rights and privileges. The efforts of male workers in this respect were assisted by contemporary gender ideology, which had difficulty reconciling middle-class notions of femininity with female wage labor. Such contradictions were ultimately negotiated via a cunning paternalism in which female workers were less employees than "daughters" of employers. This mechanism was presumably developed for the continued social control of women and for justifying blatant wage discrimination. Yet, as in most historical cases, and as Appelt's nuanced portrait shows, the operation of gender was not monolithic. Professional class interest served to erode gender solidarity among males, evidenced within the civil service by the preference for hiring females with familial ties to the bureaucracy over males with no such ties. In sum, Appelt's essay provides us with an intriguing look at how gender mediated labor supply and demand in Austria, and was in turn mediated by corporate interests.

Female labor force participation in twentieth-century Austria is analyzed by Gudrun Biffl within a comparative international framework.[19] She notes that the percentage of women in the Austrian labor force exceeded that of most European nations until the 1960s. This was true of the United States as well, where the corresponding rate lagged far behind Austria throughout most of the century (from 1910 on) and only exceeded it in the late 1960s. Both the sources of this phenomenon and its meaning for women remain problematic, tied to a host of historical variables within and among the nations in question.

In the last three decades this trend has been reversed: much of northwestern Europe (specifically, Sweden, Great Britain, France)

19. Biffl (1994) provides an expanded discussion on these themes. For historical perspectives on household and family labor in Austria see Ellmeier and Singer-Meczes (1989) and Bernold (1990).

and the United States have consistently and vigorously outpaced Austria in terms of the rate of growth of the female labor force. Biffl attributes this slackening of Austrian female labor participation to a combination of supply-side variables (fertility, life cycle choices, and education), unique demand-side features specific to the Austrian economy (a rapidly declining agricultural sector, a limited clerical and service sector, the lack of part-time work) and institutional factors (tax structures, the nature of child care facilities, and the functioning of the foreign worker system).

Biffl's most original contribution is her inclusion of domestic production within a market model. She quantifies the value of contemporary household labor as a percentage of gross domestic product, thereby allowing us to gauge women's domestic contribution to the overall economy in "hard," statistical terms. Her results indicate that Austrian women account for a significantly large share of overall production.

Biffl's methodological innovation adds an important macroeconomic dimension to a subject that feminists have more typically researched at the micro level,[20] and may be seen as a significant improvement over more standard economic models that ignore housework altogether. Not surprisingly, she finds that contemporary Austrian women tend not only to work more hours in the household than males, but work more total hours over the course of the life cycle, within the household and the labor market combined. Such statistics evoke familiar images of women's "double burden" in modern society.

Biffl's essay offers historians of gender intriguing material for speculation. The initial overrepresentation and then slackening of female labor participation underscores the ambiguous legacy of the dual burden. When the Austrian "economic miracle" of the postwar era allowed women to withdraw from the full-time labor force, perhaps their response at least in part reflected the historical experience of combining high levels of full-time paid work with full reponsibility for housework.

Or perhaps, after several generations of stagnating income levels, Austrian men encouraged women's exit from the labor force amidst the heady boom of the Austrian "economic miracle" in the postwar era. Increased status for men and increased control over women may have played a part in such behavior, or women may have opted for this return to the home in light of their previous overrepresentation in the labor force and a general experience of "hard times." In

20. For examples of important sociological studies of housework in North America, see Treiman and Hartmann (1981) and Luxton (1980). For a historical approach to housework in Germany, see Meyer (1987). Boydston (1990) offers an excellent study of the political economy and ideology of housework in early America.

each of these versions, historical experience is seen as conditioning outcomes, and gender ideology, in the sense of what women's work meant for both men and women, figures prominently.

Seeking to identify gender-linked patterns in identity formation, Gertraud Diem-Wille explores evidence garnered from interviews with successful contemporary career men and women. She plumbs these for subconscious motifs that may predispose a child to success, alongside such "external" demographic data as birth order and parental professions. Although Diem-Wille could not identify any gender-specific "inner dynamics" that led to later career success, her psychoanalytic approach yields innovative, if controversial, insights.

Taken together these essays touch upon important aspects of the synchronous operations of gender, class, and ideology in the arena of women's work. Consistent with findings in the political sphere, the essays in this section provide a sobering corrective to any superficial notions of an implicit connection between an increased female economic presence and increased female power. Scholars who are interested in the intersection of patriarchy and capitalism will find strong comparative material here, as will those who have found similar strategies of resistance among male workers (and a common defense of the family wage) in their examinations of other industrializing societies.[21] These essays suggest new methodological approaches for feminists interested in workforce issues and pose compelling questions for future historical debate.

## Female Identities

The work of Michel Foucault (1978-86) first illumined the concept that the construction of modern notions of sexuality was in large part framed by the discourse of a burgeoning medical establishment in the eighteenth and nineteenth centuries. Marie-Luise Angerer's study of the nineteenth-century medical discourse on female sexuality in Austria is set in a theoretical framework drawn from Foucault. Angerer investigates how the medical and psychoanalytical disciplines contributed to gender identities and models in their discourse on gender-specific disease in the realms of gynecology and psychoanalysis.[22] Beginning with the professionalization of Austrian gynecology in the

---

21. For evidence of the latter see Rose (1991) and Blewett (1988).
22. For an elaboration of these themes, see Angerer (1994). Comparative examples of the history of medicine and sexuality in nineteenth-century Europe may be found in Gallagher and Laqueur (1987) and Laqueur (1990).

late eighteenth century, Angerer explains the construction of a specifically female physiognomy in terms of both scientific advancements and the needs of the state to maintain control over female bodies for the purposes of social reproduction.

Freud, of course, was particularly instrumental in contributing to gendered perceptions of mental illness, especially by assigning a clear role to female sexual drive in the development of hysteria. More surprising perhaps is Angerer's report that Austrian surgeons commonly practiced ovariectomy and clitoridectomy in the second half of the nineteenth century as a cure for "symptoms which indicated healthy sexual arousal" and cases of "chronic masturbation."

Building on the work of Nike Wagner (1987) and others, Angerer locates the male project to contain female sexuality in men's mounting sense of impotency in an increasingly pluralistic age. She thus adds a unique and interesting case study to the substantial comparative literature that centers female oppression within the operations of male anxiety.[23]

Monika Bernold brings another source to bear on the history of female identity, namely, autobiography. Bernold investigates the construction of early-twentieth-century female identity by sifting these personal narratives with a special eye to their beginnings. She shows how the different ways that authors begin their life stories provides clues to their social and gender identity. In doing so she pioneers a careful and close reading of these interesting historical texts as documents with particular characteristics, that is, as examples of a genre. Her focus on language complements similar and increasingly common post-structuralist approaches to cultural history and responds to the need for such interpretive work in the Austrian setting.

Completing this section, Irene Bandhauer-Schöffmann and Ela Hornung trace the experience of Austrian women under National Socialism and in the immediate post-World War II period. Drawing on the tradition within feminist historiography that centers on women's voices and perspectives, Bandhauer-Schöffmann and Hornung organize their study around evidence from interviews with sixty Viennese women who lived through this era. The authors provide a welcome view into women's daily experience, while at the same time revealing the female side of collaboration with the Nazi regime. They also take on the thesis that women held substantial

---

23. For discussions of male anxiety and anti-female backlash as a result of economic chaos and war see, respectively, Faue (1993) and Gilbert (1983). On artistic projections of misogyny in fin-de-siècle culture, see Dijkstra (1986).

power in the immediate postwar era, which they later lost. According to the authors, such power was never as profound as originally thought, because both men and women devalued war-time female "survival labor." Bandhauer-Schöffmann and Hornung thus echo a chorus of voices within the collection that argues for a problematic relationship between increased labor and increased power for women. Here, too, women are shown to be complicit in history. As Bandhauer-Schöffmann and Hornung clearly show, it was women who primarily allowed for the reintegration of returning husbands within the fold of hearth, home, and hierarchy. Rather than exploiting the political instability of postwar Austria for their own ends, women effectively reinscribed prewar gender norms.

Collectively, these essays add much to our historicized understanding of female (and male) identity-formation. They examine this process from the perspective of both internal (familial) and external (discourse) structures, and attempt to trace the mechanisms by which prevailing cultural and gender norms enmesh themselves in the building of individual identity. In doing so they speak to wider interests concerned with the historical construction of the self. Bernold's use of autobiography and Bandhauer-Schöffmann's and Hornung's use of oral history are noteworthy for their methodological creativity, while Angerer's study of the impact of the medical community in defining female sexuality is particularly germane in addressing that subject on the very terrain of the birth of modern psychoanalysis. Finally, Bandhauer-Schöffmann's and Hornung's consideration of Austrian collaboration is a valuable addition to a growing literature dedicated to confronting Austria's National Socialist past.[24]

## Conclusion

As the contributions in this collection testify, incorporating the Austrian case into wider discussions of the experience of European women is both relevant and capable of yielding rich insights. Despite the wide multidisciplinary sweep, there are threads of commonality among these works, and a basic resonance with the agendas of scholarly feminism and gender analysis.

Within these pages, Austrian women are seen as important actors in the political and economic sphere, who nevertheless suffer under restric-

24. For important studies of Austrian women under National Socialism, see Berger (1984), Berger (1985), and Gehmacher (1994). An expanded account of the historiography of this period is provided in Saurer (1994).

tive ideologies and conditions. Women both fashion, and are fashioned by, these synchronous strategies of agency and objectification.

The nuanced nature of this finding speaks to a welcome appreciation of the complexity of women's lives and, in keeping with the highest codes of feminist scholarship, avoids the pitfalls of monolithic explanations. There are no overarching or simplistic theses, in which evidence is mustered to defend the paradigm at the expense of contradictory, if crucial, detail; nor are there any grand narratives of female emancipation or victimization. Instead, differences between and among women are highlighted, experienced within chronological outlines that roughly parallel modernity and even post-modernity. The themes are mined for their complexity, the one integrating principle of the collection.

Part of that complexity is the interaction between women and men. In each of these essays, the presence of men is either directly felt or implied through the workings of state policy and patriarchal institutions and values. This even extends to the way gender relations construct and constitute female identity.

The other side of female agency and limitations to that agency is women's responsibility for others, and for their own actions. In this volume we learn about Austrian women's social feminism and attempts at moral guardianship, as well as their complicity in the persecution of Jews. The full range of female behavior is thus explored, and superficially celebratory views are jettisoned in favor of more sincere and tempered expressions of respect as well as implicit critique. The essays are the result of careful research rather than a facile recapitulation of common understandings.

This volume thus offers compelling perspectives on the experience of women in Austria, past and present. It begins to redress the informational and methodological void that has characterized the study of Austrian gender relations, a pursuit that will undoubtedly lead to new conceptions of the historical and contemporary Austrian state, while illuminating and disrupting broader patterns of European practice and behavior. The Austrian case waits to be tapped for its full methodological and comparative potential. This volume is a preview of the conceivable richness of that enterprise.

# References

Allen, A.T. 1991. *Feminism and Motherhood in Germany 1800-1914.* New Brunswick.

Anderson, H. 1990. "Zur Beteiligung von Männern und den Bestrebungen der österreichischen Frauenbewegungen um 1900." In *"Das Weib existiert nicht für sich ...": Geschlechterbeziehungen in der bürgerlichen Gesellschaft.* Eds. H. Dienst and E. Saurer. Vienna.

Angerer, M.L., ed. 1994. *The Body of Gender: Körper, Geschlechter, Identitäten.* Vienna.

Berger, K. 1984. *Zwischen Eintopf und Fließband. Frauenarbeit und Frauenbild im Faschismus: Österreich 1938-1945.* Vienna.

———. ed. 1985. *Der Himmel ist blau. Kann sein: Frauen im Widerstand Österreich 1938-1945.* Vienna.

Bernold, M. et al, eds. 1990. *Familie: Arbeitsplatz oder Ort des Glücks. Historische Schnitte ins Private.* Vienna.

Biffl, G. 1994. *Theorie und Empirie des Arbeitsmarktes am Beispiel Österreichs.* Vienna.

Blewett, M. 1988. *Men, Women, and Work: Class, Gender and Protest in the New England Shoe Industry.* Urbana, Ill.

Bolognese-Leuchtenmüller, B. 1983. "Die Wiener Wäschermadln: Von der Kultfigur des Biedermeier zur Lohnarbeiterin." In *Wien Wirklich: Ein Stadtführer durch den Alltag und seine Geschichte.* Vienna.

Boxer, M. and Quataert, J., eds. 1987. *Connecting Spheres: Women in the Western World, 1500 to the Present.* New York.

Boydston, J. 1990. *Home and Work: Housework, Wages, and the Ideology of Labor in the Early Republic.* New York.

Bridenthal, R., Koonz, C. and Stuard, S., eds. 1987. *Becoming Visible: Women in European History.* Boston.

Dijkstra, B. 1986. *Idols of Perversity: Fantasies of Feminine Evil in Fin-de-Siècle Culture.* New York.

Duby, G. and Perrot, M., genl. eds. 1992-1994. *A History of Women in the West.* Cambridge, Mass.

Eder, F. 1990. *Geschlechterproportion und Arbeitsorganisation im Land Salzburg: 17.-19. Jahrhundert.* Vienna.

Ehmer, J. 1981. "Frauenarbeit und Arbeiterfamilie in Wien: Vom Vormärz bis 1934." *Geschichte und Gesellschaft* 7 (3/4): 438-73.

———. 1991. *Heiratsverhalten, Sozialstruktur, Ökonomischer Wandel. England und Mitteleuropa in der Formationsperiode des Kapitalismus.* Göttingen.

Ellmeier, A. and Singer-Meczes, E. 1989. "Modellierung der sozialistischen Konsumentin: Konsumgenossenschaftliche (Frauen) Politik in den zwanziger Jahren" *Zeitgeschichte* 16 (11/12): 410-26.

Faue, E. 1991. *Community of Suffering and Struggle: Women, Men, and the Labor Movement in Minneapolis, 1915-1945.* Chapel Hill.

Foucault, M. 1978-1986. *The History of Sexuality.* 3 vols. New York.

Gallagher, C. and Laqueur, T., eds. 1987. *The Making of the Modern Body: Sexuality and Society in the Nineteenth Century.* Berkeley.

Gay, P. 1984 and 1987. *The Bourgeois Experience: Victoria to Freud.* 2 vols. New York.

Gehmacher, J. 1994. *Jugend ohne Zukunft: Hitler-Jugend und Bund Deutscher Mädel in Österreich vor 1938.* Vienna.

Gellott, L. 1991. "Mobilizing Conservative Women: The Viennese Katholische Frauenorganisation in the 1920s." *Austrian History Yearbook,* 22: 110-30.

Gerschenkron, A. 1962. *Economic Backwardness in Historical Perspective.* Cambridge, Mass.

———. 1977. *An Economic Spurt That Failed.* Princeton.

Gilbert, S. 1983. "Soldiers' Heart: Literary Men, Literary Women, and the Great War." *Signs: Journal of Women in Culture and Society* 8: 422-250.

Gilbert, V.F. and Tatla, D.S., eds. 1985. *Women's Studies: A Bibliography of Dissertations 1870-1982.* Oxford.

Hahn, S. 1992. "'Als ob man bloß arbeiten tät, um einen Lehrbuben zu ersetzen': Frauenarbeit im ausgehenden 18. und 19. Jahrhundert. Am Beispiel Wiener Neustadt." In *Bewegte Provinz. Arbeiterbewegung in mitteleuropäischen Regionen vor dem ersten Weltkrieg,* 259-78. Eds. R.G. Ardelt and E. Thurner. Vienna.

Hamann, B. 1982. *Elisabeth: Kaiserin wider Willen.* Vienna.

Hanley, S. 1989. "Engendering the State: Family Formation and State Building in Early Modern France." *French Historical Studies* 16 (1): 4-27.

Harsin, J. 1985. *The Policing of Prostitution in Nineteenth-Century Paris.* Princeton.

Hauch, G. 1990. *Frau Biedermeier auf den Barrikaden. Frauenleben in der Wiener Revolution 1848.* Vienna.

Heindl, W. 1987. "Ausländische Studentinnen an der Universität Wien vor der Erstem Weltkrieg: Zum Problem der studentischen Migrationen in Europa." In *Wegenetz europäischen Geistes.* Vol. 2. Eds. R.G. Plaschka and K. Mack. Munich.

Heindl, W. and Tichy, M. 1990. *Durch Erkenntnis zu Freiheit und Glück: Frauen an der Universität Wien (ab 1897).* Vienna.

Hunt, L. 1984. *Politics, Culture, and Class in the French Revolution.* Berkeley and Los Angeles.

Jeffries, S. 1982. "Free from the Uninvited Touch of Men: Women's Campaigns around Sexuality, 1880-1914." *Women's Studies International Forum* 5 (6): 629-45.

Jušek, K. 1994. *Auf der Suche nach der Verlorenen: Die Prostitutionsdebatten im Wien der Jahrhundertwende.* Vienna.

Kann, R.A. 1950. *The Multinational Empire: Nationalism and National Reform in the Habsburg Monarchy, 1848-1918.* 2 vols. New York.

Kohn, H. 1944. *The Idea of Nationalism: A Study of Its Origins and Background.* New York.

Laqueur, T. 1990. *Making Sex: Body and Gender from the Greeks to Freud.* Cambridge.

Levy, D.G., Applewhite, H.B., and Johnson, M.D., eds. 1979. *Women in Revolutionary Paris 1789-1795: Selected Documents Translated with Notes and Commentary.* Urbana.

Loeb, K., Searing, S. and Stineman, E., eds. 1987. *Women's Studies: A Recommended Core Bibliography 1980-1985*. Littleton, Colo.

Luxton, M. 1980. *More Than a Labour of Love: Three Generations of Women's Work in the Home*. Toronto.

Mazohl-Wallnig, B. 1990. "The State of Women's History in Austria." In *Writing Women's History: International Perspectives*, 279-90. Eds. K. Offen, R. R. Pierson, and J. Rendall. Bloomington, Ind.

McLaren, A. 1983. *Sexuality and the Social Order: The Debate over the Fertility of Women and Workers in France, 1770-1920*. New York.

Meyer, S. 1987. "The Tiresome Work of Conspicuous Leisure: On the Domestic Duties of the Wives of Civil Servants in the German Empire." In *Connecting Spheres: Women in the Western World, 1500 to the Present*. Eds. M.J. Boxer and J. Quataer. New York.

Mitterauer, M. 1979. *Grundtypen alteuropäischen Sozialformen: Haus und Gemeinde in vorindustriellen Gesellschaften*. Stuttgart.

___. 1989. "Geschlechtsspezifische Arbeitsteilung und Geschlechtrollen in ländlichen Gesellschaften Mitteleuropas." In *Aufgaben, Rolle und Räumen von Frau und Mann*. Vol. 2. Eds. J. Martin and R. Zöpfel. Munich.

___ and Sieder, R. 1982. *The European Family: Patriarchy to Partnership from the Middle Ages to the Present*. Chicago.

Nautz, J. and Vahrenkamp, R., eds. 1993. *Wiener Jahrhundertwende. Einflüsse, Umwelt, Wirkung*. Graz and Vienna.

Nolte, C. 1993. "'Every Czech a Sokol!' Feminism and Nationalism in the Czech Sokol Movement." *Austrian History Yearbook* 24: 79-100.

Offen, K. 1988. "Defining Feminism: A Comparative Historical Approach." *Signs* 14: 119-57.

Rebel, H. 1983. *Peasant Classes: The Bureaucratization of Property and Family Relations under Early Habsburg Absolutism 1511-1636*. Princeton.

Roper, L. 1989. *The Holy Household: Women and Morals in Reformation Augsburg*. Oxford.

Rose, S. 1991. *Limited Livelihoods: Gender and Class in 19th Century England*. Berkeley.

Rosaldo, M.Z. 1980. "The Use and Abuse of Anthropology: Reflections on Feminism and Cross-Cultural Understanding." *Signs* 5: 389-417.

Saurer, E. 1994. "Frauengeschichte in Österreich: Eine fast kritische Bestandsaufnahme." *L'Homme* 2: 37-63.

Schiel, I. 1990. *Stephanie: Kronprinzessin im Schatten der Tragödie von Mayerling*. Munich.

Schorske, C. 1980. *Fin-de-siècle Vienna: Politics and Culture*. New York.

Scott, J. 1988. "Gender: A Useful Category of Analysis." *Gender and the Politics of History*, 28-50. New York.

Spiel, H. 1962. *Fanny von Arnstein, oder Die Emanzipation: Ein Frauenleben an der Zeitenwende 1758-1818*. Frankfurt am Main.

Strobel, P. and Miller, M., eds. 1986. *Women's History*. Vol. 3. *Selected Reading Lists and Course Outlines from American Colleges and Universities*. New York.

Tilly, L. and Scott, J. 1978. *Women, Work, and Family*. New York.

Treiman, D. and Hartmann, H., eds. 1981. *Women, Work, and Wages: Equal Pay for Jobs of Equal Value*. Washington, D.C.

Wagner, N. 1987. *Geist und Geschlecht: Karl Kraus und die Erotik der Wiener Moderne*. Frankfurt am Main.

Walkowitz, J. 1980. *Prostitution and Victorian Society: Women, Class and the State*. New York.

Wegs, J.R. 1989. *Growing Up Working Class: Continuity and Change among Viennese Youth, 1890-1938*. University Park, Penn.

Wiesner, M. 1993. *Women and Gender in Early Modern Europe*. Cambridge.

Zaar, B. 1994. "Vergleichende Aspekte der Geschichte des Frauenstimmrechts in Grossbritannien, den Vereinigten Staaten von Amerika, Österreich, Deutschland und Belgien." 2 vols. (Dissertation) University of Vienna.

Zöllner, E. 1990. *A History of Austria from Its Beginnings to the Present*. Vienna.

*Chapter 1*

❧

# THE GENDERED POLITICS OF
# GERMAN NATIONALISM IN AUSTRIA, 1880-1900

...........................

*Pieter M. Judson*

I n an address to the membership of the nationalist German School
Association *(Deutscher Schulverein)* at its annual convention in 1882,
Executive Chairman and Liberal party deputy Moritz Weitlof noted
with particular enthusiasm that "our German women and maidens
have conquered their natural aversion against appearing in public,
and are forming a substantial contingent of members in our association ... and that we have two women who are already chairmen *[sic]*
of local branches" (*MDS*, no. 7, May 1883: 3).[1]

Stressing the key contribution of women's activism to the association's success, Weitlof also singled out for special praise the fifty
women who had been elected by their local branches to serve
among the 1,250 delegates to the convention. Five years later the
same Weitlof, still an avid supporter of women's activism in the

---

1. Weitlof served as Executive Chair of the German School Association through the
    1880s. At the same time, he also served in the Austrian Parliament or *Reichsrat*, the
    Lower Austrian Diet, and on the Vienna City Council. Throughout the 1870s and
    1880s, Weitlof belonged to the more progressive and nationalist wings of the larger
    bourgeois liberal movement. During his tenure as Executive Chair of the School
    Association, he vigorously opposed any accommodation with anti-Semitic nation-
    alists (von Wotowa 1905).

School Association, joined the Liberal majority in the Lower Austrian Diet when it voted to rescind the suffrage rights of female property owners in provincial elections. Arguing that women required special protection from the increasingly unpleasant rigors of public life, Weitlof seemed to contradict the enthusiastic support he had expressed for women's activism in the German nationalist School Association (*SPLNÖ*, 2 October 1888).[2]

Both of Weitlof's positions – his enthusiasm for bourgeois women's activism in the new nationalist politics and his willingness to deprive them of the vote – capture the essence of an important ideological transformation taking place in the 1880s. They marked new ideological ventures from the more traditional Liberal notions of community citizenship that had dominated nineteenth-century Austrian public life. Austrian men had never openly encouraged their wives, sisters, and daughters to take part in specifically political activities, like those engaged in by the nationalist associations.[3] Neither had bourgeois liberals troubled themselves much over issues of gender in determining who would have a voice in governing the local community.[4]

2. Weitlof's colleague Joseph Kopp, another liberal nationalist deputy, presented this legislation with the words, "it would be completely abnormal, and would hardly conform to the dignity of the female sex, if women had to make their way into the election locale, and be exposed to the 'influence terrorism'...of our increasingly hard fought elections." Moritz Weitlof in fact reported to the Diet for the *Landesausschuß* in the following year on the progress of a law to revise voting procedures at the communal level, changes due to the recent decision to rescind the right of women property owners to vote (*SPLNÖ*, 11 June 1889).

3. Some readers may question my characterization of the German School Association and similar groups as political organizations, particularly since it was their legally non-political status that enabled them to recruit women. Nevertheless, a close examination of these associations and their activities will, in my opinion, convince even the most skeptical reader that their activities easily fall under the heading of politics.

4. See, for example, *SPLNÖ* 1861, sessions of 10 and 18 April, for the arguments made by Liberal deputy Rudolf Brestel in favor of granting women property holders the right to vote either personally or by proxy in local and provincial elections. Although it is true that the Constitutional Committee of the Kremsier Reichstag of 1848 denied women the right to vote for parliament, its justification for doing so coincided with the admission that in questions of suffrage, property ownership and not gender must remain decisive. The deputies argued that men would represent the interests of their wives (Springer 1885: 186-89). However, the actions of the Kremsier Reichstag did not necessarily typify the discussions and actions of the individual provincial diets in that year. See, for example, the discussion of women's suffrage and the community rights of women property owners in *Verhandlungen des provisorischen Landtages des Herzogthumes Steiermark*, Session of 17 June 1848. For the most part, the issue seems to have been treated as an exceptional case, deserving neither exhaustive discussion nor a principled decision.

This chapter examines how ideologies of national identity and gender identity emerged and interacted among middle-class, German-speaking Austrians during the 1880s. Ever since the 1970s, the rise of nationalist ideologies and political movements among German-identified Austrians has received significant attention from historians.[5] Yet the simultaneous development of explicit ideologies about gender and of significant levels of public activism among bourgeois women has received almost no attention. In part this lacuna can be attributed to the relatively narrow and simplistic conceptualizations of gender employed by many historians. Those studying women's activism and agency in late nineteenth-century Austria have focused too much on the politics of women's suffrage, an issue that mobilized support among far fewer bourgeois women in Austria than it did elsewhere in Europe. I argue that the needs of the early bourgeois German nationalist movement opened up different avenues for women's public activism and agency, starting in the 1880s. At the same time, the new understandings of women's possible roles in society propagated by this movement tended to discredit the kind of individualistic political goals pursued by bourgeois women activists in England or the United States.[6]

The 1880s were a decade of intense confusion, introspection, and ideological reorientation among many bourgeois Germans in Austria. The fall of the German Liberal Auersperg Cabinet in 1879, and the subsequent defeats of the Liberal party at the polls, unleashed an internal crisis of confidence among many self-styled German "Bürger." Political defeat laid bare the precariousness of their hegemony in local, provincial, and state political institutions. Defeat also revealed the growing power of Slavic, clerical, and lower middle-class groups who demanded more responsive treatment from those institutions.

German activists attempted to consolidate and protect their position against the attacks of their newly empowered opponents. They reformulated their political appeals around a more populist German nationalism, seeking to broaden their political base by mobilizing new classes for their cause.[7] Arguing that national affiliation alone

---

5. For some classic formulations of the rise of German nationalism, see among others, Charmatz (1907), Hantsch (1955), and Kann (1950). Recently, historians of the Monarchy have suggested more nuanced approaches to nationalism that focus less on the claims of German national ideology, and more on its social and economic context, and on regional differences. See for example Deak (1967), Verdery (1983), Cohen (1981).

6. For comparable discussions about the anti-individualist political focus of bourgeois women's activism in the German Reich, see Evans (1978) and Hackett (1971).

7. The essays and speeches in Knoll (1900) constitute excellent examples of this ide-

endowed the individual with a community identity, nationalist activists called upon those who shared a German identity to mobilize politically in support of that community regardless of class. This type of appeal gradually replaced the traditional liberal, cosmopolitan, notions of community that had down-played the importance of political activism and stressed deference to wealth and education.

The new nationalism did pose certain risks to those leaders of the Liberal parties accustomed to the more traditional style of politics. These leaders rightly feared that a large-scale political mobilization of the German lower classes could challenge their own hegemony in local politics, a power they exercised primarily through their tacit monopoly of leadership posts in local voluntary associations. For the party bosses, any popular mobilization had to be accompanied by guarantees to protect traditional patterns of social and political hierarchy within the community. Thus, along with the populist redefinition of community on nationalist lines came a simultaneous attempt to impose a subtle hierarchy of class within the German national community by defining Germanness as adherence to specifically bourgeois norms and behaviors (Cohen 1981: 184-232; Judson 1991: 76-95).

Earlier forms of German nationalism had not carried the same pressures for social egalitarianism implied by the new populism. Nor had they stressed the kind of ethnic or linguistic exclusivity common among the new nationalists. For traditional Austrian Liberals, the rights of active citizenship within a community had rested on the shared culture of property ownership. Property ownership and education, not privilege of birth, earned a citizen both civic rights and social status. Liberal leaders in the spring of 1848 had claimed, for example, that membership in the German nation was "based not simply on the soil of birth or language of culture, but rather on ... nobility of action and worthiness of conviction" (Schwartz-Roth-Gold 1848; Judson 1991: 81-84).[8] Thus, before 1880, community membership had remained relatively open to property owners of different linguistic, geographic, or religious origins who shared bourgeois values.[9]

---

ological transformation. See also Cohen's illuminating discussion of this process in Cohen (1981: 140-83).

8. *Schwartz-Roth-Gold* was the organ of the Liberal Association of Germans in Austria.

9. Liberals did not seek to impose a German national identity on other groups, but they did assume that progress demanded a knowledge of science, technology, and literature only available to those in the Monarchy who had mastered the German language. For an interesting articulation of this position among a provincial German bourgeoisie, see Vodopivec (1988: 85-119).

After 1880, however, the new nationalist ideologies of community increasingly emphasized the bonds that supposedly united Germans of all classes and separated them from all others. The twin needs to stake out a clear position against Slavic nationalisms and to define just what constituted Germanness for a more diverse community of German activists led to a new preoccupation with ethnic purity.[10] The need to strengthen a specific, multi-class, German identity, once pure, but long since diluted by so-called ethnic intermingling, increasingly pervaded the nationalist literature published by bourgeois voluntary associations and newspapers after 1880.[11]

Much of the responsibility for reestablishing national purity and preventing further ethnic creolization belonged to women, or more accurately, to mothers. Both the nationalists of the 1880s and the more traditional cosmopolitan liberals believed that women instilled culture and language in children within a domestic world imagined as separate from the public world of work and politics.[12] The growing concern with preserving national identity after 1880 gave a new significance to women's activities in this sphere.

By giving mothers the increasingly politicized responsibility for protecting the core identity of the nation, nationalism also created a space for women to participate in the notionally public sphere of politics. The new nationalism did not at this point require German bourgeois women to raise their birth rate (as the French natalists and British Social Darwinists required of their women). It did often require them to become active guardians of ethnic purity in the community through overt regulation of marriage habits and prohibition of intermarriage.

10. I do not wish to suggest here that earlier ideologies of community had necessarily encouraged or validated the intermingling of groups. Rather, those who saw themselves as German nationalists often assumed that because of its cultural superiority, Germanness would be adopted willingly by educated peoples of many backgrounds.

11. The emerging obsession typically insisted on establishing a kind of *ur*-endogamous national identity by purifying creolized linguistic and cultural usages. These concerns ranged from establishing proper German place names to appropriating common Central European customs and traditions, by calling them German and inventing specifically German histories for them. See for example *MDB*, no. 2, July 1885. A General German Language Association, formed in 1885 to fight the "spreading plague of foreign words," also urged its members never to "use a foreign word for anything which can be expressed in good German!" *MDS*, no. 17, December 1885: 3.

12. On ideologies about separate spheres, their historical construction, and their function in early capitalist and industrializing Central European societies see for example, Ehmer (1986: 195-218), Frevert (1988: 17-48), and Kaplan (1991). For an excellent British comparison, see Davidoff (1987).

For example, number five of the "Ten Commandments of the German Peasant," which appeared in various popular almanacs, commanded the peasant to marry his daughter to a German-speaking husband (*Deutscher Volkskalender für die Iglauer Sprachinsel* 1887: 156).

The need to define and propagate specifically German behavior after 1880 created new opportunities for bourgeois women to assume influential roles within male voluntary organizations. Activists like Moritz Weitlof took pains to demonstrate that nationalist issues, unlike other political questions, were intrinsic to female domestic and cultural concerns. They encouraged women to join nationalist organizations and to become more actively involved in all aspects of public associational life. Yet, if women were to be mobilized publicly because the national issue involved the domestic sphere, then it followed that they should be excluded from those political situations that did not involve them as women. Even as it opened up some new spaces for women in public, German nationalism in Austria systematically closed off other opportunities for public expression that were traditionally available to them, for example, the right of female property owners in Lower Austria to vote.

The fact that nationalist activists increasingly spoke of women purely as mothers or as potential mothers reflects the shape of this new public discussion in the 1880s. In an 1881 "Appeal to German Women," the editors of the *Deutsche Zeitung* explained just why all females should take an active interest in the German School Association. Claiming that a child learns its first words – in fact its language – from its mother, the newspaper addressed the German woman as Mother, asking, "won't your heart tremble in pain if your children have schoolbooks in a language you don't understand? No one should find this association more important than women and German mothers!" ("Mahnruf an die deutschen Frauen" 1881). Appeals to women in their "unselfish" and their "natural" capacities clearly posed far less of a threat to the social order than one made to them as individuals or as citizens.

Calls to action addressed to women carefully delineated very different justifications for male and female forms of political activism. A *School Association Almanac* published in 1884 clarified the potential confusion of male and female roles inherent in this new situation, using arguments drawn from history and nature:

> Men alone fight for issues of freedom; these questions are too distant from the concerns of women. But when the enemy threatens the most precious of national possessions, the holiest legacy of our ancestors, our mother tongue, then the mother's heart is also affected (*Schulvereinskalender für 1884*: 6-7).

This call to arms assigned a specifically female (*qua* mother) identity to the endangered object, "the mother tongue." It used the gender of this threatened object to justify mothers' public activism – an activism that, taken out of this particular context, would certainly extend beyond established norms. To banish any lingering doubts about the propriety of this motherly activism, the almanac also described in detail (as colorful as it was historically dubious) just how the wives of the ancient and warlike German tribes had fought beside their husbands to preserve their nation from Roman conquest. Nature and history, two favorite sources of authority for nineteenth-century positivist liberals, were called upon first to revise, and then to strengthen, the new ideological boundaries separating the sexes. Another pamphlet from the same year managed this reconceptualization more succinctly: "A German woman never lags behind when it is a question of the welfare of her dear children" (*Ein ernstes Wort ... Priester* 1885).

The discussion within nationalist circles about mothers and their more public role represented a significant departure from previous norms. Like the earlier, more open forms of German nationalism, attitudes about women and gender role division had also been much less fixed in the mid-nineteenth century. Beliefs about women's particular nature had traditionally influenced the role division that characterized the bourgeois family, work, and public life. Yet these beliefs seem rarely to have required explicit articulation. Before 1880, as long as women did not confront the contradictions in their public status by engaging in symbolically male activities, open-ended public discussion could take place periodically about a woman's roles and her capabilities, with no particular resolution. Depictions of women in 1848, for example, portray them in a variety of roles: as heroic mothers of the revolution, as helpmates to their men on the barricades, or, occasionally, as individuals deserving citizenship.[13]

Two characteristics of public discussions about women in the years before 1880 should be stressed. First, after 1867 these discus-

13. The imagery of women during the 1848 revolutions in the Habsburg Empire reflects some variation and a tolerance of ambiguity regarding women's roles. Yet explicit attempts by women themselves to discuss citizenship often elicited some male opposition. When a group of women met in August 1848 to found the First Viennese Women's Democratic Association, they faced male hecklers and a press that caricatured them as somehow unfeminine in dress and habit. For contemporary accounts of this incident, see *Neue politische Strassenzeitung*, no. 2, 31 August 1848, and the pamphlet "Der Frauenaufruhr im Volksgarten oder die Waschenanstalt der Wiener Damen" (Vienna 1848). In general on 1848, see Hauch (1990). See also Häusler (1848: 363-64) and Weiland (1982: 208-09, 286-87).

sions were part of an expanding liberal culture of discussion and information, which could be attributed by contemporaries to the successful implementation of the liberal education reforms. Secondly, discussions in bourgeois circles on the "Women's Question" (*Frauenfrage*) during the liberal 1860s and 1870s elicited a multiplicity of viewpoints, not limited to clearly progressive, conservative, or socialist positions. The pages of the *Politische Frauenzeitung* in 1870, for example, assembled all kinds of contradictory claims, suggestions, and calls for reform, all gathered together for the interest of the reading public. Fifteen years later, this diversity of views would no longer be acceptable in middle-class circles.[14]

If the conception of woman purely as national mother specified and limited the scope of her public activism in the 1880s, it was also meant to attract women of all social groups, even those normally excluded from participation in local bourgeois association life. The journal of the German School Association, for example, repeatedly linked its nationalist mission to classless images of community:

> We will never accomplish our mission until all social strata of the people take an active part, until those who inhabit the German palaces as much as those who inhabit German peasant huts make a claim to their Germanness (*MDS*, no. 5, November 1882).[15]

The comparable appeal to women that down-played their social differences while highlighting their commonalities did so by stressing their identity as mothers.

All these appeals had a noticeable impact on Austrian bourgeois society. The School Association alone succeeded in drawing over 10,000 Austrian women into its 982 local branches by 1885. These branches, when added to its 100,000 male members, made the organization one of the largest bourgeois voluntary associations in Central Europe. In 1883, a group of women in Graz led by Nina Kienzl, wife of the Liberal mayor of that city, organized the first all-female local branch (*Frauen- und Mädchen-Ortsgruppe*). In a short time, this branch

---

14. See *Politische Frauenzeitung*, particularly the following issues for articles on women, politics, and social issues from differing points of view: 1869, 1, 2; 1870, 1, 6, 7, 14, 16, 23. For a fascinating discussion of the *Frauenfrage* from a later period, heavily influenced by the new nationalism, see Hruschka (1890). While Hruschka developed an argument that endorsed bourgeois women's secondary and university education along with their employment in public, she did so in the narrower context of a woman's duty to the nation, not in terms of her development as an individual.

15. An article in the same edition also pointed proudly to the diversity in occupation of its male activists, a variety that made this solidly bourgeois organization appear to reflect and to represent the diversity within the universal German community.

became one of the largest and financially most successful, with over 1,300 members. Women all over the Monarchy followed suit, and by 1885 there were 83 such women's branches in existence.[16]

This successful mobilization of over 10,000 women activists in less than five years might have discredited notions that women's very nature prevented them from attaining competence in the conceptually male realm of politics. Yet the new context of nationalist politics had created an appropriately discrete niche for women's activism, giving women the task of renewing the national community.

Many women took advantage of these new opportunities and their nationalist activism soon brought a number of them to prominence.[17] Among the first women to gain public recognition in the German School Association was Therese Ziegler. As the first woman to be elected president of a local branch with both male and female members, Ziegler became a popular favorite at School Association conventions. The organization presented her as a role model for female nationalist activists. Whenever she spoke, Weitlof intentionally introduced Ziegler to the membership as "my colleague," thereby emphasizing her equal public status; and after her first speech, the association began selling her autographed picture. The School Association Almanac of 1883 went so far as to compare her favorably to a Norse goddess of Wisdom.[18] Yet Ziegler's understanding of her own activism was redolent with the new, more explicit articulation of gender difference, which made it safer for her to appear on the same platform with male colleagues. In her first speech to the German School Association she reminded her audience that:

> she considered it no achievement on her part, but rather the duty of every German woman to use her abilities to work for the School Association. A woman's major concern [however] should remain her house and family, where she could achieve great successes, by giving her

16. For general membership statistics, see Wotowa (1905: 72). On Kienzl's group in Graz, see *MDS*, no. 11, June 1884: 7. The records of the association leave no indication of why women in some communities decided to organize their own branches, while in other communities they joined men to form mixed groups. Some sexual division of labor between mixed and female branches is occasionally evident, particularly in the interest shown by delegates from the latter for girls' schools and kindergartens at some School Association conventions. Nevertheless, there was never any statutory difference between the two types of branches.

17. I am not suggesting that women were simply coopted into the School Association. In addition, it should be clear from the following discussion that women not only contributed funds and energy to these associations, but often accomplished much of the ideological work required to build an effective mass nationalist movement.

18. *Schulvereinskalender für 1884* (1884: 6-7). For the sale of Ziegler's picture, see *MDS* no. 7, May 1883: 25.

daughters a good example and by raising her sons to be exemplary German men (*MDS*, no. 7, May 1883: 24).

The nationalist crisis also required more conscientious work from women in their roles as nurturers within the home, school, or charitable institution. Women of all classes who joined nationalist associations were subjected to a barrage of prescriptive literature that specified the German virtues they should strive to embody and disseminate. Much of this barrage was intended to convey a tangible conception of just what it meant to live as a German. These materials helped to enforce specifically urban bourgeois norms of behavior among the more marginal classes of Germans who now belonged to the community.

Pamphlets, almanacs, and, particularly, newsletters published by nationalist associations, offered a variety of useful hints on how German parents could instill German virtues in their children, dress them in specifically German garb, provide them with inspirational German stories and pictures on the wall, and cook them German food. These prescriptions encouraged individuals to join in the process of community purification, to restore their lapsed sense of national identity, and to give specific bourgeois meanings to the concept of Germanness.[19] In Bohemia, for example, these kinds of prescriptions also aimed to prevent socially marginal German speakers from gradually adopting Czech identities for socio-economic survival.[20]

These trends reflect the interrelatedness of class and gender concerns among bourgeois German nationalists. If class relations seemed in doubt or in flux, it was a combination of nationalist and gender constructs that were called upon to reinforce them. Layered into the more explicit discussions of just what constituted Germanness can be found many references to the different behaviors appropriate to the two sexes, both at home and in public.

A typical article, published in 1888 by the German League for the Bohemian Woods, warned its readers that

> the seed of national education must be planted immediately at birth. Give your children real German names, you German mothers; a name reminds the youth and the man, the maiden and the woman for their

19. See, for example, the diagnosis offered by Lippert (1882: 1-3). For a discussion of the concepts of national authenticity and cultural purity, see Judson (1996).
20. The German League for the Bohemian Woods repeatedly articulated this goal throughout the period 1885-1895, in its publication, *MDB*. See also Hainisch (1892). For an interesting discussion of ethnic attrition from German identity to Czech identity in Prague, see Cohen (1981: 86-139).

entire life, that they are a part of the German tribe, and that their duty is to think and act like Germans (*MDB*, no. 17, 1889: 188).

The same writer reminded the reader that raising this German child was a German woman's primary responsibility. If she required a maid (a problem the bourgeois writer assumed that German home-makers of all social classes might at any moment encounter), she should certainly hire a German-speaking domestic, and never a Czech-speaking one. This particular piece of advice aimed, in part, to slow the migrations of German working-class or peasant men and women from Bohemia in search of better employment by offering the Bohemian women jobs as local domestics.[21] This prescription also prevented the German mother from inadvertently allowing her children to learn a second language before the age of fourteen, another danger of hiring Czech-speaking domestic help.

German national journals were obsessed with the idea that exposure to a second language bore primary responsibility for the problem of creolization. They tended to view "cultural mixing" as an unfortunate by-product of being exposed to a "foreign" culture at too early an age, something the vigilant mother must avoid at all costs. One article chided German mothers for their frequent reliance on Czech-speaking wet nurses, explaining that "along with the milk of a Czech nurse, the child imbibes her language" (Lippert 1882: 1-3). Learning a second language could only confuse a child, and therefore should be avoided before the child reached the age where he or she had already internalized a solid consciousness of national identity.

Such articles assigned to the mother other aspects of German (bourgeois) homemaking and child rearing as well, including the responsibility for instilling in her children the behavioral virtues appropriate to their sex. For girls, German virtues meant "modesty and chastity in dress and manner, in word and glance, in feeling and actions; a German maiden should be sensitive and emotional, but never weak and overly sweet." The mother must be certain to adorn her walls with artwork that depicted German heroes, German rulers, and most important (perhaps because of their conspicuously small number), historical "examples of German community unity." A mother must avoid unnatural French fashions in dressing herself and her children, resorting rather to the trusted German traditional costume *(Tracht),* and accent-

---

21. The organization sought to find other forms of employment for women of the lower middle and working classes, as well as to prevent the spread of alcoholism and illegitimacy.

ing the child's individuality (sexual identity) by dressing boys and girls in differing colors (*MDB*, no. 17, 1889: 188).[22]

If this ideological barrage limited the ways in which women's life alternatives could be discussed in public, it did not prevent some bourgeois women from putting this discourse to their own uses, for instance, Therese Ziegler and other women active in the nationalist associations. Women also often appropriated this ideology to justify their own employment in such "nurturing" professions as teaching and social work. And ironically, the increasing public employment of single bourgeois women, justified by the emerging ideology of particularly feminine abilities, occasionally led women to challenge existing gender-based professional disparities between themselves and their male colleagues.[23] Here I will mention one suggestive example of how bourgeois women used the newly accented ideology of sexual difference to justify an activism that eventually led them to challenge the very limits placed on them by nationalist ideologies of community.

The Liberal school reforms of 1868 and 1870 had increased employment opportunities for women in primary education, and in 1870 a group of Viennese teachers had founded the Association of Female Teachers and Educators in Austria. In its early years, the association sponsored lectures on pedagogy and held social events for its members. Gradually, however, the teachers began to use the organizational and political skills they were developing to identify and promote their individual professional interests. By the 1880s, the club's lecture series still emphasized the special nurturing role of female teachers, but it increasingly focused on ways of promoting equality within the teaching profession.[24]

The organization began to lobby for greater state pension coverage for women, for equal consideration with male colleagues for posts as school principals, and against laws that barred married women from teaching. The women formulated resolutions and sent petitions to the Lower Austrian Diet. On occasion, they invited a sympathetic parliamentary deputy or city councilor to their meetings. Finally, the frustration they experienced as professionals led

22. One almanac article enjoined peasants to "Honor your Tracht." *MDB*, no. 17, 1889: 189-90.

23. Professional employment for bourgeois women from less well-to-do families often offered them a measure of improved class status. See the chapter by Erna Appelt in this volume.

24. See the *Mittheilungen des Vereines der Lehrerinnen und Erzieherinnen in Österreich* (*MLVEÖ*), particularly those issues starting in 1887.

some of these women openly to abandon the ideologies of separate spheres and nationalist duty. In 1893, these pioneers founded a small organization whose main purpose was to campaign for women's suffrage. Gendered ideologies of nationalism had originally justified many of these bourgeois women's work in public. Yet the very experience of that work had presented them with a series of on-the-job contradictions that increased their consciousness as individual professionals rather than as nurturers of the nation.[25]

My goal here has been to connect the rise of a specifically nationalist community identity among bourgeois Germans to a new and stronger public articulation of sexual difference in late nineteenth-century Austria. Since the eighteenth century, bourgeois liberalism had generally worked against traditional hierarchic social norms to realize an ideal society peopled by fundamentally equal individuals distinguished only by their differing ability to gain property. Both sex differences and ethnic differences within this community might be important, but were rarely decisive because the community viewed itself as a universal one. In this universe, women did not normally own property, and Slavs could advance themselves by adopting German culture.

The crises of the 1880s changed all of this. By 1895, a person's ethnic identity and gender role appeared to have replaced wealth and education as the fixed ideological determinants of political status. Yet if, in the 1880s, the nationalist cause mobilized politically a more socially heterogeneous group of people on the basis of a shared ethnic identity, it rarely distributed access to political power on that same basis. Asserting a common German identity often enabled bourgeois German-speaking Austrians to co-opt competing classes and social groups for the sake of preserving national unity.[26]

The development of language and images that combined nationalism with a heightened awareness of sexual difference brought a

---

25. *MVLEÖ*, articles from January, February, and June 1887; February and March 1888; March 1889; March 1891. In 1893, a number of bourgeois women including members of the teachers' association led by Auguste Fickert, founded the General Austrian Women's Association (*Allgemeiner österreichischer Frauenverein*), which worked to achieve women's suffrage. I am indebted to Renate Flich for her insights on this association and its leader. See Flich's excellent work on the early feminist activist teacher August Fickert (Flich 1990: 1-24). See also the articles in *Aufbruch in das Jahrhundert der Frau? Rosa Meyreder und der Feminismus in Wien um 1900* (1989) and Judson (1992). For an excellent discussion of comparable British examples, see Vicinus (1985: 1-45, 121-210, 247-292).

26. Lower-middle-class activists often turned to anti-Semitic German nationalist ideologies, partly to subvert the iron hold that bourgeois professionals exercised over political and professional associations. See Judson (1991: 92-94).

variety of outcomes. By assigning sex-related identities to concepts like patriotism or national culture, bourgeois Austrians attempted to co-opt women's mobilization in order to help create a sense of common identity among increasingly diverse social groups. They did this by using a nationalist ideology that worked normatively to endow the newly important social categories of "German" and "non-German," "male" and "female," with stability. It stressed the naturalness and timelessness of these social categories, as well as their applicability to all individuals within the imagined community. In doing so, nationalism preempted and even denied the possibility that conflict might break out among classes or between the sexes within the "German nation."

From another vantage point, however, it is clear that the very ideological nature of these categories made them highly unstable. Ultimately they could not contain the contradictions between their universal explanations and the individual's actual experience of real social relations of power. And just as power relations within the German national community constantly shifted during this period, so these categories, however stable they may appear to have been, were constantly contested and revised. For example, women who became active in the nationalist movement shaped and directed their own actions, often molding nationalist ideologies in new ways to fit their own purposes.

In 1893, the nationalist writer Ella Hruschka observed that, "women should protect their difference, and develop themselves within, not outside the boundaries of this difference," adding that, "whether they have chosen the domestic or the public sphere, all [women] have the duty to strive for a noble femininity" (Hruschka 1890: 39). Yet by attempting to fix those boundaries of difference more clearly, and by legitimating certain political roles for women at the same time, the new nationalist politics actually contributed to a decisive de-stabilization of those boundaries. Any attempt to define femininity with precision and finality only unleashed new struggles by women themselves. The Viennese teachers and the nationalist activists of the 1880s had actually created a way for bourgeois women to enter the imagined public sphere legitimately.[27] Within that limited space, they might debate the reasons justifying their

---

27. Some bourgeois women activists made a virtue of feminine difference, claiming that their moral qualities made them better qualified to direct politics than morally and physically corrupted men. As Christabel Pankhust expressed it in 1909, "Votes for women and chastity for men!" Quoted in Vicinus (1985: 278). For Austrian examples, see the work of Karin Jusek in this volume.

presence in public, and thereby expand the limits of "noble femininity." By 1900, with one foot in the door ideologically, these middle-class women could take up the struggle to conquer all areas of public life for themselves.

The research for this article was facilitated by generous grants from the National Endowment for the Humanities and from the Pitzer College of the Claremont Colleges. I would like to thank Jane Caplan, Laura Downs, Miranda Pollard, Marsha Rozenblit, Laurie Schrage, and Diane Shooman for their valuable comments on various versions of this piece.

# References

## Contemporary Sources

*Mittheilungen des deutschen Böhmerwaldbundes. (MDB)*
*Mittheilungen des deutschen Schulvereins. (MDS)*
*Mittheilungen des Vereines der Lehrerinnen und Erzieherinnen in Österreich. (MVLEÖ)*
*Stenographische Protokolle des Landtages für das Erzherzogthum Österreich unter der Enns. (SPLNÖ)*

## Books and Articles

*Aufbruch in das Jahrhundert der Frau? Rosa Meyreder und der Feminismus in Wien um 1900.* 1989. Exhibition catalog of the Historical Museum in Vienna. Vienna.
Charmatz, R. 1907. *Deutsch-österreichische Politik.* Leipzig.
Cohen, G.B. 1981. *The Politics of Ethnic Survival: Germans in Prague.* Princeton.
Davidoff, L. and Hall, C. 1987. *Family Fortunes: Men and Women of the English Middle Class, 1780-1850.* London.
Deak, I. 1967. "Comments." *Austrian History Yearbook* 3/1: 303-8.
*Deutscher Volkskalender für die Iglauer Sprachinsel.* 1887. Iglau.
Ehmer, J. 1986. "The Artisan Family in Nineteenth-Century Austria: Embourgeoisement of the Petite Bourgeoisie?" In *Shopkeepers and Master Artisans in Nineteenth-Century Europe.* Eds. G. Crossick and H. Haupt. London.

*Ein ernstes Wort über den deutschen Schulverein von einem katholischen Priester.* 1885. Vienna.

Evans, R. 1978. "Liberalism and Society: The Feminist Movement and Social Change." In *Society and Politics in Wilhelmine Germany.* Ed. R. Evans. New York.

Flich, R. 1990. "Der Fall August Fickert-eine Lehrerin macht Schlagzeilen." *Wiener Geschichtsblätter.* 1: 1-24.

Frevert, U. 1988. "Bürgerliche Meisterdenker und das Geschlechtsverhältnis: Konzepte, Erfahrungen, Visionen an der Wende vom 18. zum 19. Jahrhundert." In *Bürgerinnen und Bürger.* Ed. U. Frevert. Göttingen.

Hackett, A. 1971. "The German Women's Movement and Suffrage, 1890-1914: A Study of National Feminism." In *Modern European Social History.* Ed. R. Bezucha. Lexington, Mass.

Hainisch, Michael. 1892. *Die Zukunft der Deutsch-Österreicher: Eine statistische-volkswirtschaftliche Studie.* Vienna.

Hantsch, H. 1955. *Die Nationalitätenfrage im alten Österreich.* Vienna.

Hauch, G. 1990. *Frau Biedermeier auf den Barrikaden: Frauenleben in der Wiener Revolution 1848.* Vienna.

Häusler, W. 1848. *Von der Massenarmut zur Arbeiterbewegung: Demokratie und soziale Frage in der Wiener Revolution von 1848.* Munich.

Hruschka, E. 1890. *Der Wirkungskreis des Weibes: Ein Beitrag zur Lösung der Frauenfrage.* Vienna.

Judson, P. M. 1991. "'Whether Race or Conviction Should Be the Standard': National Identity and Liberal Politics in Nineteenth-Century Austria." *Austrian History Yearbook* 22: 76-95.

_____. 1992. "Die unpolitische Bürgerin im politisierenden Verein: Zu einigen Paradoxen des bürgerlichen Weltbildes im neunzehnten Jahrhundert." In *Bürgertum in der Habsburgermonarchie.* Vol. 2. Ed. E. Bruckmüller, et al. Vienna.

_____. 1996. "Frontiers, Islands, Forests, Stone: Mapping the Geography of a German Identity in the Habsburg Monarchy. In *The Geography of Identity.* Ed. P. Yaeger. Ann Arbor, forthcoming.

Kann, R. 1950. *The Multinational Empire.* New York.

Kaplan, M. 1991. *The Making of the Jewish Middle Class: Women, Family and Identity in Imperial Germany.* New York.

Knoll, P. 1900. *Beiträge zur heimischen Zeitgeschichte.* Prague.

Lippert, J. 1882. "Die Erziehung auf nationaler Grundlage." In *Sammlung Gemeinnütziger Vorträge.* Prague.

"Mahnruf an die deutschen Frauen." 1881. *Deutsche Zeitung,* 3 March.

*Neue politische Strassenzeitung.* 1848. No. 2, 31 August.

*Politische Frauenzeitung.* 1869; 1870.

*Schulvereinskalender für 1884.* 1884. Vienna.

*Schwarz-Roth-Gold.* 1848.

Springer, A., ed. 1885. *Protokolle des Verfassungs-ausschusses im Österreichischen Reichstage 1848-1849.* Vienna.

Verdery, K. 1983. *Transylvanian Villagers: Three Centuries of Political, Economic, and Ethnic Change.* Berkeley.

*Verhandlungen des provisorischen Landtages des Herzogthumes Steiermark.* 1848. Session of 17 June.

Vicinus, M. 1985. *Independent Women: Work and Community for Single Women 1850-1920.* Chicago.

Vodopivec, P. 1988. "Die sozialen und wirtschaftlichen Ansichten des deutschen Bürgertums in Krain vom Ende des sechziger bis zum Beginn der achtziger Jahre des 19. Jahrhunderts." In *Geschichte der Deutschen im Bereich des heutigen Slowenien 1848-1941.* Ed. H. Rumpler and A. Suppan. Vienna.

Weiland, D. 1982. *Geschichte der Frauenemanzipation in Deutschland und Österreich.* Dusseldorf.

Wotowa, A. v. 1905. *Der deutsche Schulverein 1880-1905.* Vienna.

*Chapter 2*

⟢

# THE LIMITS OF FEMALE DESIRE
The Contributions of Austrian Feminists to the
Sexual Debate in Fin-de-Siècle Vienna

...............................

*Karin J. Jušek*

Much has been written about turn-of-the-century Vienna (John-ston 1972; Janik and Toulmin 1973; Schorske 1980) but it has not always provided us with new or deeper insights. Often enough, the author's fantasy has been so ignited by the material that Peter Gay's comment that fin-de-siècle Vienna was not a real city, but rather an invention of cultural historians, seems justified (Gay 1984: 4). But perhaps this imaginary Vienna, the Austro-Hungarian Empire in its last throes, is less the creation of historians than of con-temporaries. Freud himself cautioned one writer with the words, "Perhaps the land you are describing has never existed, and we are just fooling ourselves" (Lothar 1961: 37). The contemporary con-troversy over whether psychoanalysis could have been developed in any other city was already suffused with well-known clichés por-traying Vienna as voluptuous, sensual, the *Porta Orientis* of the unconscious, and the world capital of neuroses. However, the ques-tion of how real the differences were between "Catholic, sensual Vienna" and the "proud cities of the west and north" (Freud 1960) has never been seriously addressed.

Undoubtedly, together with the generally deplorable social conditions of the era and the problems of multinationality, the "sexual crisis" figures as one of the "great questions" of the time.[1] Indeed, the extent to which the so-called "question of morality" occupied bourgeois society at the end of the nineteenth century could lead to the conclusion that a general immorality was the most urgent problem of the time.

Throughout Europe, moralists and scholars produced an endless stream of books, articles, and tracts that tirelessly recounted the dreadful state of the nation, and offered the alarmed reader particular suggestions for improving conditions. Seduction, illegitimacy, adultery, promiscuity, in short, all forms of "moral straying," were thoroughly and passionately discussed. No subject, however, aroused tempers as much as prostitution.[2]

The "discovery" of prostitution as a social problem can be traced to the first half of the last century. Recurrent outbreaks of epidemic typhus spurred interest in the hygienic and social conditions of the poor. Research into these conditions confronted hygienists and physicians with prostitution. The French physician, Parent-Duchatelet, was the first in his profession to undertake a large-scale empirical study (Parent-Duchatelet, 1836), earning him the title: "the Newton of Prostitution." His work was followed by a spate of publications that were, as a rule, far below the standards he set.

Discussions of morality and prostitution (the lack of a "moral" context was generally considered offensive at the time) were initially confined to medical circles. Eventually, however, the number of self-proclaimed experts greatly expanded as jurists, economists, theologians, and feminists joined the passionate debate (Schulte, 1984; Walkowitz, 1980; Corbin, 1978).[3] In the following discussion, I will concentrate on the attitudes of Austrian bourgeois feminists, and their contributions to this debate. Until these women joined it (uninvited, of course), the Austrian debate over prostitution had been an unquestioned male province. Although the subject had received increasing press attention and had become a popular social concern, the participation of women in the discussion was considered extremely improper.

The bourgeois women's movement was much more concerned with prostitution than was its social-democratic counterpart. The

---

1. The expression stems from G. Meisel-Hess (1909).
2. Richard J. Evans (1976) and Judith Walkowitz (1980) have noted the symbolic function of prostitution.
3. I use the term feminist, despite its inherent problems, as a covering term for those women who perceived themselves to be part of the bourgeois or social democratic women's movement.

interest of the latter was principally directed at the inhumane working conditions of women, and for them, a radical change in relations between the sexes was not a high priority. This is not to say, however, that they ignored its importance: Therese Schlesinger-Eckstein, one of the leading women in the social-democratic movement, published a clear and incisive analysis of prostitution (Petition 1897: 23).[4] Although differences between bourgeois and social-democratic women repeatedly surfaced, they were able to work together effectively in this area. By contrast, the topic of prostitution aroused no interest among the Christian Socials, the remaining segment of the women's movement (Jušek 1990a).

## The Women's Movement and Prostitution: A Difficult Relationship

Even for bourgeois women, however, the "sexual question" was not an easy one. I will first describe the difficulties that feminists had in confronting this topic, and then discuss the texts of two authors, Irma von Troll-Brostyáni (1848-1912) and Rosa Mayreder (1858-1938), both of whom published extensive works on the "sexual question." Mayreder took the lead in the political fight against prostitution, and the publications of the Allgemeiner Österreichischer Frauenverein on this topic are from her pen. Troll-Borostyáni criticized bourgeois sexual morality at a time when this topic was not recognized as a problem for the women's movement (Troll-Borostyáni 1878, 1884, 1893, 1896). However, she wrote as a private person, whereas Mayreder wrote in the name of the Allgemeiner Österreichischer Frauenverein.[5]

4. For additional information on Social Democratic and bourgeois attitudes towards prostitution see Jusek (1994).
5. Other feminist authors concerned with the "sexual question" whose work I cannot treat here because of space limitations are Else Jerusalem (Jušek 1990b), who wrote a 700-page novel about a Viennese brothel that was published in Berlin in 1909, and Grete Meisel-Hess, whose book on "sexual crisis" I have mentioned above. It is questionable whether Meisel-Hess should be counted as an Austrian author as she lived the greater part of her life in Germany and her activities were concentrated there. She was, for example, an active member of the German "Bund für Mutterschutz," founded in 1905 by Helene Stöcker. Meisel-Hess also clearly differs from the Austrian feminists formally, in the shrill tone that her writing assumes, and substantially, in her fanatical interest in racial hygiene. Her penned reactions to Otto Weininger's "Gender and Character," for example, share with Rosa Mayreder's the criticism of his concept of femininity as abstruse, but Meisel-Hess goes on to judge homosexuality in sharp terms as degenerate and decadent (Meisel-Hess 1904).

It required civil courage for a woman to address publicly such topics as sexuality and prostitution. Marianne Hainisch, a pioneer of the Austrian women's movement, complained, "It is only recently that women have taken part in the fight against sexual immorality at all" (Hainisch 1901: 180), and went on to describe the lack of interest that women still brought to the topic. The bourgeois women's movement did not initially view prostitution as a problem: it had to be convinced by Mrs. Flora Carnegie (a friend of the famous English abolitionist, Josephine Butler) that the fight against prostitution should be an important goal of the women's movement. While she was living in Vienna, Mrs. Carnegie distributed leaflets on the subject, an action which, according to Hainisch, was "initially offputting. Only a few understood their obligations arising out of public morality" (Hainisch 1901: 180). Mrs. Carnegie did not give up, and was finally able to convince the leadership of the Allgemeiner Österreichischer Frauenverein of the importance and significance of the "fight against the toleration and legitimation of vice." This would prove to be the easier part of the battle for legitimation; winning over the members of the association to this "great cultural task of the women's movement" was much harder (Hainisch 1901: 181).

The need to overcome resistance within the rank and file is demonstrated in a speech by Auguste Fickert delivered at a meeting devoted to the topic of prostitution. She declared that in the "present economic situation," the level of prostitution was growing

> as never before. Our ignorance, our indolence with respect to this terrible phenomenon, is tantamount to complicity for all the social evils arising therefrom. Just as the traveler who has left the path does not hesitate to wade through a morass or cross the wilderness in order to reach solid ground and open roads, we women must not shrink back from learning about the deplorable state of social affairs if we are to save society from becoming a total swamp. With energetic, purposeful action we can accomplish this, because we address these evils impersonally and objectively. We must no longer allow our criminal silence to sanction a social structure that dismisses prostitution with a shrug of the shoulders as a necessary evil. We must not allow our silence to sanction conditions that enfeeble our youth and poison children in the womb (Petition 1897: 5).

In her address, she even had to explain and justify the fact that no warnings had been posted at the door to keep younger girls away from the meeting (Petition 1897: 6).

The Austrian feminists' "discovery" of prostitution as a problem came late in comparison to other countries; fully twenty years after the laws regulating the institution were introduced in Vienna. Representing the Allgemeiner Österreichischer Frauenverein, Marie Lang was the first and only Austrian delegate to the Abolition Congress held in London in July 1898. Both her address, which stressed the social aspects of prostitution, and the fact that she was from Austria, raised interest. She received encouragement from many of the delegates, and the president of the Abolitionist Federation "expressed his joy that Austria had joined the fight against prostitution" (Sparholz 1986: 50).

In the Austrian context, however, the reaction of the women's movement was not really late. Official registration of prostitutes had been introduced in 1873 on the occasion of the World's Fair, when approximately two thousand women were registered. The measure did not receive much public attention at the time. Only in succeeding years, as perceptions of the effects of registration crystallized and agitation for stricter measures, particularly from the press, continued to mount, did prostitution become an important issue. It was at this point that the Austrian women's movement began to enter the discussion, which had until then been the exclusive domain of male "experts." A clear political stance on the question of prostitution was taken by the Allgemeiner Österreichischer Frauenverein within a year after its founding on 28 January 1893 (Petition 1897).

The Austrian feminists' position was in keeping with the abolitionist view, which ascribed prostitution to both social and economic factors. In this, they distanced themselves from the Catholic clergy – who were also against registration – as pointedly as the latter had distanced themselves from the feminists (Jušek 1990a). Rosa Mayreder spoke of "two tendencies that must not be confused with one another. The one, based on Christian ideas, hopes to rid the world of prostitution through religious upbringing and a reawakening of religious feelings – an assumption which, in all the centuries of Christian-dominated culture, has failed to justify itself." In contrast to this position, the women's movement insisted "that a realistic and comprehensive fight against prostitution must be based above all on a reorganization of economic life, but that new moral influences that are capable of changing the behaviorally relevant moral views of individuals must also come forth" (Petition 1897: 12-13).

These differences symbolized not only a difference in priorities – the church stressing the moral factors and the feminists social and economic issues – but also an ideological rift. Where the church called for piety, the feminists called for a new relation between the sexes. In the name of the Allgemeiner Österreichischer Frauenverein, Rosa Mayreder called for "the economic and social emancipation of the female sex as a significant and necessary means for improving the prevailing conditions." She attacked the Public Health

Police as "an insufficient, one-sided and unjust institution that only cripples a comprehensive and effective fight against prostitution. No form of registration can influence the unregistered, medically uncontrolled prostitution, which is everywhere in the terrible majority, as long as so many working women are compelled to turn to prostitution to keep from starving" (Petition 1897: 13). This radical official position cost the association many members (Hainisch 1901: 181).

Under Mayreder's leadership, the fight against registration became a guiding principle, because the women subjected to this system were "reduced to the status of mere things." However, it was clear from the beginning that the abolition of registration could only be a first step. The ultimate goal would have to be the abolition of prostitution itself, for its essence was seen as the reduction of women to the status of objects, a situation that was irreconcilable with the views of the women's movement. Mayreder described the particular significance of the fight against prostitution for the women's movement as follows: "The women's movement is fighting for the individual rights of the woman; if we do not have the courage to fight for our fundamental principles there, where difficulty and responsibility are greatest, we will lose all hope of eventual success" (Petition 1897: 13).

At a meeting on 9 December 1893, the Allgemeiner Österreichischer Frauenverein voted to sponsor a national petition for the prohibition of brothels and the abolition of registration. The petition was introduced in the imperial legislature (Reichsrat), by the social-democratic representative Pernerstorfer, on 26 April 1894.

There is a key difference between the Austrian women's movement and the women's movements in England (Walkowitz 1980), the Netherlands (Huitzing 1983), and the United States (DuBois & Gordon 1983). Although the Austrian feminists took part in the public discussion concerning general morality and prostitution in particular, their fight was restricted to the level of discourse. No demonstrations were held, nor were leaflets distributed (as mentioned above, Mrs. Carnegie's behavior was considered aberrant), brothels were neither picketed nor were their windows smashed as in other countries.[6] It would appear that, in contrast to their shining example, the English feminists, Austrian women saw their struggle as more or less hopeless from the beginning. When, after a three-year delay, Parliament rejected the above-mentioned petition with the curious recommendation that feminists should give up their fight for the vote and concentrate on charitable activities, Rosa Mayreder proclaimed:

---

6. Such actions were carried out, for example, in the Netherlands.

"We have never nurtured the illusion that our petition could have had any other fate. It was an attempt, within our weak powers, to fight against the indifference of those conditions to be found [in Parliament]..." (Petition 1897: 10).

The fight against prostitution in Austria was essentially carried on by writers, through the primary means at their disposal, namely, the text.

## The Burning Desires of the Heart in Man and Woman

Irma von Troll-Borostyáni had engaged in moral criticism in various books and had offered suggestions for improving the social conditions she described. In so doing, she gave free reign to her anger. Her indictments were passionate and not always free from pathos, her vision relentless, the measures she proposed were drastic, and over time, she became increasingly radical.

She viewed "*Erbkapitalismus* and the subjugation of women" as the basic causes for the sexual misery of the time (Troll-Borostyáni 1896: 57).[7] The emphasis of bourgeois morality on material aspects had reduced the relations between men and women to the level of barter, not just to the disadvantage of the woman, but to that of the human race:

> Overindulgence in a disorderly life of pleasures, a tired longing for domestic ease, for solicitous care in illness and at the beginning of old age, consideration for his social position or his business interests, his wife's money or the social contacts of her family that could accelerate his career: these are the motives leading the average man to the altar or to the justice of the peace. From the abysses of the civilized world up to the heights of society, the motives are based on material, not ideal interests.... and it is no different among women. A great number give their hand to an unloved suitor in order to gain material security, others to attain social standing, and all this, because she was taught that marriage is the purpose of a woman's life, that she must not end up a spinster (Troll-Borostyáni 1896: 10).

One should not be surprised that infidelity is the rule in such marriages, rather than the exception. "Infidelity will play a major role in our society as long as marriage is not a union of those two humans who are most strongly attracted to one another. It is natural that peo-

---

7. By *Erbkapitalismus*, Troll-Borostyáni meant the bequeathing of accumulated property. According to her, any person should be free to accumulate property and wealth, but in the event of death everything must fall to the state; bequeathing property and wealth was to be forbidden. In this, she appealed to John Stuart Mill and modern Social Democracy.

ple who share a bed with someone who is unloved yearns for a happy embrace. A free and spontaneous desire for love, must replace the 'marital duty'"(Troll-Borostyáni 1896: 28).

Troll-Borostyáni repeatedly emphasized the intimate connection between bourgeois marriage and prostitution. Mothers who "trained" their daughters for a husband could just as well enroll them in a brothel. Troll-Borostyáni held a heart-felt contempt towards so-called respectable people. "In truth, you have no right, you worthy women, and you men who anxiously protect the virtue of your wives and daughters, you have no right to shower with contempt and ignominy, those women who prostitute themselves! For your morality is not worth much more than their shame" (Troll-Borostyáni 1896: 11-12). It was not just in the realm of morals, according to Troll-Borostyáni, that civilization had reached such an extremely dubious level, but also with respect to the health of the populace. A "life-awakening union of the sexes without the sanction of love is a violation," and nature cannot be violated without consequences: an increasing incidence of "physical and psychological degeneration" was the result (Troll-Borostyáni 1896: 29).

Although Troll-Borostyáni expressed alarm about the increasing degeneration of the race in all her texts, she was a moderate follower of the racial hygiene movement. She was convinced that people cannot be bred like horses and dogs, and so set her hopes on a form of "natural" selection that would develop spontaneously, once immoral conventions were abolished. "The first and unavoidable condition for the promotion of the positive development of mankind, for the psycho-physical improvement of the human race is: free choice in love" (Troll-Borostyáni 1896: 30). The genetically and infectiously ill were, however, to be excluded from this future freedom. Above all, syphilitic men who infected their wives and children incensed her to the extreme. "The state, which metes out stiff punishments for infanticide and abortion, looks with folded arms on the poisoning of the generations by the reproduction of unscrupulous egotists. Compared to the indescribable misery of congenital invalidity, the killing of an embryo that is devoid of feeling or even a living child should be considered a lesser crime than the poisoning of life from conception" (Troll-Borostyáni 1896: 41).

She considered irresponsibility of the male in sexual matters to be criminal. Her scorn for the scandalous "failure of the man to observe his responsibilities toward the woman who serves as a vehicle for his sexual pleasure and toward the children he sires" (Troll-Borostyáni 1896: 21-22) was not restricted to the syphilitic. The male had "shoved the whole burden and suffering that the sexual problem entails onto the weaker sex – the female – and in part also on to the still weaker 'children of love [*Kinder der Liebe*]'" (Troll-Borostyáni 1896: 24).

Troll-Borostyáni considered the female sex to be as sensual as the male, and thus considered it a grave injustice for women who engaged in sexual behaviour as men did to face condemnation. Such conditions were only possible because men, by virtue of their physical superiority, had usurped control. "By using his superior muscle and bone strength, man has made himself ruler over woman, whom he allows only the roles of servant for his domestic needs and tool for satisfying his sexual desires" (Troll-Borostyáni 1896: 36). By excluding women from public life, the male was able to create a moral dogma which cannot sustain itself in the forum of justice and reason: that sexual morality is a duty of the woman, not the man. He attained two goals with the establishment of this illogical article of faith: "firstly, that his wife is obliged to marital fidelity whereas his violations are tolerated. Secondly, that in his extramarital sexual relations, all responsibility for infractions against morality and the social order is deflected onto his partner in sexual pleasure, the woman" (Troll-Borostyáni 1896: 36-37). Thus, it is the "fallen" woman who, whether she be an unwed mother or a prostitute, is subject not only to moral scorn, but also to the full force of harsh laws.

Troll-Borostyáni conscientiously differentiated between unwed, abandoned mothers and prostitutes. The former were to be helped by making the father co-responsible for child-rearing so that the full burden did not fall on the woman alone. The latter were to be helped through offers of alternative employment and thus gradually become reintegrated into society. For Troll-Borostyáni it was self-evident that prostitution must be abolished. She categorically rejected any suggestion that amounted to a rehabilitation of prostitution as a profession, because she considered prostitution equally dangerous to both sexes. Prostitution was always a "moral, physical and social degradation" of the woman and an "encouragement and constant temptation" for the man that could only result in physical and moral degeneration (Troll-Borostyáni 1896: 55).

Although Troll-Borostyáni described the problems of her time in great detail, in contrast to Rosa Mayreder, understanding their causes did not interest her. She was satisfied with noting that the stronger exercised power at the expense of the weaker. The basis for her critique of these more or less "natural" conditions was that, in a civilized society, such primitive mechanisms should no longer be tolerated.

# The Problematic Weakness of Woman's Will

Rosa Mayreder's writings are comprehensive and voluminous. A large part, which was published only in the 1920s, will not be considered here. She expressed her ideas in a political, theoretical, and literary manner. Her great theme was the development of a free and individual "personality." She analyzed and criticized the cultural barriers to this goal for women, always seeking the causes. In her preface to *Critique of Femininity*, which appeared in 1905, she spoke of a three-pillared foundation of the women's movement consisting of economic, social, and ethical-psychological components. She expressed the opinion that social and economic problems had acquired more importance in recent years, but asserted that the greatest contribution of the women's movement was that it posed idealistic demands. In her works she was almost exclusively concerned with "ethical-psychological" problems. "For my part, I have treated the economic not at all, and the social only in passing" (Mayreder 1905: 2).

Mayreder scorned the material basis of bourgeois morality, and commented exactly as Troll-Borostyáni did on the different standard used to judge men's and women's sexual behavior.

> Bourgeois morality requires of women that they grant sexual favors only in exchange for marriage and all associated social and economic advantages … . This assumes sexual integrity on the part of the woman. If marriage is to be the price of sexual surrender, the moment that the barter object upon which the marriage contract rests no longer exists, the man, who is to pay a high price for it, must feel taken advantage of if another before him has gotten it for free (Mayreder 1912: 157; Mayreder 1982: 47).

Besides economic and religious motives, Mayreder suspected that a man's interest in fatherhood was a source of unequal relations. "Sexual and social instincts are fused inseparably" (Mayreder 1912: 159; Mayreder 1982: 49) in the feelings of a man. How else could the fact be explained that "the normal man does not value the free, that is, the uninterested [non-pecuniary – KJ] sexual surrender of a woman; contrary to his own sexual interests, he considers only that woman as morally wholesome, who extracts the highest price for surrender he has to offer – his commitment through marriage" (Mayreder 1912: 159; Mayreder 1982: 48). "The sexual surrender of a woman without commitment...offends the paternal feelings of a man" (Mayreder 1912: 159; Mayreder 1982: 49).

Despite the extent to which nature had favored the man as sexual being, Mayreder saw the contestable nature of fatherhood as his

Achilles heel, for every man was completely dependent on the fidelity and reliability of the woman who was to bear his child. Since the emotionally primitive man did not want to rely only on the feelings and will of a woman, he instituted physical and psychological coercion – a moral double standard – that secured his freedom, but tightly bound the woman (Mayreder 1912: 160; Mayreder 1982: 49).

Mayreder had great sympathy for the insecurity of men. Since they were so completely dependent on women in this matter, it was a woman's responsibility to prevent even the slightest suspicion of contested fatherhood.

> The woman has no means of meeting the natural inequality in matters of progeny other than to combine individual rights with a profound consciousness that the content of her honor with respect to man must be the securing of his paternity: there is nothing more damaging for the position of the female personality than a falsification in these matters. As little as the preservation of virginity really has to do with the concept of female honor, so inseparable from it is the preservation of her fidelity. If women are to succeed in achieving recognition of new norms which do justice to the interests of the female personality, generative reliability must become strongly anchored in the consciousness of the female sex (Mayreder 1923b: 103; Mayreder 1982: 208).

Mayreder thus demanded the sexual "integrity" of the woman with the same vehemence as did bourgeois society. To be sure, for her it was a matter of ideals (as part of the development of the female personality), not material considerations. For women, however, the difference was unimportant. What Mayreder was recommending was the internalization of a morality that was even more rigid than that prevailing in society, for there were husbands who were willing to close an eye to their wives' extra-marital transgressions. In such cases, wives were able to fulfill romantic and sexual desires within a socially condoned framework. Under the morality propagated by Mayreder, such freedom was unacceptable: even if a husband was generous in the matter, a woman's sexual infidelity represented a threat to society, and a threat to the social position of all women, because her irresponsible behavior could only serve to aggravate the male sense of insecurity.

Mayreder made women not only responsible for the level of civilization, but also for the cultural changes that she deemed necessary for its evolution. These changes had to be effected by women exclusively, and at their cost. "If the right to free personal development is to be realized in the social position of women, then woman herself must refrain from any behavior that would contradict this personality and allow men to justify, emotionally or rationally, the old concept of woman as an object" (Mayreder 1923: 105; 1982: 209).

Mayreder was proposing tightrope walk – even the most virtuous woman cannot prevent her virtue from being questioned – and making women's whole future dependent on its questionable outcome. It is likely that she was unaware of the full consequence of her demands. In any case, she never modified this concept in later years.

Like her contemporaries, Mayreder viewed men as the physically superior sex. Nature had given women a heavy burden, motherhood. Thanks to greater mobility, men had secured domination over civilization (Mayreder 1905: 63). However, while Troll-Borostyáni assumed that the sex drive was equally strong in men and women, Mayreder posited an aggressive drive in men, and, in contrast, a "peculiar suggestibility and weakness of will" among women that led to their subjugation by men. For Mayreder, this suggestibility was a trick played by nature in order "to bring women more easily under the power of men than would be possible with equal strength of will" (Mayreder 1905: 50). That is, in order to ensure procreation, nature made the female polygamous. In this context, Mayreder speaks of the "teleological weakness of women" (Mayreder 1905: 51), as she could not consider female promiscuity an asset.

As Mayreder saw it, the transformation of women from natural to cultural beings was one of the most important tasks of the women's movement. However, to the great misfortune of women, prevailing ideology exploited every cultural possibility for keeping women fixed at the lowest stage of their primitive nature. The emphasis on sex-specific character traits poses a great danger for the women's movement.

> For the same teleological characteristics that make the female fit for reproduction – the weakness of will that subjugates itself to outside influences without resistance, the inferior intellect that does not reach beyond immediate sensuality, the predominance of the vegetative life in the psycho-physical constitution, in short, all those characteristics subsumed under the concept of female passivity – contribute to a woman's acceptance of the condition in which she remains no more than a sexual tool for serving the most base instincts of the man. In other words, the bright side of her teleological sexual nature disposes a woman to motherhood, the dark side of that same nature to prostitution (Mayreder 1905: 53-54).

A comparison of Mayreder's ideas with those of her contemporary, the sexologist Richard von Krafft-Ebing, reveals that their conclusions are amazingly similar despite contrary assumptions. In his *Psychopathia sexualis*, Krafft-Ebing started from the assumption that man is polygamous and woman monogamous by nature. "In any case, the psychic leaning of the woman is monogamous, whereas the man tends toward polygamy" (Krafft-Ebing 1888: 11). Indeed, this man of learning found that the difference preserved order, for if a woman is "normally developed and well brought up, her sensual desires are weak. If this were not the case, the whole world would be a brothel, and marriage and family would be unthinkable" (Krafft-Ebing 1888: 10).

Both authors saw prostitution as a direct threat to civilization, and both took it for granted that women are responsible for the general morality. With respect to nature, however, Mayreder is much more critical than Krafft-Ebing. She is quite able to see late nineteenth-century bourgeois morality in relative terms, and to differentiate it from the reproductive goals of nature. Where the famous doctor is content to rely on "normal development" and "good upbringing," Mayreder sees a need to outwit nature. For her, the female's morality cannot be assumed to be natural. On the contrary, it is a cultural achievement.

Mayreder's idea of the natural condition of the female was not complimentary to women; in this, she followed in some respects the views of her male contemporaries, but she insisted that the condition was changeable. Her idea that women had a teleological weakness of will echoes Freud's notion of a weaker superego in females. But for Mayreder the condition was not immutable; it was the starting point for her vision of human development. She argued that supporting the development of women is one of the most important tasks of civilization. Unimpeded by pregnancy, men had been able to advance beyond their natural condition; it was now women's turn. There could be no further cultural advancement if only men were allowed to develop their potential while women were held back on every front.

Mayreder's theories were firmly anchored in bourgeois ideology. Her belief in progress through slow but steady improvement was unshakable. She did not question the cultural values of her day, but criticized injustice within that system of values. She took the madonna-whore dichotomy for granted, as did the majority of her contemporaries. She was convinced that "Contradictory values cannot simultaneously prevail. If the model of woman as wife, mother, and virgin are accorded the highest status for the female in social life, then the model of the promiscuous female cannot enjoy the same favor" (Mayreder 1923: 177; Mayreder 1986: 138). Additionally, individual development for the Western woman was closely bound to her sexual behavior (Mayreder 1923: 177; 1986: 139). That is, a woman who makes, or lets herself be made, into a sexual object cannot attain individuality in the rest of her social life. And it is just this kind of virtuous personality, which is wholly dependent on her sexual behavior, that she must develop if she wants to attain equality with men. If she fails, she becomes a danger to all other women, for a woman "who makes herself into an object provokes all those primitive and elementary impulses in the male psyche that are foreign to the female personality. She brings the relations between the sexes down to a level where the woman is only a meek tool of male domination" (Mayreder 1923: 105; 1982: 209).

What is interesting about this view is that Mayreder takes antagonism between the sexes entirely for granted. She was convinced that the primitive and elementary impulses of men were necessarily directed against women. And as Mayreder held women to be the inherently disadvantaged sex – motherhood placed a heavy burden on women – it followed for her that women must be the losers in the fundamental fight for existence.

Mayreder's commitment to fighting prostitution becomes understandable in the context of her moral position. Prostitution was to be abolished because the women's movement could not tolerate an institution that reduced a woman to a "mere thing." Mayreder roundly rejected proposals that would socially rehabilitate prostitution.

> Any measure that aims at raising the status accorded to prostitution by the populace must be considered a dangerous experiment. It is beyond doubt that prostitution is a destructive element in the political order because the women who fall prey to it are cast into an excessive style of life which disposes them to many crimes, and because the men who fall prey to it are led into depravity, which destroys any sense of natural obligation among the sexes (Petition 1897: 38).

## Visions of the Future

Troll-Borostyáni's (1884) tract is a concrete and detailed catalog of measures for improving prevailing conditions. In her opinion, it was urgently necessary to "order the sexual act" such that the conflict between the individual and society was resolved for the benefit of both (Troll-Borostyáni 1884: 12). To this end she proposed the following measures:

– complete social and political equality of the sexes
– free and unrestricted divorce
– abolition of prostitution as a legal or tolerated institution
– fundamental reform in the education of both sexes
– the upbringing of children in institutions under the direction of, and paid for by, the state (Troll-Borostyáni 1884: 50).

If the sexes were equal, they would work with and alongside each other, "support each other like party members or feud like antagonists." Although women would have to struggle for their existence, they would also gain influence in matters of state. Men would finally recognize that women were not created solely for their comfort and pleasure, and would respect them more than ever before. As a lively and rich exchange of ideas began to inhibit the awakening of sensual feelings, the sexual attraction between the sexes would decrease, and women would have better things to do than flirt with men. Thus, two important things would be accomplished with the equalization of the sexes: the social injustices based in the traditional male-female relationship would end, and the sex drive would be moderated in the interests of culture.

Troll-Borostyáni did not want to abolish marriage as an institution, but she did want to reform it fundamentally. Only marriages of love should be entered into, and since even such liaisons have no lifetime guarantee, the free availability of divorce was a moral necessity. No one can be expected to remain bound to a person who is no longer loved, as this would become "an unbearable yoke" that would lead to "the most gruesome moral and even physical suffering" (Troll-Borostyáni 1884: 160). Reform of marriage, however, would have to await the economic and social independence of women. As long as inequality persisted, easy access to divorce would only increase women's dependency on men (Troll-Borostyáni 1884: 162-63).

The emancipation of women would also lead to a great decrease in prostitution because the majority of those now involved were forced into it by economic circumstances. Prostitution might even disappear altogether, because in this case supply creates its own demand. The starting point of the author was that the two sexes are equal in sensuality. Since women were well able to control themselves, the explanation for the male weakness in this respect must lie in an upbringing that encourages debauchery and the continual stimulation of the senses (Troll-Borostyáni 1884: 194). For this reason, a thorough reform of education was of the utmost importance.

For Troll-Borostyáni the central problem was that women had sole responsibility for the moral level of society. "The ax has never been taken to the root of this social evil. The demand has never been made that the man rein in his desires" (Troll-Borostyáni 1884: 235-36). She was not, however, satisfied simply to broaden responsibility to include men, prescribing in addition, draconian measures for both sexes. Poor eating habits (too much meat), lack of exercise (ideally twice a day, but most importantly in the evening just before bed and carried out to the point of fatigue), and ignorance about the human body and the laws of nature were responsible for the prevailing loose living and must be fought in the interest of cultural progress (Troll-Borostyáni 1884: 237-38). Her willingness to turn over child-rearing to state-run institutions suggests that she did not have much confidence in the general acceptance of her pedagogic measures.

Rosa Mayreder's visions of the future were much less concrete. She was enthusiastic about the ideal of free love, the complete fusion of souls, and an unreserved merging between lovers. She rhapsodized on the "exchange of souls in which every trace of strangeness melts in the warmth of soulful communion and the desire to possess each other in the most intimate and complete closeness, to penetrate to the depths of the soul of the loved one in order to offer oneself in unreserved abandon." This was the way for a woman to become a subject rather than an object in love (Mayreder 1982: 225). She cited numerous letters between famous lovers to illustrate her ideas.

She contrasted domineering erotic males, whom she sharply criticized as wanting to keep women down at their lowest developmental stage (Mayreder 1982: 143), with highly gifted erotic lovers. Although her description of domineering erotic males sounds fully plausible (she had without a doubt encountered this type with great regularity), the picture she paints of the gifted lovers remains pallid. It is questionable whether she ever met one. In any case, her diaries make no mention of this (Mayreder 1988).

Mayreder was, of course, well aware that the ideal condition she imagined would not be easy to achieve, but she made no attempt to outline how this ideal could be reached. As mentioned above, she had little interest in the socioeconomic conditions of her time. She never explained under which social and economic conditions her views could be realized.

## Defensive Strategies

What insights can we gain from the texts of these two authors? Both criticized sexual morality and behavior. Troll-Borostyáni argued that women and men have equally strong sexual desires. The "rules of sexual conduct" that she developed would lead to a certain equilibrium between the sexes. Her insistence on diminishing sexual desires, however, would appear to us as very problematic. Mayreder, too, did not aim at loosening bourgeois morality. On the contrary, in order to achieve social respectability, women must be absolutely "trustworthy" in their sexuality. It was not that Mayreder was a killjoy. She did declare herself for free love, but believed that passion must remain restricted to the one true love.

I think it significant that neither Austrian author developed a theory of feminine "passionlessness." The theory that women have a weaker sex drive was often used by nineteenth-century bourgeois feminists for strategic purposes, but this does not apply to Austria. According to Nancy Cott (1978), by propagating feminine passionlessness, American women were attempting to dislodge the old picture of the lustful woman. The idea that women are determined by their sexuality is very risky for women in a patriarchal society; for Cott, this partly explains why women were attracted to the new ideology of "passionlessness." It not only provided a means for attaining good social standing, it also legitimated women's claim to moral responsibility and control. Further, these ideas strengthened the solidarity among women through their emphasis on a common aversion to "male" sexuality, and it gave women a means of avoiding undesired sex. Cott recognized that these women had to pay a price – the loss of female sexuality – but she was of the opinion that this strategy brought more than it cost.

Cott's ideas, which are shared by others (Jeffreys 1985; Meyer-Renschhausen 1985), are important because they reveal that turn-of-the-century women were not at all the yielding and defenseless victims of a Victorian ideology, but rather sought to make the best out of a bad situation. The gains that they were trying to achieve become perceptible and their actions understandable. This thesis is by no means uncontroversial, and the disadvantages of the strategy have received little attention.

Subsequent research (DuBois and Gordon 1983; Ryan 1984) has substantially changed our ideas about the power of women in the nineteenth century, and the drawbacks of the idea that females have a weaker sex drive have become much clearer.

In their brilliant article, Ellen Carol DuBois and Linda Gordon (1983) have analyzed all important aspects of this strategy. Where Cott, for example, points out the unifying character of an aversion to "male" sexuality, Gordon and Dubois argue that not all women reject "male" sexuality, and that those women who do become the new outsiders. "Social purity feminists not only accepted a confining sexual morality for women, but they also excluded from their sisterhood women who did not or could not go along" (DuBois and Gordon 1983: 16).

Mary Ryan, analyzing the strategy and tactics of the "American Female Moral Reform Society," which was founded in Utica, New

York, in 1837, comes to a similarly pessimistic conclusion. The Society contributed to the establishment of a Victorian sexual morality emphasizing female purity. In the end, its members used their social power to create a moral codex that required particularly strong sexual repression of their own sex. The Austrian writers, however, ended up at a similar dead end, but started from the opposite viewpoint; they stressed rather than minimized the sexual needs of women (Ryan 1984: 287-88).

Nancy Cott's claim that the ideology of the weaker female sex drive was successfully exploited and that women gained more through it than they lost is quite problematic. It is difficult enough to weigh the material aspects against each other. In personal matters such as sexual desires, comparisons seem to me to be totally impossible from the outset. In the end, we have no good basis for the supposed gender-specific difference in sex drive. The concept of the weaker female sex drive is a typical product of the nineteenth century. In contrast, the idea that women have greater sexual needs is much older. Then there is also the third possibility: that lust and desire are evenly distributed between men and women. This, of course, says nothing about the truth of any of these theories.

The denial of female desire implies that women are fundamentally less demanding sexually. One does not have to be a convinced proponent of psychoanalysis in order to find this viewpoint questionable. We should recognize that the price paid by women for propagating the image of their passionlessness may have been very high indeed.

A very interesting and balanced viewpoint has been presented by Philip Rieff (Rieff 1973). In this study, Rieff argues that "within the nineteenth-century panorama of moral attitudes there were always *two* viable forms of misogyny. One was the Victorian form in which Americans were once schooled, which idealized women as natively innocent and above sex. The other view still in the ascendant, partly because of Freud's influence, in which women are conceived (by both women and men) as naturally more sensual" (Rieff 1973: 182; emphasis in the original). According to Rieff, the French, English, and Americans were more inclined to exalt women, whereas the Germans and Russians tended to patronize them as anti-intellectual. He leaves no doubt that he finds women in both cases to be disadvantaged.

> The first misogynistic attitude is based on the *sexual* deficiency of women (the Victorian image): women are considered more delicate emotionally and more cultivated, in contrast with the crude, earthy energies of the male. The second misogynistic attitude is based on the *intellectual* deficiency of women: the child-bearing female represents the natural heritage of humanity, while the male carries on in spite of her enticements the burden of government and rational thought (Rieff 1973: 182-83; emphasis in the original).

Rieff's characterization of national idiosyncrasies is fascinating and, in many respects, apt. He insists with reason that both views are misogynistic, and that women are denied something in each case: either sexuality or intellect.

When we compare the theories of American and Austrian feminists, we find that, regardless of whether they were convinced of their own lack of sexuality or took female desire to be natural and normal, they had the feeling that they had to choose between body and mind. In both cases, the mind was favored at the expense of the body. We have to respect this choice, but should by no means idealize it. As long as women accept that such a choice is extracted from them, they will not have gained much.

# References

Allgemeiner Österreichischer Frauenverein, ed. (cited as Petition 1897).
  *Zur Geschichte einer Petition gegen die Errichtung öffentlicher Häuser in Wien: Protokoll über die am 20. Februar 1897 im Sitzungssaale des alten Rathhauses zu Wien stattgehabte allgemeine Frauenversammlung.* Vienna.
Cott, N. 1978. "Passionlessness: An Interpretation of Victorian Sexual Ideology, 1790-1835." *Signs* 4: 219-36.
Corbin, A. 1978. *Les filles de noce: Misère sexuelle et prostitution aux 19e et 20e siècle.* Paris.
DuBois, E. and Gordon, L. 1983. "Seeking Ecstacy on the Battlefield: Danger and Pleasure in Nineteenth-Century Feminist Sexual Thought." *Feminist Studies* 9: 7-25.
Evans, R.J. 1976. "Prostitution, State and Society in Imperial Germany." *Past and Present* 70: 106-29.
Freud,"Zur Geschichte der psychoanalytischen Bewegung." *Gesammelte Werke* 1960, Vol. 10.
Gay, P. 1984. *The Bourgeois Experience, Victoria to Freud: The Education of the Senses.* New York.
Hainisch, M. 1901. "Die Geschichte der Frauenbewegung in Österreich." In *Die Geschichte der Frauenbewegung in den Kulturländern.* Vol. 1. Ed. H. Lange and G. Bäumer. Berlin.
Huitzing, A. 1983. *Betaalde Liefde: Prostituées in Nederland 1850-1900.* Bergen.
Janik A. and Toulmin, S. 1973. *Wittgenstein's Vienna.* New York.
Jeffreys, S. 1985. *The Spinster and her Enemies: Feminism and Sexuality, 1880-1930.* London.
Johnston, W.M. 1972. *The Austrian Mind: An Intellectual and Social History.* Berkeley and Los Angeles.

Jušek, K.J. 1990a. "Die Erneuerung des Staates durch die sittliche Kraft der Untertanen: Kirchenpolitik und Sexualmoral zur Zeit Kaiser Franz Joseph I (1848-1916)." *Groniek* 107: 79-91.

___. 1990b. "Ein Wiener Bordellroman: Else Jerusalems 'Heiliger Skarabäus.'" In *"Das Weib existiert nicht für sich."* Ed. H.Dienst and Edith Saurer, 139-47. Vienna.

___. 1994. *Auf der Suche der Verlorenen: Die Prostitutionsdebatten im Wien der Jahrhundertwende.* Vienna.

Krafft-Ebing, R.v. 1888. *Psychopathia sexualis, Mit besonderer Berücksichtigung der conträren Sexualempfindung: Eine klinisch forensische Studie.* Stuttgart.

Lothar, E. 1961. *Das Wunder des Überlebens: Erinnerungen und Ergebnisse.* Vienna.

Mayreder, R. 1905. *Zur Kritik der Weiblichkeit.* Leipzig.

___. 1912. "Mutterschaft und doppelte Moral." In *Mutterschaft. Ein Sammelwerk für die Probleme des Weibes als Mutter.* Munich.

___. 1923. *Geschlecht und Kultur. Essays.* Jena.

___. 1982. *Zur Kritik der Weiblichkeit.* Ed. H. Schnedl. Munich.

___. 1986. *Wider die Tyrannei der Norm.* Ed. H. Bubeniček. Vienna.

___. 1988. *Tagebücher, 1873-1937.* Ed. H. Anderson. Frankfurt am Main.

Meisel-Hess, G. 1909. *Die sexuelle Krise.* Jena.

Meyer-Renschhausen, E. 1985. "Radikal, weil sie konservativ sind? Überlegungen zum 'Konservatismus' und zur 'Radikalität' der deutschen Frauenbewegung vor 1933 als Frage nach der Methode der Frauengeschichtsforschung." In *Die ungeschriebene Geschichte.* Ed. Wiener Historikerinnen: 20-36. Vienna.

Parent-Duchatelet, A.J.B. 1836. *De la prostitution de la ville de Paris.* Paris.

Rieff, P. 1973. *Freud: The Mind of the Moralist.* Chicago.

Ryan, M.P. 1984. "Mief und Stärke. Ein frühes Lehrstück über die Ambivalenzen weiblicher Moralisierungskampagnen." In *Listen der Ohnmacht: Zur Sozialgeschichte weiblicher Widerstandsformen.* Ed. C. Honegger and B. Heintz: 278-300. Frankfurt am Main.

Schorske, C.E. 1980. *Fin-de-Siècle Vienna: Politics and Culture.* New York

Schulte, R. 1984. *Sperrbezirke: Tugendhaftigkeit und Prostitution in der bürgerlichen Welt.* Frankfurt am Main.

Sparholz, I. 1986. *Die Persönlichkeit Marie Lang und ihre Bedeutung für die Sozialreformen in Österreich im ausgehenden 19. Jahrhundert.* Dissertation, University of Vienna.

Troll-Borostyáni, I.v. 1878. *Die Mission unseres Jahrhunderts: Eine Studie über die Frauenfrage.* Leipzig.

___. 1884. *Im freien Reich: Ein Memorandum an alle Denkenden und Gesetzgeber zur Beseitigung sozialer Irrtümer und Leiden.* Zürich.

___. 1893. *Die Prostitution vor dem Gesetz: Ein Apell ans deutsche Volk und seine Vertreter.* Leipzig.

___. 1896. *Die Verbrechen der Liebe: Eine sozial-pathologische Studie.* Leipzig.

Walkowitz, J. 1980. *Prostitution and Victorian Society: Women, Class and the State.* Cambridge, Mass.

Worbs, M. 1983. *Nervenkunst: Literatur und Psychoanalyse im Wien der Jahrhundertwende.* Frankfurt am Main.

*Chapter 3*

FEMALE EDUCATION IN
GERMAN-SPEAKING AUSTRIA, GERMANY,
AND SWITZERLAND, 1866-1914

............................

*James C. Albisetti*

Organized women's movements in Europe and North America
struggled for women's access to secondary and higher education and to careers in the liberal professions during the second half
of the nineteenth century. The upsurge of interest in women's
history during the last two decades has led to detailed studies of
these struggles not only in the English-speaking countries, but also in
many continental European states (Johanson 1987; Margadant
1990; Albisetti 1988).

The fight by Austrian women for increased educational and employment opportunities during the age of Franz Joseph, however, has
not been as thoroughly documented. Women's history in general has
not made as great an impact in Austria as in many countries; in the
words of Brigitte Mazohl-Wallnig: "As has always been the case in our
history, Austria has again fallen behind" (Mazohl-Wallnig 1991: 287).
Except for a recent study of feminism in turn-of-the-century Vienna
by Harriet Anderson (1992), scholars publishing in English have
done little to remedy this. Document collections, anthologies of articles, and survey texts give little or no coverage to the women of the

Habsburg Monarchy[1]. Those historians who do deal with this theme tend to focus on working-class and socialist women or on the more radical middle-class reformers, but to ignore education (see Riemer and Fout 1980; Evans 1977; Anderson and Zinsser 1988).

Several older works by Austrians outline the development of schooling for girls and women, but offer little analysis (Braun et al. 1930; Mayer 1952; Forkl and Koffmahn 1968). The same holds true for Helmut Engelbrecht's comprehensive history of Austrian education (Engelbrecht 1984, 1986). Much of the more specialized research on female education in Austria is found in unpublished dissertations (Lind 1961; Göllner 1986; Steibl 1986), including several not available in the United States (Hutterer 1978; Kronreif 1985). Even the best of recent publications provide little comparison of developments in Austria to those elsewhere in Europe (Heindl and Tichy 1990).

Despite the lack of comparative studies, however, leading scholars have applied notions of "Austrian backwardness" not just in the field of women's history, but also in the history of educational opportunities for women in the Dual Monarchy. For Engelbrecht, it is clear that "Austria lagged behind western developments" (Engelbrecht 1986: 279). Waltraud Heindl is slightly more circumspect, noting that "along with most of the German states Austria was the last European country that allowed women to study" (Heindl 1987: 317). One of the few explanations offered for this alleged "backwardness" has been the multinational character of the Habsburg Empire. According to this interpretation, ethnic conflict made cooperation among feminists of different nationalities extremely difficult and caused non-German feminists to subordinate their goals to the nationalist movements (Freeze 1985: 53).

Yet even the most cursory glance at Russia during the second half of the nineteenth century suggests that economic and political "backwardness" and ethnic diversity do not adequately explain the restricted educational opportunities for Austrian women. Russian girls and women in this era had more secondary schools, more "higher courses," and greater access to medical training than did their Austrian sisters; they also studied abroad in significantly greater numbers (Johanson 1987).

Here I evaluate claims of Austrian "backwardness" in educational and employment opportunities for women by comparing Austria with Germany and Switzerland. My examination of the status of

1. Bertha von Suttner and Sigmund Freud are the only Austrians included in Bell and Offen (1983). There are no references to Austria in Boxer and Quataert (1987), and very few in Bridenthal, Koonz, and Stuard (1987).

female teachers, the growth of secondary schools for girls, and the struggles for access to the Matura (certificate received after completing a course of study at a Realgymnasium), the universities, and the professions, indicates that the general picture of an Austrian lag is much more complicated and nuanced, and suggests an agenda for future research.

The creation of the Austro-Hungarian Empire in the Compromise of 1867 came at a time when issues of women's education and employment were receiving an unprecedented level of public attention throughout Europe. In providing job training for girls and young women from the middle classes who needed to support themselves, Austria mirrored the European-wide concern in the 1860s with "redundant" or "surplus" women.

The foundation in 1866 of the Women's Employment Association *(Frauenerwerbsverein)* in Vienna followed by less than a year, and to some extent imitated, the creation of the Lette Association in Berlin. Both organizations were modeled ultimately on the English Society for Promoting the Employment of Women (Engelbrecht 1986: 280; Witzmann 1984: 22-23). Within five years, both German and Czech women in Prague had started similar associations to train middle-class girls for "respectable" occupations; other Austrian cities soon followed suit (Wiechowski 1903: 11; Volet-Jeanneret 1988: 78, 221-23).

The most important improvement in job opportunities based on education came in the wake of the school law of 1869, which for the first time led significant numbers of lay women into elementary teaching (Braun et al. 1930: 174-91). In creating normal schools for such teachers, Austria trailed most of its European neighbors except for Russia, but not as drastically as it might appear. The first state-supported seminars for women teachers in Prussia dated back to 1832, but the city of Berlin hired its first female elementary teachers only in 1863. The first regulations for such teachers were introduced in Württemberg in 1858, Saxony in 1859, Baden in 1863, and Braunschweig in 1868 (Albisetti 1988: 60-67). In Switzerland, women supplied 24 percent of elementary school teachers in the canton of Bern as early as 1861, but the city schools of Zurich did not hire women until 1874 (Schraner 1938: 82; Zehender 1883: 49). That women supplied over 43 percent of elementary teachers in Vienna by 1896 (Engelbrecht 1986: 439), whereas a few years later their Prussian sisters provided only 25 percent of teachers in the cities and 9 percent in the countryside, suggests a relatively successful development of this new professional opportunity for women in at least part of the Habsburg Monarchy (Hardt 1905: 10-11).

As in all the German states, women teachers in Austria were for many years required to abandon their careers if they married.[2] In contrast to their German sisters, however, Austrian women working in the elementary schools began to earn the same salaries as their male colleagues as early as the 1870s (Engelbrecht 1986: 280; Volet-Jeanneret 1988: 272). This provision of equal pay for equal work so astounded the American Theodore Stanton when he learned of it in the early 1880s that he assumed the information was mistaken (Stanton 1884: 452n). In this area, at least, Austrian backwardness is a myth.

At the time of the Compromise of 1867, schooling for girls beyond the elementary level was, to the extent it was regulated at all, treated separately from secondary education for boys; but this was true in all other European countries as well. In Austria, parents who wanted their daughters to learn more than the rudiments of reading, writing, arithmetic, and religion that were taught in elementary schools had to choose between convent schools run by various Catholic teaching orders and secular private schools (Mayer 1952: 13-14; Engelbrecht 1984: 27-30, 38-39, 292; Witzmann 1984: 56-57). There is little research on the clientele and curricula of such schools, which certainly had their equivalents throughout most of western and central Europe at that time.

State support for advanced education for Austrian girls was limited to two institutions for special groups, both of which dated back to the late eighteenth century. The *Offizierstöchter-Erziehungs-Institut,* founded in 1775, and the *Zivil-Mädchen-Pensionat,* opened in 1786, provided daughters of officers and civil servants with both general education and preparation for employment as governesses (Engelbrecht 1984: 165-166). These schools were older than a number of similar foundations in other German states, the most famous of which was the Luisenstiftung established in Berlin in 1811 (Friese 1890).

What Austria lacked in 1867 were any equivalents to the state- and city-sponsored higher girls' schools (*höhere Mädchenschulen*) found in many parts of Germany and Switzerland. Such sponsorship, even if it did not involve significant financial contributions, gave important public recognition to the need for special educational facilities for girls of the middle and upper classes. Austrian backwardness in this area can be exaggerated, however, for at the time of Bismarck's partition of the German Confederation, such cities as Hamburg, Bremen, Lübeck, Essen, Cologne, Düsseldorf, Dresden, and Leipzig

---

2. A mistaken view that Austria did not have this celibacy requirement *(Zölibat)* was put forward in Schirmacher (1912: 162), and it has been repeated in works such as Gahlings and Moering (1961: 77).

did not yet have any public secondary schools for girls (Albisetti 1988: 27-30, 37-41, 52-54). Italy, France, Belgium, and England also had no such institutions as of the late 1860s.

The first major public demand for improving the secondary education of Austrian girls came from Marianne Hainisch at a meeting of the Women's Employment Association in 1870. Her call for the city of Vienna to found a *Realgymnasium* for girls fell on deaf ears, however, even though, in 1871, the lower house of the Reichsrat recommended that the government consider creating some form of secondary schooling for girls. The Women's Employment Association itself decided to start a four-year private school for girls between the ages of twelve and sixteen, to which classes for ten- and eleven-year-olds were added in 1877. This extension to six years came in imitation of what is often considered to have been the first Lyzeum for German-speaking girls, which opened in Graz in 1873 – ten years after such a school had been founded for Czech girls in Prague. Beginning in the mid-1870s, the government began to give subsidies to these and similar secondary schools for girls. The school in Graz, which was taken over by the municipality in 1885, was the first to achieve public status (Braun et al. 1930: 15-16; Mayer 1952: 16-29; Volet-Jeanneret 1988: 239-240).

As was the case in Prussia, the six-year girls' Lyzeen and the smaller, three- to five-year higher girls' schools developed without any curriculum dictated by the state. All devoted more attention to modern languages and less to the classics, science, and mathematics than did the secondary schools for boys; and all ended at least two years earlier than did the eight-year Gymnasium. These schools spread rather slowly through German-speaking Austria. A higher girls' school that opened in 1880 in Klagenfurt remained that city's only such institution in 1901. Linz did not have any secular school for girls until 1889, Innsbruck not until 1898 (Machan 1901: 22; Mayer 1952: 30; Engelbrecht 1986: 284). Local studies are needed to show who supported these institutions and how they competed for pupils with existing convent and private schools.

Two contrasts with conditions in the similar but much more numerous higher girls' schools of Prussia in the last third of the nineteenth century are worth noting. One is the even more limited role played by women secondary teachers in Austria. Whereas Prussian regulations adopted in 1874 provided for the certification of women teachers for either the elementary or the higher girls' schools, no such higher certification existed in Austria. Until after the turn of the century, male teachers dominated the Lyzeen except for subjects such as needlework, drawing, and singing (Mayer 1952: 31; Braun et al. 1930: 122). Yet these male teachers (especially the minority who had university degrees) appear to have been much less aggressive than their Prussian counterparts in pursuing the upgrading of their schools into true secondary institutions, with a concomitant increase in salaries and prestige (Albisetti 1988: 108-10, 113-14, 147-49).

Not until the late 1890s did the Austrian government move to regulate the girls' Lyzeen, and then it responded to pressure more from women's organizations than from male teachers. The Prussian regulations for the higher girls' schools of 1894 served in many ways as a model for the Austrian reform: the Ministry of Education even commissioned Johann Degn, director of the Linz Lyzeum, to undertake a fact-finding trip to Germany. As had the Prussian regulations, the Austrian "provisional statute" of December 1900 introduced a fixed structure for the first time, standardizing the Lyzeum as a six-year school. Although still given a "feminine" slant, the curriculum devoted more time to academic subjects than had previously been the case in most schools. In direct imitation of the Prussia regulations, the "provisional statute" required that every male director should appoint a woman as his special assistant *(Directionsadjunctin)*. In both countries, however, this stipulation was frequently ignored (Mayer 1952: 41-49; Engelbrecht 1986: 285-86, 604-5).

The Austrian regulations went farther than the Prussian by placing the Lyzeen under the same administration and inspection as the boys' secondary schools. They also leapfrogged past the Prussian rules with regard to training for female secondary teachers. Whereas Prussia, in 1894, had created an advanced certification for women teachers *(Oberlehrerinnenprüfung)* to be taken by experienced teachers who had spent two or three years in special courses taught mostly by university professors, Austria allowed young women who had graduated from either a girls' Lyzeum or an elementary teachers' seminar to attend the philosophical faculties of the universities as full time auditors *(ausserordentliche Hörerinnen)*. After three years of study, these women could be certified to teach in all grades of the Lyzeen. Hundreds of them took advantage of this opportunity, despite the fact that their educational backgrounds left them much less prepared for university studies than the graduates of boys' secondary schools (Engelbrecht 1986: 291; Braun et al. 1930: 122).

The final restructuring of girls' secondary education before the war, the reforms of 1912, also imitated Prussian models to a certain degree. Prussia, in 1908, had created fixed curricula for courses leading to the secondary diploma, or Abitur, and had provided for links between the regular girls' schools – which now adopted the Austrian name of Lyzeen – and the Abitur programs. Austria did more or less the same thing in 1912, creating a situation where a four-year lower level for pupils aged ten to fourteen could be followed by either a three-year upper Lyzeum or a four-year Reformrealgymnasium that led to the Matura. Most existing and new schools chose the eight-year structure, and by 1927 no seven-year girls' Lyzeen were left in Austria (Mayer 1952: 59, 70-78). As of that date, there were still no Austrian state-run schools leading to the Matura, however, whereas in Prussia the government had moved immediately in 1908-9 to add Abitur courses to the four girls' schools that it operated, two in Berlin and one each in Trier and Posen (Albisetti 1988: 278).

This reluctance to support institutions that would prepare young women for the Matura is all the more surprising because the examination leading to the Matura had been open to Austrian women since 1872. Those who passed did not, however, gain the right, as did men, to matriculate at Austrian universities. This was made clear in a decree issued in September 1878. This undoubtedly limited the number of women who were willing to put forth the effort needed to prepare privately for the Matura; as of 1895, about twenty-five had passed the Matura examination (Mayer 1952: 28-29, 35). Although several Austrian scholars have stressed the tight restrictions on women's access to the Matura and the small numbers who attempted it (Engelbrecht 1986: 284; Heindl and Tichy 1990: 22-23), they have failed to note that no German woman was allowed to take the Abitur examination until 1895 (Albisetti 1988: 208).

German women began popular petition campaigns aimed at gaining access to both the Abitur and matriculation in the universities in the late 1880s. Two new organizations of Austrian women launched similar drives in 1890, with the Minerva Association, a Czech group from Prague, being followed almost immediately by Vienna's Association for Expanded Women's Education *(Verein für erweiterte Frauenbildung)*, which had been established in 1888. Without receiving any clear-cut assurance from the authorities that women with the Matura would be allowed to matriculate, both organizations moved more quickly than their German counterparts to create private Gymnasium courses for girls. The course in Prague opened already in the fall of 1890, as the first such school in central or western Europe, and it produced its first graduates in May 1895. The *gymnasiale Mädchenschule* in Vienna enrolled the first pupils in its six-year course in 1892, with the first graduation coming in July 1898. Despite repeated requests for assistance, the school did not receive a government subsidy until 1920 (Volet-Jeanneret 1988: 248-51; Freeze 1985: 57-59; David 1991: 29; Braun et al. 1930: 128; VfeFW 1892ff.).

In Germany, Gymnasium courses for girls opened in Berlin, Karlsruhe, and Leipzig in 1893 and 1894, stimulated in part by the new schools in Austria. At that time, the states of Prussia, Baden, and Saxony had not yet guaranteed that graduates would be allowed to take the Abitur, much less enroll in the universities. In these and most other German states, admission of women to this examination was clearly linked to the first graduates of such courses. In Baden in 1900, and in Bavaria and Württemberg a few years later, admission of women to matriculation followed directly on access to the Abitur; but in Prussia and Saxony opposition from professors and other officials delayed this step for a decade. Once women could take the Abitur, though, many state and city governments began to subsidize or even to create schools that could prepare them for it (Albisetti 1988: 206-17, 242-50). The situation in Austria – a twenty-year delay between the opening to women of the Matura and the creation of the first girls' Gymnasium, followed by a nearly thirty-year delay in the provision of state aid to this institution – thus did not closely resemble developments in Imperial Germany. Much greater similarities existed with conditions in France, where women gained access to the baccalauréat examination in the 1860s, but where no state-supported classical courses for girls were established until after World War I.

Higher education for women was in its infancy at the time of the creation of the Dual Monarchy. Vassar College had opened its doors two years earlier; Girton College was still in the planning stage. A handful of women had begun to audit lectures at a few German universities, and in Zurich the first European woman to earn a regular university degree in this era, the Russian medical student Nadezhda Suslova, was preparing to graduate in December 1867. That a significant portion of the research for Suslova's dissertation was completed during the summer and fall of that year at the physiological institute of the University of Graz indicates that Austria was not entirely unreceptive to these first stirrings of higher education for women (Tuve 1984: 20).

Similar opportunities for informal or unofficial study also existed at other Austrian universities or their associated clinics. Early in 1869, the young Russian mathematician Sofia Kovalevskaia found that she could get help at the University of Vienna from a physics professor named Lange but not from any specialists in her own field, so she soon moved on to Heidelberg and Berlin (Koblitz 1983: 87). In the same year, the American Mary Jane Safford arrived in Vienna to spend fifteen months studying at the General Hospital. Three years later, Anna Broomall, a graduate of the Women's Medical College of Pennsylvania, studied obstetrics in the Austrian capital. At one time in the early 1870s, as many as six women associated with the New England Hospital for Women and Children were pursuing advanced medical studies in Vienna.[3]

In the early 1870s as well, the German-language University of Prague admitted several women as auditors. Among them was Susanna Rubinstein, who was from the Bukovina and spent time in Prague before moving on the University of Leipzig, where, in 1874, she received a doctorate in philosophy – twenty years before any native German woman (Wiechowski 1903, 20; VfeFW 1896, 53). Emilie Lehmus, the first German woman to earn a medical degree at Zurich, did postgraduate work in the clinic of a Professor Weber at Prague in 1875-76 (Lange, 1900-1901).

For Austrian as well as many German universities, the question of allowing women to matriculate as regular students was first raised by Russian women who were told by their government in the spring of 1873 that they had to leave the University of Zurich – seen as a hotbed of radicalism – or face permanent exile. Some of these Russian women applied for admission to Graz, where the academic authorities were unwilling to make a decision and requested a ruling from the Ministry of Education. When the Ministry in turn asked the medical faculty at Vienna for its views regarding the possible admission of women students, the professors bluntly rejected the idea, in much the same terms as did their colleagues at German universities (Heindl 1987: 327-28; Heindl and Tichy 1990: 19-20; Lind 1961: 42; Forkl and Koffmahn 1968: 18; Albisetti 1988: 126-28).

This rejection of matriculation for women in 1873 came despite the opening of the Matura to them in the previous year. A young woman named Rosa Welt, who passed the Matura in 1873, was refused admission at the University of Vienna just as were the Russians at Graz. She chose to go to the University of Bern, where in 1878 she became the first female subject of Franz Joseph to earn a Swiss medical degree. Welt belonged to a remarkable family from Czernowitz: her sisters Sarah and Leonore received medical degrees from Zurich in 1885 and 1888, respectively, and their youngest sister Ida, after graduating from Vassar College, earned a doctorate in

3. See entry on Mary Safford in *Biographical Cyclopedia of Homeopathic Physicians*, ed. E. Cleave (Philadelphia, 1873): 466; P. S. Ward, "Anna Elizabeth Broomall," in *Notable American Women*, 3 vols., ed. E. T. James (Boston, 1971) 1: 246; Vietor (1924: 359).

chemistry from the University of Geneva in 1895 (VfeFW 1895: 47-48; Heindl and Tichy 1990: 218-19).[4]

The next consideration of admitting women to Austrian universities came a few years later and resulted, in May 1878, in a decree allowing women to audit courses on an individual basis only in "exceptional circumstances." Among the first women to try to take advantage of this opportunity were Rosa Welt, with her Swiss degree in hand, and her sister Leonore. The philosophical faculty at Vienna, faced with applications from these two and from the German Cläre Schubert, decided to make the Matura a prerequisite for female auditors. Both Welt sisters had already obtained this diploma in Czernowitz; Schubert, who studied art history, had to pass a special examination in Greek before being allowed to continue attending lectures (Volet- Jeanneret 1988: 251; Engelbrecht 1986: 583-84; Forkl and Koffmahn 1968: 18-19, 24).[5]

Historians have tended to view the regulations of 1878 as extremely restrictive. Yet the Austrian policy was less restrictive at the time than that of any German university except Leipzig. Within two years, new female auditors would be barred from Leipzig, something that never happened at the University of Vienna. Under the policy adopted in 1878, women such as Gabriele Stadler, Siddy Eisenschitz, and Josefine Kammerling were able to receive part of their higher education at home before moving to Switzerland to obtain degrees (Albisetti 1988: 128-29; VfeFW 1895: 41; VfeFW 1899: 42-43).

Being able to audit courses in exceptional circumstances was not, of course, a satisfactory long-term solution for Austrian women. Yet during the 1870s and 1880s, very few chose the alternative of pursuing degrees at Zurich or Bern. Russian, American, and English women were, in fact, more numerous at Swiss universities than Austrian, German, or even Swiss women.[6] Women from the Habsburg Empire who did study in Switzerland tended to come, as did the Welts and Susanna Rubinstein, from the periphery, not from the core German lands. Among the few who studied the humanities, for example, was Eugenie Nussbaum (Schwarzwald), who had been born in Galicia and

---

4. Leonore Gourfein-Welt, who later settled in Geneva, contributed an article on women's education there to Schweizerischer Verband der Akademikerinnen, *Das Frauenstudium an den Schweizer Hochschulen* (Zurich, 1928).

5. See also "Cläre Schubert-Feder," in *Lexikon deutscher Frauen der Feder*, 2 vols., ed. S. Pataky, (Berlin, 1898) 2: 276-277.

6. Only two of the first twenty-eight female physicians to graduate from Zurich were Swiss (Rohner 1972: 78-82). No native Swiss woman enrolled at the University of Geneva from 1872 until 1890. See S. Woodtli, *Gleichberechtigung: Der Kampf um die politischen Rechte der Frauen in der Schweiz,* 2nd enl. ed. (Frauenfeld, 1983): 59.

raised in Czernowitz (Göllner 1986: 37-43). Others who pursued medical degrees included the Hungarian Vilma, Countess Hugonnay and the Czech Bohuslava Keck (Keckova), who graduated from Zurich in 1879 and 1880, respectively. Keck's countrywoman Anna Bayer (Bayerova) earned her medical degree from Bern in 1887. The first German-Austrian woman to complete medical training in Switzerland was Georgina von Roth, an officer's daughter born in Slovakia, who graduated from Geneva in 1892. At Zurich the first German-Austrian female physician was Gabriele von Possaner-Ehrenthal, a bureaucrat's daughter who was born in Budapest and moved to Vienna only at the age of twenty; she finished her studies in 1894. She was followed two years later at the same university by Anna Fischer-Dückelmann, born in Galicia as the daughter of a military physician (Heindl and Tichy 1990: 216-19; VfeFW 1895: 39-42; VfeFW 1896: 45-52). Such cases may not be numerous enough to constitute a general pattern, but they do raise questions about how geographical and/or ethnic "marginality" may have affected women's decisions to challenge convention by pursuing higher education.

A second possible alternative for women barred from matriculation at the men's universities, creation of a separate institution for women, aroused even less interest in Austria than in Germany during this period (Lind 1961: 45). Perhaps one reason was the lack in Vienna of an institution like the Victoria Lyzeum in Berlin, which the Crown Princess Victoria and some of her circle of supporters envisioned in the 1880s as the core of a German university for women. The Anglophilia of the Crown Princess's circle, many of whose members had visited Girton and Newnham Colleges at Cambridge, does not appear to have affected Austrian women to a similar degree (Albisetti 1988: 151, 155-57).

Only with the creation of the Athenäum in Vienna in 1900, after matriculation in the philosophical and medical faculties had been opened to women, did Austria possess an institution that provided the same type of academic lectures for women as the Victoria Lyceum. That the government provided a subsidy to the Athenäum from the beginning, in contrast to its repeated refusal to aid the *gymnasiale Mädchenschule*, suggests that educational officials may have seen this institution as a way to divert women from the Matura and study at the university. According to Günter Fellner, in the years before World War I more women attended courses at the Athenäum than enrolled as students or auditors at the University of Vienna (Fellner 1986: 99-115).

As was noted above, petition campaigns aimed at opening Austrian universities to women began in 1890. Central to the campaigns was an argument put forward frequently in Germany: female physicians were needed to provide medical treatment to women (Albisetti 1988: 160, 183). Several developments at this time gave Austrian women some reason to hope that the practice of medicine would soon open to them. Until 1890, German women with foreign medical degrees had enjoyed somewhat more freedom to practice their profession than their Austrian counterparts, but now this situation began to change. In 1890 Franz Joseph granted to the Russian-born and Swiss-educated physician Rosa Kerschbaumer special permission to continue operating an eye clinic in Salzburg that had been run by her husband, who had recently died. The following year, the Austrian government hired the Czech physician Anna Bayer to treat Muslim women in Bosnia; two years later she was replaced by her countrywoman Bohuslava Keck. In 1895, Georgina von Roth was hired to be the school physician for the girls attending the *Offizierstöchter-Erziehungs-Anstalt*, even though, as one skeptic pointed out, no Moslems who refused to be treated by men were enrolled there (Forkl and Koffmann 1968: 25-26; Freeze 1985: 58). Public debate over admitting women to the universities, and over female physicians in particular, became much more heated following the publication in 1895 of a notorious pamphlet by the professor of surgery Eduard Albert, which asserted, among other things, that "men have produced all human creations that you see surrounding you" (Albert 1895: 1). In response to this provocation, the recently formed Austrian Women's Association decided to begin a mass petition asking the lower house of the Reichsrat to support the opening of the medical profession to women. The house did respond positively, urging the government to take action (AöF 1895: 11; Engelbrecht 1986: 290). The graduation of the first class from the Minerva Gymnasium in Prague in 1895 also made resolving the question of matriculation for women more urgent.

The first step taken by the government, however, was to allow female physicians trained abroad to gain the right to practice, not by special dispensation on an individual basis, but by taking all the necessary Austrian examinations, a process known as "Nostrifikation" of their foreign degrees. The first woman to submit to this form of double jeopardy was Gabriele von Possaner, who passed in April 1897 (Sablik 1968: 817; Heindl and Tichy 1990: 189-219). That no one else sought such recognition of a foreign degree until 1902 suggests how unimportant a reform this really was.

In contrast to the general practice in the German states of opening all faculties except for Catholic theology at the same time, the Austrian universities allowed women to matriculate in the various faculties at different times. Women with the Matura were accepted as regular students in the philosophical faculties in 1897, three years before Baden became the first German state to allow matriculation for women. In the first year, only three women entered the philosophical faculty at Vienna, but the graduation of the first class from the *gymnasiale Mädchenschule* in 1898 brought a substantial increase in their numbers. The pioneer in obtaining a Ph.D. from Vienna was Gabriele von Wartensleben, born in Austria but educated largely in Germany, who received her degree in classics in 1900, despite not having studied there (Lind 1961: 57; Braun et al. 1930: 194; Harper 1985: 118-23). By that time, many German universities, including Berlin, had granted doctorates to women on the basis of audited courses and a dissertation, a practice not followed in Austria.

Closely related to matriculation of women in the philosophical faculties was their admission to certification as secondary teachers on the same basis as men. In 1898, two women received special permission to take the certification examination. Both passed. Josefine Kammerling opened a private Gymnasium course for girls in Lemberg, while Frau Sembor began to teach at the Minerva Gymnasium in Prague. Two years later, Cecilie (Böhm-)Wendt, who received all of her higher education in Austria, became the first woman to work as a probationary teacher at the *gymnasiale Mädchenschule* in Vienna. Seraphine Puchleitner, who in 1902 was the first woman to earn a Ph.D. at Graz, passed her certification the following year, when women no longer needed special permission to take the examination. These developments in Austria preceded by a few years the admission of women to the Prussian certification for secondary teachers, the examination *pro facultate docendi* (VfeFW 1897: 6; 1898: 12; 1899: 40; and 1900: 13; Braun et al. 1930: 295; Forkl and Koffmahn 1968: 75; Aigner 1977: 119-22; Albisetti 1988: 250-53).

Admission of Austrian women to the medical faculties came only in 1900, four years after the decree on Nostrifikation of foreign degrees, and one year after the German Bundesrat had allowed certification of female physicians on the basis of audited courses taken at German universities. At Vienna, several women already enrolled in the philosophical faculties immediately took advantage of the opportunity to transfer to the study of medicine. At Graz, the first medical student, Maria Schuhmeister, also switched from the philosophical faculty in 1900. At Innsbruck, however, the pioneering female medical student did not enroll until 1911 (Sablik 1968: 817-18; Aigner 1979: 45-70; Steibl 1987: 39, 92).

The law faculties remained closed to Austrian women until after World War I, though students enrolled in the philosophical faculties could take courses in the Staatswissenschaften. This ban continued despite the strong support for the admission of women expressed by the law professor Edmund Bernatzik, who at the turn of the century even rallied a narrow majority of the faculty at Vienna behind his position. The most frequently advanced explanation for the resistance to female law students is that the government feared it could not prevent women with law degrees from claiming positions in the civil service (Lind 1961: 87-88; 30 Jahre 1927: 9). Yet in Prussia similar fears, expressed by the then Minister of the Interior Theobald von Bethmann Hollweg and others, helped to delay matriculation in all faculties until 1908, but did not keep the legal faculties closed when others finally did open (Albisetti 1988: 247-48). A more thorough examination of the resistance to female law students in Austria thus seems necessary.

Only one woman, Elise Richter, became a *Privatdozentin* in Austria before World War I; but this was one more than in Germany. Richter had passed the Matura in 1897 at the age of thirty-two and had been one of the first three women to matriculate at the University of Vienna. She received her doctorate in French in 1901 and published what she hoped would be her *Habilitationsschrift* in 1904. A three-year struggle ensued, during which other universities were consulted on the question of female instructors, before she finally gained approval from the university and the Ministry of Education (Pulgram 1986: 425-32; Christman 1980; Heindl and Tichy 1990: 221-31; Steibl 1987: 71). Similar debates took place around the same time in Prussia, where Marie von Linden sought the *Habilitation* at the University of Bonn. She did not succeed in becoming a *Privatdozentin*, but the Prussian government did grant her the title of Professor and appointed her to the directorship of a university laboratory (Albisetti 1988: 255).

As was the case in Germany, a high percentage of the first generation of women students in Austria came from the educated middle classes: Engelbrecht estimates that half of them had fathers with university degrees. In contrast to the German case, the early female students in Austria, despite exceptions such as Elise Richter, were not significantly older than their male colleagues. The main reason for this appears to have been the lack, in Austria, of the large numbers of women teachers who entered the German universities relatively late in life once the opportunity to do so became available (Engelbrecht 1986: 292; Cohen 1987: 313). Particularly striking, though not mentioned at all by Engelbrecht, was the high percentage of Jewish girls and women among those Austrians pursuing secondary and higher education in the years before World War I. As Marsha Rozenblit has noted, in Vienna "in 1895/96, 57 percent of all Lyzeum students were Jewish, and in 1910 the figure was still 46 percent" (Rozenblit 1983: 121). It would also appear that many of the Austrian women who studied in Switzerland came from Jewish families. Among female physicians trained in Austria, eleven of the first eighteen graduates at Vienna, and six of the first twenty at Graz, were Jewish. So was Elise Richter, who was to die in a concentration camp. As of 1911/12, Jewish women comprised 37 percent of female students at Vienna (Sablik 1968: 818; Aigner 1979: 69; Heindl 1987: 337). Jewish women were also over represented at Prussian universities in this era, although they supplied a more modest 21.7 percent of the women students at Berlin and 12.9 percent overall in 1913/14 (Albisetti 1988: 290).

Over representation of Jewish girls and women mirrored, of course, an under representation of their Catholic counterparts in the secondary schools and universities. Until now, scholars working on Austrian women's history, concerned primarily with secular reformers and institutions, have not seriously addressed the impact of Catholicism on female education or the feminist movement in the Dual Monarchy. The major research projects currently under way in Austria, as described by Brigitte Mazohl-Wallnig, also do not appear to be examining this issue (Mazohl-Wallnig 1991: 283-86). A sharper focus on the impact of Catholicism on German-Austrian women in this era, similar perhaps to Bonnie Smith's (1981) work on France, would appear to be the most fruitful approach to more nuanced explanations of both Austrian "backwardness" in women's education and the large percentages of Jewish and ethnic minority women among the first generations of women students.

The recent article by Katherine David offers a promising start to rethinking Austrian women's history. David attributes the relative strength of Czech feminism in part to Czech "ambivalence about the Catholic church" (David 1991: 39). Research by David and others on Czech women also suggests that the nationalist movement did not hinder the pursuit of feminist goals, but tended to support or even to stimulate demands for women's rights (David 1991; Volet-Jeanneret 1988). That ethnic tension in the Dual Monarchy was not always detrimental to women's interests is also seen in the productive competition found in Gymnasium courses for girls in the early 1890s, and in the way the needs of Muslim women helped to open medical practice for Austrian women.

How well does the picture of Austrian backwardness painted by Engelbrecht and Heindl hold up? In several general policy areas, such as the minimal public support given to secondary education for girls, the long delay in allowing women to teach academic courses in the Lyzeen, and the refusal to open the legal faculties to women until 1919, Austrian practices were more restrictive than those of Prussia or the German Empire. Yet Austria pursued less restrictive policies with regard to several issues – the opening of the Matura in 1872, the toleration of auditing by women after 1878, the hiring of female physicians by the government, the permission granted to women to take the certification examination for male secondary teachers, and the *Habilitation* of Elise Richter. In giving women elementary teachers equal pay with their male colleagues, Austria was more progressive than of any of the German states and the vast majority of European countries and American states as well. There is clearly a need for additional research into the origins and implementation of government policies, the growth of private and public secondary schools for girls, the influence of the Catholic Church on attitudes toward female education, and the activities of women's groups outside Vienna. Such research, when combined with comparative studies, especially of other Catholic countries, will illuminate further the issue of Austrian "backwardness" with respect to educational and employment opportunities for women.

Since the completion of this essay, the two works listed below have appeared in Austria. Based on archival sources, they provide more detailed and regionally differentiated information on the girls' schools and conidtions for women teachers, but they do not offer a major challenge to the views expressed.

Mazohl-Wallnig, B., ed. 1995. *Bürgerliche Frauenkultur im 19, Jahrhundert.* Vienna, Cologne, and Weimar.

Simon, G. 1993. *Hintertreppen zum Elfenbeinturm: Höhere Mädchenbildung in Österreich. Anfänge und Entwicklungen.* Vienna.

# References

Aigner, R. 1977. "Seraphine Puchleitner: Der erste weibliche Student und Doktor an der Universität Graz." *Blätter für Heimatkunde* 51: 119-122.

———. 1979. "Die Grazer Ärztinnen aus der Zeit der Monarchie." *Zeitschrift des historischen Vereins für Steiermark* 70: 45-70.

Albert, E. 1895. *Die Frauen und das Studium der Medizin.* Vienna.

Albisetti, J.C. 1988. *Schooling German Girls and Women: Secondary and Higher Education in the Nineteenth Century.* Princeton.

Allen, A.T. 1991. *Feminism and Motherhood in Germany.* New Brunswick.

Allgemeiner Österreichischer Frauenverein (cited as AÖF). 1893ff. *Jahresbericht.* Vienna.

Anderson, B.S. and Zinsser, J.P. 1988. *A History of Their Own: Women in Europe from Prehistory to the Present.* Vol. 2. New York.

Anderson, H. 1992. *Utopian Feminism: Women's Movements in Fin-de-Siècle Vienna.* New Haven.

Bell, S.G., and Offen, K., eds. 1983. *Woman, the Family and Freedom: The Debate in Documents.* 2 vols. Stanford.

Boxer, M. and Quataert, J., eds. 1987. *Connecting Spheres: Women in the Western World, 1500 to the Present.* New York.

Braun, M.A., et al., eds. 1930. *Frauenbewegung, Frauenbildung und Frauenarbeit in Österreich.* Vienna.

Bridenthal, R., Koonz, C. and Stuard, S., eds. 1987. *Becoming Visible: Women in European History.* 2d ed. Boston.

Bund Österreichischer Frauenvereine. 1908. *Die Unterrichtsanstalten für die weibliche Bevölkerung der im Reichsrate vertretenen Königreiche und Länder der österreichisch-ungarischen Monarchie.* Vienna.

Christmann, H.H. 1980. "Frau und 'Jüdin' an der Universität: Die Romanistin Elise Richter." *Abhandlungen der Geistes- und Sozialwissenschaftlichen Klasse, Akademie der Wissenschaften und Literatur.* Vienna.

Cohen, G. 1987. "Die Studenten der Wiener Universität von 1860 bis 1900." In *Wegenetz europäischen Geistes.* Vol. 2. Eds. R.G. Plaschka and K. Mack. Munich.

David, K. 1991. "Czech Feminists and Nationalism in the Late Habsburg Monarchy." *Journal of Women's History* 3: 26-45.

*30 Jahre Frauenstudium in Österreich.* 1927. Vienna.

Engelbrecht, H. 1984. *Geschichte des österreichischen Bildungswesens.* Vol. 3, *Von der frühen Aufklärung bis zum Vormärz.* Vienna.

———. 1986. *Geschichte des österreichischen Bildungswesens.* Vol. 4, *Von 1848 bis zum Ende der Monarchie.* Vienna.

Evans, R.J. 1976. *The German Feminist Movement, 1894-1933.* Beverly Hills and London.

———. 1977. *The Feminists: Women's Emancipation Movements in Europe, America, and Australasia, 1840-1920.* London.

Fellner, G. 1986. "Athenäum: Die Geschichte einer Frauenhochschule in Wien." *Zeitgeschichte* 14: 99-115.

Forkl, M. and Koffmahm, E., eds. 1968. *Frauenstudium und akademische Frauenarbeit in Österreich.* Vienna.

Friese, M. 1890. *Chronik der Luisenstiftung zu Berlin.* Berlin.

Freeze, K. J. 1985. "Medical Education for Women in Austria: A Study in the Politics of the Czech Women's Movement in the 1890s." In *Women, State, and Party in Eastern Europe.* Ed. S.L. Wolchik and A.G. Meyer, 51-63. Durham, N.C.

Gahlings, I. and E. Moering. 1961. *Die Volksschullehrerin.* Heidelberg.

Göllner, R. 1986. "Mädchenbildung um Neunzehnhundert: Eugenie Schwarzwald und ihre Schulen." Ph.D. dissertation, University of Vienna.

Hardt, W. 1905. *Die Lehrerinnenfrage.* Lissa.

Harper, R.S. 1985. "Gabriele Gräfin von Wartensleben and the Birth of *Gestaltpsychologie.*" *Journal of the History of the Behavioral Sciences* 41: 118-23.

Heindl, W. 1987. "Ausländische Studentinnen an der Universität Wien vor dem ersten Weltkrieg: Zum Problem der studentischen Migrationen in Europa." In *Wegenetz europäischen Geistes.* Vol. 2, Eds. R.G. Plaschka and K. Mack. Munich.

Heindl, W. and Tichy, M., eds. 1990. *"Durch Erkenntnis zu Freiheit und Glück ...": Frauen an der Universität Wien (ab 1897).* Vienna.

Hutterer, W. 1978. "Mädchen- und Frauenbildung in Österreich seit 1900: Aufgezeigt am Beispiel der Mittelschulbildung." Ph.D. dissertation, University of Salzburg.

Johanson, C. 1987. *Women's Struggle for Higher Education in Russia, 1855-1900.* Montreal.

Koblitz, A.H. 1983. *A Convergence of Lives: Sofia Kovalevskaia.* Boston.

Kronreif, M.A. 1985. "Frauenemanzipation und Lehrerin: Ein Beitrag zur Sozialgeschichte der Pflichtschullehrerin in Österreich." Ph.D. dissertation, University of Salzburg.

Lange, H. 1900-1901. "Aesculapia Victrix." *Die Frau* 8: 346.

Lind, A. 1961. "Das Frauenstudium in Österreich, Deutschland und der Schweiz." Law dissertation, University of Vienna.

Machan, A. 1901. *Über Frauenbildung und Frauenbewegung in Kärnten zu Ende des 19. Jahrhunderts.* Klagenfurt.

Margadant, J. 1990. *Madame le Professeur: Women Educators in the Third Republic.* Princeton.

Mayer, A., ed. 1952. *Geschichte der österreichischen Mädchenmittelschule.* Vienna.

Mazohl-Wallnig, B. 1991. "Women's History in Austria." In *Writing Women's History.* Ed. K. Offen, R.R. Pierson, and J. Rendall, 279-90. Bloomington, Ind.

Pulgram, E. 1986. "In Pluribus Prima: Elise Richter (1865-1943)." *Cross Currents* 7: 425-32.

Riemer, E. and J. Fout, eds. 1980. *European Women: A Documentary History, 1789-1945.* New York.

Rohner, H. 1972. *Die ersten 30 Jahre des medizinischen Frauenstudiums an der Universität Zürich, 1867-1897.* Zurich.

Rozenblit, M.L. 1983. *The Jews of Vienna, 1867-1914.* Albany.

Sablik, K. 1968. "Zum Beginn des Frauenstudiums an der Wiener medizinischen Fakultät." *Wiener medizinische Wochenschrift* 118: 817-19.

Schirmacher, K. 1912. *The Modern Women's Rights Movement.* New York.

Schraner, E. 1938. *Hundert Jahre Lehrerinnen- und Arbeitslehrerinnenbildung im Kanton Bern, 1838-1938.* Bern.

Smith, B.G. 1981. *Ladies of the Leisure Class: The Bourgeoises of Northern France in the Nineteenth Century.* Princeton.

Stanton, T., ed. 1884. *The Woman Question in Europe.* New York.

Steibl, M. 1987. "Frauenstudium in Österreich vor 1945, dargestellt am Beispiel der Innsbrucker Studentinnen." Ph.D. dissertation, University of Innsbruck.

*30 Jahra Frauenstudium in Österreich.* 1927. Vienna.

Tuve, J. 1984. *The First Russian Women Physicians.* Newtonville, Mass.

Verein für erweiterte Frauenbildung in Wien (cited as VfeFW). 1888ff. *Jahresbericht.* Vienna.

Vietor, A., ed. 1924. *A Woman's Quest: The Life of Marie E. Zakrzewska, M.D.* New York.

Volet-Jeanneret, H. 1988. *La femme bourgeoise à Prague, 1860-1895: De la philanthropie à l'émancipation.* Geneva.

Wiechowski, W. 1903. *Frauenleben und -Bildung in Prag im 19. Jahrhundert.* Leipzig.

Witzmann, R., ed. 1984. *Die Frau im Korsett: Wiener Frauenalltag zwischen Klischee und Wirklichkeit, 1848-1920.* Vienna.

Zehender, F. 1883. *Geschichtliche Darstellung des öffentlichen Unterrichtes für Mädchen in der Stadt Zürich von 1774 bis 1883.* Zurich.

*Chapter 4*

⤫

# WOMEN IN AUSTRIAN POLITICS, 1890-1934
## Goals and Visions

...........................

*Birgitta Bader-Zaar*

## Introduction

Woman shall stimulate politics with her fresh and unexpended strength, ennoble it with her higher morality and her stronger feelings for social responsibility, with the gifts which form the essence of her femininity, especially with her motherliness and her instinct for the home, she shall complement the work of man in the community (Urban 1919: 1).

The terms "social responsibility," "motherliness," and "instinct for the home" evoke images that have effectively relegated women to the field of social and family legislation in politics to this very day. Through these concepts, women have been and are still discouraged from fully utilizing their political rights. For Gisela Urban, however, who published the above statement after the introduction of female suffrage in Austria, the qualities she ascribed to women were essential for her vision of a society endowed with social harmony, social justice, and peace.

How women's role as voter and politician should be modeled once they achieved political equality was one of the main issues of the campaign for female suffrage in Austria. In pressing for the emancipation of women and formulating visions of women's profound moral influence on politics and society, both male and female proponents of female suffrage attached great hopes to women's right to vote. Similar patterns can also be observed in the history of women's suffrage in other countries.

The idea that giving women the vote would enhance the general welfare and promote a new, more moral society constituted the basis of what has been called the "expediency argument" in the history of American women's suffrage. Some studies on the female suffrage campaign in the United States tend to view this strain of the suffrage argument primarily as a strategy in reaction to the changed political environment, as a response to opponents who protested the dissolution of separate spheres for men and women, or as mere "rhetoric" (Kraditor 1971: 43-44; Baker 1984: 642; Cott 1987: 100). Felice D. Gordon, however, concluded from her study of suffragist activities in New Jersey in the period following the women's enfranchisement, that some individuals in the women's movement in the United States genuinely believed the argument for a specifically female role in promoting social welfare (Gordon 1986). Karen Offen has emphasized the need to reconsider the history of suffrage arguments based on the idea of a "distinctive contribution" of women to society as childbearers and nurturers in contrast to the individualist mode of argumentation (Offen 1988: 135-36, 153). She has defined this approach as relational ("women's rights as women in relation to men") thus avoiding terms like "strategy" and "self-interest," which are implicit in "expediency arguments". Austrian and German historians have also basically dealt with the political visions of suffragists as genuine opinions to be taken seriously (Schöffmann 1986a; Bussemer 1988: 199-203; Clemens 1988: 78-89). In the suffrage movements of the German-speaking countries, "relational" views on the political qualities of women were widely accepted, not only in the moderate liberal movement but also among several social democratic women. Indeed such views were far more important to their cause than were arguments based on the natural rights of women.

My essay examines the goals and visions of Austrian suffragists in the context of the circumstances they faced in attempting to realize those goals and visions after the introduction of women's suffrage in 1918. It also points out differences and similarities between the Austrian case and the experience of the United States. As elsewhere, the realization of Austrian women's goals proved to be difficult. To begin with, the political and social realities of a post-World War I society had to be coped with. In addition, parties tended to be more interested in women's voting behavior than in their political integration, while women themselves failed to vote solidly for the goals of the women's movement. While the Social Democratic, Catholic, and liberal women's movements did not relinquish their views on women's positive value for politics, their evaluation of women's position vis-à-vis politics and the state was increasingly negative towards the end of the 1920s. The debate over whether an autonomous organization of women outside party structures might be a solution to the general absence of female power within the political arena resulted in the creation of an independent women's party by a group of liberal women. The end of democracy and the installation of an authoritarian regime in 1933/34, however, signalled the end of all such dreams of enhancing the political influence of women.

## The Suffrage Movement, 1890-1918

While the women's movement in the United States had focused on the participation of women in the political arena from the middle of the nineteenth century on, Austrian women took up the demand for the right to vote much later. The budding women's movement in Austria was more interested in educational and occupational opportunities for women. Asking for political rights was an extremely difficult undertaking, considering the political repression following the revolution of 1848 and the dominant ideology of separate spheres, which regarded politics as the preserve of men and was advocated by the powerful Catholic church. The restraint of the suffrage campaign itself reflects the idiosyncratic nature of Austrian conditions. As Irma Troll-Borostyáni, a seminal theorist of the liberal women's movement, put it, the Austrian women's movement purposely distanced itself from the "vigorous espousal" of suffrage rights voiced by American and English suffragists. Troll-Borostányi attributed this to the limited interest of Austrian women in political life, their scanty political knowledge, and the very different political context, one which required "wise restraint" (Troll-Borostyáni 1902: 5). There was also a practical reason for the belated demands of Austrian women for political rights: some women already possessed the vote. But in accordance with the suffrage laws relating to municipal councils, provincial diets, and the lower house of parliament (Reichsrat), women were allowed to vote, although usually only by male proxy, if they paid a certain amount of taxes on real estate or income from employment and business, and did not live in major cities such as Vienna or Prague (Zaar 1994: 351-64, 368-70).

This changed towards the end of the nineteenth century in some provinces and municipalities. As men began to demand universal male suffrage and the franchise began to be expanded, the premise of linking the right to vote to property holdings and income gradually became obsolete. Instead, the vote came to be viewed as an inherent right of the individual. In the course of this evolution, gender gained significance as a qualification for enfranchisement. The belief that women's place was not in politics led several provincial diets henceforth to exclude women from suffrage. For example, tax-paying women in Lower Austria, with the exception of the few women who possessed real estate, lost their right to vote for the provincial diet in 1888. One year later, discussions in the diet about also excluding tax-paying women from the municipal franchise served as the incentive for women to launch the suffrage campaign (Guschlbauer 1974).

The campaign operated on a far smaller scale than the American or British suffrage movements, and was also devoid of any militant action. The first Austrian suffragists were mainly teachers already active in a female teachers' association that stood in the liberal middle-class wing of the women's movement. They hoped to win support for their goal through public meetings and petitions to the Reichsrat and the government. A few years later, in 1892 and 1893, the Social Democrats also took up the demand for women's suffrage.

Neither movement was able to achieve much until 1905 and 1906, when universal and equal suffrage for men was discussed in parliament. While the Social Democratic women's movement obeyed its party's ruling that it should suppress its claims in order to let the universal male suffrage bill pass without any problems, a moderate group of liberal women viewed this as a favorable occasion to demand women's suffrage and founded a women's suffrage committee. An official association registered with the authorities was never possible in the Austrian half of the Habsburg Empire because women were forbidden to be members of political associations by the Association Law of 1867. The law inhibited the organizing potential of the liberal women's movement, which, unlike the Social Democratic women's movement, worked outside party structures.

After universal and equal parliamentary suffrage for men had been introduced at the beginning of 1907, both the liberal and the Social Democratic movements stepped up their campaign for women's enfranchisement. The latter held street demonstrations on 1 May (workers' day), and, from 1911, on international women's days; the liberal women crusaded in a quieter manner, with meetings and deputations. Differences in strategy and ideology were impediments to cooperation between the two organizations, and caused a deep split that ran roughly along class lines. Ethnicity and nationalism were additional divisive elements: Czech, Polish, Slovenian, and Hungarian women formed their own movements and conducted suffrage activities apart from the German-speaking organizations.

In Austria women's suffrage was a popular cause neither among the population nor in the legislatures. Of the parties represented in the Reichsrat the Social Democrats were the only ones that grafted this demand onto their platform, but their support was hardly overwhelming. Motions for women's enfranchisement by Liberal, Czech or Social Democratic deputies in the Reichsrat were either met with laughter or not debated at all. Only with the collapse of the Empire at the end of World War I did profound changes in the state make women's enfranchisement possible.

As alluded to earlier, some of the strongest arguments of the suffrage movement emphasized how women could influence or even change political life once they achieved the vote. Essentially such reflections were predicated upon, and worked in conjunction with, the prevailing gender ideology of the nineteenth century, according to which women and men had distinct but complementary qualities. The women's movement, however, modified this ideology and harnessed it to their own ends. Instead of attributing passivity to women and aggressiveness to men, and declaring therefore that women did not belong in politics, suffragists took a positive view of women's alleged "inherent" qualities. These not only made women fit for politics but enabled them to solve all human problems.

The radical suffragists at the beginning of the movement propagated more practical arguments, according to which women's needs would direct their possibilities in politics. To the radicals, suffrage was the means for the emancipation of women. More pressing objectives were a thorough reform of the educational system (especially, better schooling for girls), and attention to the economic and social interests of women, including better and healthier working conditions, prenatal care for mothers, and a reform of the marriage law.[1] Initially the middle-class women's movement, however, did not think that it could realize its goals within the party system. Liberal at heart, and opposing the conservative Christian Socials openly at every election (*Neues Frauenleben* 1902, 14/10: 21) it preferred to leave its organiza-

---

1. See Auguste Fickert's demands in *Zum Frauenstimmrecht* 1894; see also *Neues Wiener Tagblatt*, 23 March 1899: 4.

tion, the *Allgemeiner Österreichischer Frauenverein* (General Austrian Women's Society) founded in 1893, politically neutral. "Political constellations," as Auguste Fickert, the president of the Frauenverein declared, ought to be used for the claims of the women's movement. The main task, however, was "the moral reorganization of the world," which was only to be accomplished if women "stand free from one-sided party interests, above the daily bustle of politics, [and] overlook the whole with a serene eye, become absorbed in themselves, study the nature of mankind and the needs of society with a scrutinizing mind and a just heart" (Fickert 1898: 1). Thus, once women had gained the franchise, Fickert envisioned them working initially in the field of general welfare: supporting better financing for education, less money for military expenditure, new nursery schools in the municipalities, more hospitals, and improved street cleaning (*Neues Wiener Tagblatt*, 23 March 1899: 4).

The moderate middle-class suffrage movement of the early twentieth century reflected Fickert's views in part, but stressed the concept of woman as the "better" sex. Notions of women's innate qualities took the place of earlier beliefs that women would diligently apply themselves to studying the ways and means of furthering the moral development of civilization. Several statements in a commemorative volume of an international conference on women's suffrage in Vienna in 1913 underline this point: Gisela Urban argued that woman wished "to complement the work of man and to make it more fruitful for both sexes, especially through the victory of the idea of motherhood in all the walks of life for the future generations" (*Das Frauenstimmrecht* 1913: 4). In the field of politics women would introduce new values into Parliament, as the president of the *Bund Österreichischer Frauenvereine* (League of Austrian Women's Societies), Marianne Hainisch, stated (*Das Frauenstimmrecht* 1913: 15). Daisy Minor believed that women would fight against egotism, prejudice and hatred, all elements of the male political world. Against these principles, female values such as morality, devotion, motherliness, reconciliation of the antagonisms between races and ideologies as well as between specific interests and social problems, would be arrayed (*Das Frauenstimmrecht* 1913: 18). During World War I, Maria Klausberger also criticized male politics as the politics of power and interest, "which can of course confront the existing with what ought to be, but only destroys the given and cannot build up anything because political personalities and creative forces, dissipated in tedious party politics, are missing" (Klausberger 1917: 3).

The contempt that these women showed for male politics was a result of the discord that social and national antagonisms had sown in Austrian politics and which had all but paralyzed parliamentary life. This climate of dissension was also one of the reasons their goals, especially that of women's suffrage, were not realized. Stopping short of attempting to analyze the political problems of the day, the moderate liberal women's movement simply expressed a general wish for peace and unity. In their eyes, women's qualities were the perfect panacea for Austrian politics. Only women were equipped with the necessary values to achieve a peaceful and united state and a better, more just society.

Unlike liberal women, Social Democratic women did not locate the source of Austria's political problems or their subordinate status in male actions. Predictably, their enemy was capitalism, and together with their male comrades, they strove for a socialist society in which equal rights and economic justice would be realized. Women's suffrage was a step towards this new world. As Therese Schlesinger explained:

> Equal suffrage for all men and women is certainly not our highest and ultimate goal, but it is one of the most important and indispensable means to get nearer to our goals. It shall help us to bring the exploitation of the working class and the special oppression of the working-class woman to an end, it shall pave the way on which we will march forward, out of a condition which is an unhealthy one for all people and signifies misery and humiliation for the largest part of the population, especially for most women, towards intellectual and moral completion, liberty and happiness (Schlesinger 1910: 26-27).

Despite their belief in the primacy of class over gender solidarity, Social Democratic women often shared the middle-class movement's views on the unique values of women. Adelheid Popp, the leader of the Austrian Social Democratic women's movement, demanded suffrage "exactly because we are womanly and motherly" (*Arbeiter-Zeitung*, 20 March 1911). Municipal suffrage was the field in which women's special suitability for political life could best be demonstrated. Popp pointed out that public relief, housing, and schooling, which were all elements of local administration, required an understanding for social work and a sensitive heart – in short, female qualities (Popp 1918: 3). In Emmy Freundlich's view the municipality was a big household that needed "the helping hands" of homemakers (Freundlich 1908: 2). Around the idea that housewives were better qualified than men to deal with municipal concerns, Social Democratic and liberal opinions coincided perfectly. Liberal women also believed that local administration, insofar as it governed schooling, poor-law administration, housing, traffic, street cleaning, and supplies, had to do with the same kind of work that housewives did (on a smaller scale) at home (Gerber 1912: 89).

A few male proponents of women's suffrage actually agreed that women could have beneficial effects on the state. However, they customarily referred to women as mothers in this respect, rather than as active politicians. Their better understanding of public life would put enfranchised women in a better position to impart the values of a civic education to their children.[2] Ideas about women's actual work in politics reflected commonly held views of beneficent feminine qualities. Women would protect the weak and those in need of help and would guarantee the absence of war in the future.[3]

Neither female nor male proponents of women's right to vote found widespread approval for their visions of a new society purified by politically active women. Opponents exhorted women not to invest their "feminine" qualities in the public sphere, but rather to infuse them into family life, thereby assuring a peaceful home. Should a woman leave home to pursue political activities, the realm nature (or God) had assigned her would suffer and the family would be destroyed. This would, in turn, endanger the state, which rested upon the family.[4]

The Catholic church especially sustained the belief that women were destined to fulfill their duties in life only at home (Schindler 1906: 96-97). Interestingly, it nevertheless tolerated women campaigning at elections for the Christian Social party. Towards the end of World War I, when it became clear that women's suffrage would be realized in the near future, both the church and its political representatives, the Christian Socials, slowly began to forgo their hostility to the participation of women in political decision making. Ideally, however, women were to remain among themselves, and vote only for their own representative body in a state in which the interests of all occupational interest groups of society were safeguarded (Seipel 1930: 36).

Another line of attack employed by opponents to female suffrage was to use biology as an argument. Women were declared physically

---

2. Gemeinderat Umlauft, in *Protokolle der Sitzungen des Gemeinderathes* der k.k. Reichshaupt- und Residenzstadt Wien 1872, vol. 2, 19 November 1872, 2159; see also the liberal deputy August Kaiser, in *Stenographische Protokolle über die Sitzungen des Hauses der Abgeordneten*, 17th session, 14 November 1906: 39864; or the Social Democrat Adolf Braun (Braun 1912: 3).

3. See August Kaiser as in note 1. Popper-Lynkeus 1913, 157; the Social Democrat Karl Seitz, in *Stenographische Protokolle über die Sitzungen des Hauses der Abgeordneten*, 22nd session, vol. 1, 13 June 1917: 185.

4. Gemeinderat Friedmann, *Protokolle der Sitzungen des Gemeinderathes der k.k. Reichshaupt- und Residenzstadt Wien 1872*, vol. 2, 19 November 1872: 2159; Ettel 1890: 23.

and psychologically unfit for political activity. Their brains were alleged to be lighter and more finely organized, and their nerves weaker than men's (Ettel 1890: 17). They were excitable, emotional, soft in feeling, and tender of soul, qualities quite unsuitable for the rational and tough world of politics.[5]

As the debates in Parliament were to demonstrate, especially when women's suffrage was close to success, the impact of women's votes upon *party power* was the real sticking point for those responsible for changing franchise laws. Foremost in their minds was the question of how women would use their votes and who would profit. In the opinion of the conservatives, women were radicals at heart and would align themselves with the Social Democrats. Yet according to male members of both the Liberal and Social Democratic parties, women stood under the whip of the clergy and would therefore favor the Christian Socials. As one participant of the Social Democratic party conference in 1903 bluntly put it: "Women are being led so nicely by the fool's rope of the priests that we have to be careful in our agitation for women's suffrage" (*Protokoll Gesamtparteitag 1903*: 130). Evidently, such convictions were widespread within the Social Democratic party, although, as mentioned above, that part had already adopted women's suffrage as part of its platform as early as 1892.

Women repeatedly argued against these claims. Already in 1886, Irma von Troll-Borostyáni identified the Catholic church and its influence as a formidable foe in the fight for women's enfranchisement. She was convinced that the vote would educate women politically and thus lessen the church's influence over women (Troll-Borostyáni 1886: 4). Similarly, the Social Democrats Adelheid Popp and Therese Schlesinger attempted to convince their party comrades that suffrage would not only offer women valuable political training, but would also enhance their capacity to think independently (*Verhandlungen Gesamtparteitag 1899*: 129; *Frauenwahlrecht und Arbeiterinnenschutz 1908*: 29). The subject was to reach its climax during the debates over women's enfranchisement in the newly founded First Republic shortly after World War I.

Similar strategic and ideological chords were struck in the American suffragist campaign.[6] The first national women's convention in 1852 hailed woman as "the redeemer, the regenerator of the world"

---

5. Alois Bahr, in the provincial diet of Upper Austria, 16 October 1889, cit. in Slapnicka and Marckhgott (1987: 57); Schindler (1906: 98). The idea of the intellectual superiority of men as a result of brain size remained popular among persistent opponents after the introduction of women's suffrage (Eberhard 1927: 94).
6. See also Elshtain (1981: 231-39).

(Stanton, Anthony, and Gage 1981: 524). Early suffragists, such as Elizabeth Cady Stanton, accused male-dominated government of

> civil, religious, and racial disorganization. The male element is a destructive force, stern, selfish, aggrandizing, loving war, violence, conquest, acquisition, breeding in the material and moral world alike discord, disorder, disease, and death ... ."[7]

Stanton espoused "a new evangel of womanhood ... exalt[ing] purity, virtue, morality, [and] true religion" as the means to lift mankind to higher levels of civilization. In more concrete terms, crusading women called for the abolition of prostitution, the curtailment of the abuse of liquor, and improved conditions for women at home and at work.

In the new phase of the suffrage movement (around 1910) the role of women in enhancing the general welfare and protecting the home became important elements of argument. The reforms demanded by the Progressive movement found support among suffragists who willingly took up the fight against the vested interests of big business and the political machines (Kraditor 1971: 48) and the ills of modern urban life. As Jane Addams wrote: "unsanitary housing, poisonous sewage, contaminated water, infant mortality, the spread of contagion, adulterated food, impure milk, smoke-laden air, ill-ventilated factories, dangerous occupations, juvenile delinquency, unwholesome crowding, prostitution and drunkenness" were "enemies" of the modern cities (Jane Addams cited in Hinding 1986: 46). Converging on Austrian women's opinions, city administration in her eyes was simply "enlarged housekeeping." Finally, with the outbreak of World War I, a consensus among members of the women's movement held that women would always raise their voices for peace (Kraditor 1971: 50).

That women would bring a "gentle and refining" influence into practical politics was also a popular view among senators and representatives supporting the Nineteenth Amendment (Sen. W.L. Jones 1913, 63 Congress, vol. 50/5: 5120). However, they did not expect any sudden "panacea for all ills," but a gradual change in the economic and social conditions of the country (Sen. H. F. Ashurst 1914 and M. C. Kelly 1915, 63 Congress, vol. 51/2: 2025; vol. 52/2: 1411).

As in Austria, however, some opponents of American women's enfranchisement denied that women would have a positive effect on political life. A female member of the movement opposing women's

---

7. Speech at the first women's suffrage convention in Washington, 1869, cit. in Scott and Scott (1982: 63). Socialists advanced similar ideas later (Malkiel n.d.: 12-13).

suffrage mused: "Give her the ballot and she will of necessity ally her-self with one party or the other and thus become but another spoke in the wheel of our political machinery. We seek to conserve the Ameri-can home and family life...."(Chittenden 1914: 6). That the home was "the realm over which woman is best fitted to reign" (Sen. J. K. Var-daman 1914, 63 Congress, vol. 51/5: 4338) was the standard argu-ment among those members of Congress opposed to female suffrage.

Thus, the impact of female enfranchisement on party power was also an issue in the United States. This was especially true of southern Democrats, who did not relish the idea of a vastly expanded Afro-American electorate. Additionally, in the 1860s and 1870s a few voices protested that women's suffrage would enhance Catholicism. Somewhat later, German-American socialists repudiated the vote for women on the grounds of women's alleged conservatism. The oppo-site view, that women were radical and would surely promote bol-shevism, was popular among female opponents and Democrats at the outset of the Red Scare.

Although political, socio-economic, and cultural differences did exist between the United States and Austria, expectations about women's enfranchisement were basically the same. The ideas of the suffrage movement spread easily as women's movements established wide international contacts and kept abreast of developments in other countries. For example, the refining influence of women in the few American states that had already introduced women's suffrage, such as Wyoming in 1869 or Colorado in 1893, received wide atten-tion in Austria.

The dissolution of the Habsburg Empire and the creation of the new Austrian Republic after World War I presented the opportunity for women's enfranchisement. While some Social Democrats still believed that women's right to vote meant a setback for them, party leaders felt obliged to fight for universal suffrage for both sexes as the foundation of the Republic's suffrage laws. Women's enfranchise-ment was, after all, part of the party platform, and female members of the party were pressing for it. Pulling back from this pledge would have made the party appear insincere in the wake of elections.[8] Their political opponents, especially the powerful Christian Socials, were uncomfortable with the prospect of a constituency consisting of a majority of women, but they yielded to the Social Democrats' new power. Nevertheless, they searched for outlets that would lessen the impact of women voters.

8. See also Renner n.d.: 307-11.

Consequently, it was not the issue of whether women should be allowed to vote that ruled post-war debates, but rather the problem of how to manipulate women voters to party advantage.[9] Strategies included raising the number of male voters until their number equalled that of female voters. The most explosive proposal, setting off numerous debates and igniting fiery newspaper commentaries, concerned the *Wahlpflicht*, the legal obligation to go to the polls. This was an idea advanced by the Christian Socials who feared that women who held a less activist interest in politics, and were therefore more liable to vote conservative, would stay away from the polls, were they not forced to vote. This, in turn, would leave the field to what the Christian Socials imagined to be the enormous number of radical women. The quarrel was finally resolved by leaving it to the provinces to decide if they wanted obligatory elections or not. On 18 December 1918 nearly all Austrian women over the age of 20 were granted the franchise. One group, however, remained unenfranchised until 1923 – prostitutes.[10]

## The Impact of Women on Politics, 1919-1934

"Will she be liberal, clerical, or socialist: will a new element of passion be carried into politics by her, does she want the consolidation of democracy or relentless upheaval?" (*Neue Freie Presse*, 23 November 1918: 1). Politically untried and virtually an unknown factor at their enfranchisement, Austrian women soon lost any threatening aspects their political influence might have held. As voters, women tended to be conservative; as representatives, they were never able to gain enough numerical strength or power to accomplish profound changes, leading to a discussion within the women's movement about the choice between party integration and autonomous organization.

### Women as Voters

The percentage of Austrian women actually going to the polls was fairly high, ranging from 82.1 percent in the first elections on 16 February 1919, with a dip in 1920 to 77.04 percent, and a rise to 89 per-

---

9. See Zaar 1984: 108-116.
10. According to the constitution of October 1920 and enacted in the law of 11 July 1923, prostitutes were not excluded from suffrage any longer (Ucakar 1985: 416). Nevertheless, the Catholic women's movement, for example, protested against prostitutes' right to vote (Paul-Sajowitz 1987: 49; *Wiener Stimmen*, 8 April 1925).

cent in 1930.[11] The disparity between female and male rates of participation decreased from a difference of 4.67 percentage points in 1919 and 6.31 in 1920 to only 2 percentage points in 1930. Women, however, always supplied the majority of voters, approximately 52 to 53 percent. Regional differences in female turnout were considerable. Carinthia, Lower Styria and Burgenland had lower turnouts, while Vienna and, predictably, the two provinces with compulsory voting, Tyrol and Vorarlberg, had high voting rates.

How women voted was of special interest to all parties, but especially to Social Democrats, who carefully analyzed election results with regard to the impact of women. This was made easier by a directive of 30 July 1920 (*Staatsgesetzblatt*, no. 352, § 59) that called for men's and women's votes to be cast in differently colored envelopes – light gray for men and blue-gray for women. Results of the elections of October 1920 conclusively demonstrated that women preferred the conservative Christian Socials (*Beiträge zur Statistik 1921*, nos. 10, 31, and 33). A law of 11 July 1923 finalized the separate counting of women's and men's votes. At the parliamentary elections of 1927 and 1930, the majority of women again tended to favor conservative parties, while about 40 percent voted for the Social Democrats. Substantial regional differences, however, continued to prevail. For example, 57 to 58 percent of all enfranchised Viennese women voted for the Social Democrats, while at least two-thirds of the women in the western provinces of the Tyrol and Vorarlberg cast their votes for conservative parties (*Statistisches Handbuch* 1927, 8: 192; 1931, 12: 210).

It is difficult to compare the data given above with that from other countries, as few statistics were published on the subject.[12] Female voter turnout seems to have been just slightly lower than male in several countries. Specific conditions make comparisons even more difficult. In the United States, for example, several southern states either did not allow Afro-American women to vote, or introduced requirements that were impossible for them to fulfill, such as poll

11. *Statistisches Handbuch für die Republik Österreich*, 1 (1920): 2, 4 (1924): 140, 8 (1927): 190; 12 (1931): 208; Danneberg 1927, table II.
12. In the United States only fragmentary figures exist, for example for Chicago and Pennsylvania (Cott 1987: 319 n. 30). Numbers from Illinois for the presidential elections in 1920 show 70 percent of all women voters supporting the Republicans and reveal a strong inclination by women to support such "moral" issues as prohibition and the rejection of left-wing parties (Cott 1987: 319-20, n. 32). Although the data are fragmentary, the German conditions seem to have been similar to those in Austria. There, too, women tended to vote conservatively (Hofmann-Göttig 1986: 28-29, 31-33).

taxes, literacy tests, or proofs of birth. (Aptheker 1982: 75-76). In other states, similar provisions were directed against immigrants. Furthermore, voter participation in the United States seems to have declined generally from the end of the nineteenth century, due to a sense of inefficacy created by a two-party system in which the parties were securely established in specific regions (Cott 1987: 101-2).

Drawing generalizations from data on women's voter turnout and voting behavior is problematic because a focus on gender tends to disregard the fact that political attitudes also reflect class, ethnic, racial, and, religious alliances, as well as individual economic and social interests. Nevertheless, the myth of a female bloc held sway over all parties, both before and after women's enfranchisement. However, in some American states, efforts to consolidate women's voting power were successful. In New York, for example, where women were enfranchised in 1917, four state legislators were defeated in 1918 because they opposed such social legislation as the minimum wage for women, and child labor laws (Cott 1987: 105).

By contrast, Austrian women turned solely to existing parties to represent their interests within wider-ranging agendas. While the Catholic movement could be satisfied with the large number of women it was able to mobilize for the Christian Socials (Gellott 1991: 118-20), the Social Democrats, the next most powerful group, took pains to interest women in politics and in the goals of their party. The structural obstacles to this aim soon became clear, however, and served to hone the program of Social Democratic women. At the Social Democratic women's conference of 5 November 1920, several participants argued that women needed more free time in order to be active in politics. Thus, kindergartens, collective laundries, and common kitchens in apartment buildings all became demands of the social democratic movement, in order to relieve women of their triple burden as mothers, housewives, and gainful employees, and to give them time for their political interests. As a further help, men were exhorted to share in housekeeping "at least one hour a week"(!) (*Arbeiterinnen-Zeitung*, 21 December 1920: 5-6). Finally, more ade-quate propaganda and its efficient dissemination were called for. As Rudolfine Fleischer, a delegate from the eighth Viennese district, argued, cold, detached newspaper reports did not readily render Social Democratic ideas accessible to women (*Arbeiterinnen-Zeitung*, 21 December 1920: 5-6).

In response to pleas at the women's conference of 1921 that agita-tion be stepped up at women's meetings, at political schools for women, and in newspapers and pamphlets (*Arbeiterinnen-Zeitung*, 6

December 1921: 5), Social Democrats founded a new women's journal, *Die Unzufriedene* (The Discontented). This magazine, inaugurated in 1923, presented easy-to-digest Social Democratic propaganda concerning social legislation (including child welfare, better housing, pensions for old-age and illness) and specific feminist goals such as abortion rights, prenatal care for mothers, marriage and family law reform, higher female employment, and closing the wage gap between women and men. It condemned the Christian Social government in the wake of rising prices and rents, and growing social misery. *Die Unzufriedene* also warned that women could only be good wives and mothers if they kept up with their husbands' interest in politics (*Die Unzufriedene*, 4 October 1924: 2). This was interwoven with articles on homemaking, fashion, and novels. The traditional *Arbeiterinnen-Zeitung* (Women Workers-Newspaper) also changed its appearance. It was renamed *Die Frau* (The Woman) in 1924 and, for some years, dropped its emphasis on critical political articles.

Although female membership in the Social Democratic party rose from 70,000 in 1919 to 223,000 in 1932, or 34 percent of total party membership (Hönigschmied 1952: 63), Social Democrats grew exasperated toward the end of the 1920s with what they considered their meager success in interesting more women in politics. The increase of civil strife in Austria, which was rooted in insurmountable hostilities between Social Democrats and Christian Socials and culminated in confrontations between the military organization of Social Democrats – the *Republikanische Schutzbund* – and the right-wing *Heimwehr*, represented a major obstacle for the Social Democratic women's movement. As noted at the women's conference of 1929, it was especially difficult to recruit followers in rural areas because people known to be left wing were often treated as outlaws by their neighbors (*Die Frau*, 1 November 1929: 13, 26-27). Marianne Pollak, the editor of the *Kleines Blatt*, however, found consolation in women's participation in the unrest of mid-July 1927. After members of the right-wing *Frontkämpfervereinigung* (Veterans Association) who had killed a child and a disabled soldier at a Social Democratic meeting in Schattendorf (Burgenland) in January 1927, had been acquitted by a jury, workers organized a strike and demonstrations. In the course of these demonstrations, the Central Law Court (*Justizpalast*) had been set on fire, and police had been ordered to crush the disturbances, which left 86 workers, women and children as well as four policemen, dead. For Marianne Pollak, the compassion women had demonstrated for their fellow workers through donations and letters of protest had proven that women, whose interests in the party always seemed to lie a little apart from the decisive political questions, have, beyond all problems of welfare, education, sanitation, housekeeping and the co-operatives, *become mature for politics*. It only has to be human, comprehensible, real-life politics. Politics that lays hold of them and which they experience first hand (Pollak 1927: n.p.).

In Pollak's mind, the areas in which women had assumed political responsibility were palpably not those where power and decision-making ability really lay. She was also of the opinion that women needed a specific access to politics, convincing and full of life. Three years later, Sophie Schuler provided a more ideological explanation for women's reluctance to enter politics, while at the same time counseling her fellow comrades not to give up hope:

> He [i.e. Karl Marx] teaches [us] that intellectual views progress much more slowly, always lagging behind economy... No doubt: the economic position of woman has changed fundamentally. But the customs and habits of former times still haunt the brains of the people as if there were no women's work, no double burden, no political equality of the sexes yet (Schuler 1930: n.p.).

The solution was to repeatedly storm this "firm bulwark" which "*will* fall because life is fighting on our side.*" Pollak's emphasis on gender difference and Schuler's emphasis on orthodox ideology articulates the dilemma of the Social Democratic women's movement in failing to integrate ideas on gender and politics into socialist theory.[13] In general, women's movements in Austria continued to stress the concept of gender difference when attempting to win women for politics. The Catholic movement, for example, underscored the family as women's place of life and work, apart from appealing to their wish to uphold Catholic ideals (Schöffmann 1986b: 236; Gellot 1991: 114-116, 128-130).

### Women's Numerical Strength in Legislatures

As was typical among industrialized nations, the number of Austrian women elected to the National Assembly was small. From 1919 to 1934, the number of female members ranged between six and thirteen, or 3.6 to 7.4 percent of all representatives.[14] Most female

13. See also Bandhauer-Schöffmann 1989: 405.
14. Fallmann 1989: 224; Hauch 1995: 92. These figures include women nominated to the National Assembly after elections. Compared to Austria, percentages of female deputies in Germany were a little higher shortly after the introduction of women's suffrage on 30 November 1918 (9.6 percent), but female representation decreased quickly after 1920 to an average of 6.2 percent, and dropped to 3.8 percent in 1933. In absolute numbers, Germany was one of the countries with the highest

deputies were Social Democrats, their number ranging from six to nine, depending on the legislative session. Between one and three women representatives were Christian Socials, and Pan-German female deputies numbered one to two.

Compared to the United States, these figures are relatively high. Only one woman was elected to the House of Representatives in the elections of November 1920. This number rose towards the end of the 1920s, reaching a peak of nine in the Congressional session of 1929-30. Two women were appointed to the Senate, filling seats vacated by deceased husbands or fathers. In the state legislatures, 33 women were representatives in 1921 and 149 in 1929, rising from nearly 0.3 percent to 1.5 percent of all legislators (Chamberlin 1973: 356-63; Cott 1987: 110, 321 n. 38; Chafe 1972: 38).

Political parties ensured that not many women would be elected by placing their names in unfavorable positions on the election lists. Thus, in the first Austrian elections, over one hundred female candidates were listed, but only a handful were successful. Furthermore, the number of female nominations was considerably lower in the provinces than in Vienna (Hawlik 1971: 194-195). As Nancy Cott has argued for the American case, parties did not see any political need to nominate women because women "did not control powerful economic interests or have political debts to redeem" (Cott 1987: 110). Women usually could only become candidates if they showed full loyalty to the party, or if the party anticipated defeat. Women functioned at campaigns primarily as precinct workers and poll watchers, "party housekeepers" as Sara Evans and Harry Boyte have termed them (1986: 95).

The reluctance of Austrian parties to back women for the National Assembly was a major source of criticism among all Austrian women's movements. Social Democratic women, however, abandoned the idea of a quota system for the representation of women in 1919 (Bandhauer-Schöffmann 1989: 404). At the Social Democratic women's conference of 1921, a motion proposed that the number of Social Democratic seats in the National Assembly, provincial diets, and municipal councils allotted to women should be proportionate to the number of Social Democratic women voters (*Arbeiterinnen-Zeitung,* 6 December 1921: 3-4). This motion, however, was later withdrawn without any recorded debate, implying that the women's executive council did not wish to have this question discussed. Only in October

---

rates of female deputies throughout this period, with between 21 and 41 representatives (Strecker and Lenz 1984: 117; Koonz 1976: 667).

1926 did the Social Democratic women's conference resolve that it was necessary,

> in times in which the share of women in all organizations of the working class [had] risen immensely, to take the needs of the female proletariat into account by enlisting women in an appropriate number... and appointing them to influential and responsible positions in the state, the provinces, and the municipalities, [and] in all organizations and institutions directed by workers (*Die Frau,* 1 December 1926: 4).

Yet, as became clear a few months later, attaining more seats within legislatures was not necessarily a priority of the Social Democratic women's movement. Some criticism did erupt after the elections of 1927 because one less female Social Democratic representative had a seat in Parliament; but the preeminent demand of Social Democratic women was greater female influence in worker's organizations. To achieve this sought-for enlarged influence, *Die Frau* called for raising women's party membership and overcoming women's sense of inferiority (1 June 1927: 4-5). Similarly, Adelheid Popp pleaded at the party conference of 1930 to include more women in party positions. They were to be viewed not as women but as equal comrades when party offices entailing responsibility were distributed (Parteitag 1930: 18; Pollak 1931: 12).

In contrast, the Catholic women's movement does not seem to have addressed the issue of women's power within the party structure of the Christian Socials until the 1930s. It was satisfied so long as at least one female held a Christian Social seat in the National Assembly. However, there were no female delegates in the 1927-30 session, and the Catholic women's newsletter *Frauen-Briefe* commented with annoyance after the elections of 1930, when the party did concede one seat to a woman, Emma Kapral:

> We will now not wheedle a sympathetic ear out of male representatives any longer, we need not canvass any more for understanding where we already know beforehand that none is to be expected. ... These elections have again clearly indicated where party loyalty lies, on which sections of the population the Christian Social party can rely. May the intention follow from this realization that the Christian Social party will never again enter a newly elected national assembly without a female representative (no. 60, 1 December 1930).

The *Frauen-Briefe* also expressed anger that no woman had been put in a secure position on the election lists (no. 61, 1 January 1931).

The liberal women's movement had the least success in entering the National Assembly. No member ever became a representative. The liberal women's movement, embodied in the nationwide organization of the *Bund Österreichischer Frauenvereine*, was not affiliated with a particular party. Many members individually joined one of the small democratic liberal parties. These, however, were either not successful at elections or, again, women were placed in unfavorable positions on the election lists (Hawlik 1971: 559-67, 595-97).

### Women as Legislative Representatives

Once female candidates succeeded in winning a seat in Parliament, they concentrated on women's issues and social problems. The speeches they made were chiefly on financial, welfare, and educational topics (public health, child welfare, girls' schooling, food) as well as on criminal law (Fallmann 1989: 230). With respect to parliamentary committees responsible for discussing motions and preparing bills, women representatives were mostly active on those dealing with education and schooling, social administration, finances and budget, and justice. Also, women were well represented on the committee for food, which dealt with the food shortages caused by the war that existed until 1923. Hardly any women participated on the committees dealing with constitutional reform, agriculture, traffic, housing, and rules of procedure (Fallmann 1989: 231-242).

Women worked actively only on laws relating to social reform, for example the ban on night work for adolescents and women in industrial and commercial firms; the employment, working hours, and Sunday rest of adolescents and women in mines; the eight-hour workday, workers' and agricultural workers' insurance, social insurance and welfare for the unemployed, and midwifery (Hauch 1995). A law on improvements in the working conditions and hours of domestic servants guaranteed, for instance, nine hours a day for sleep, two hours for meals, eight hours off every second Sunday, and a paid vacation of one to three weeks. In the field of marriage and family law, some bills on the reform of alimony were successful, but Adelheid Popp's demand for full equality in family law was not realized until 1975.

One of the central demands of the Social Democratic women's movement, the repeal of Article 144 of the criminal code concerning the prohibition of abortion, was first initiated in 1920, but was also not successful in the First Republic.

In contrast, the work of women in the Congress of the United States differed significantly from that of women in the Austrian Parliament. The few women elected to Congress or nominated into party positions on the national level were not strong supporters of the goals of the women's movement (Cott 1987: 97-99, 111; Chafe

1972: 28-29). Thus the Republican representative Alice Robertson (Oklahoma) in 1921 voted against the Sheppard-Towner bill on infant and pre-natal maternity care out of loyalty to her party. Still, a member of the New Jersey League of Women Voters declared women to be especially suitable for state legislatures and Congress because of their "motherly instincts" and their pride in keeping their homes "spic and span" (Gordon 1986: 40-41). On the other hand, the political system of the United States offered several possibilities of practicing pressure on legislatures apart from sitting inside them; many members of the American women's movement chose to continue the means of political pressure that women's organizations had used successfully before the Nineteenth Amendment on women's right to vote: lobbying.[15] Several organizations, among them the League of Women Voters, the Women's Trade Union League, and the Woman's Christian Temperance Union, formed the Women's Joint Congressional Committee. This committee initiated laws such as the Sheppard-Towner Act of 1921 that allocated federal funds for infant and prenatal maternity care. It also lobbied on behalf of independent citizenship for married women, which was partially achieved in the Cable Act of 1922 and fully at the beginning of the 1930s; and it advocated the prohibition of child labor as an Amendment to the Constitution in 1924. However, this last campaign was not successful, and its failure marked the beginning of the dissolution of the committee (Flexner 1975: 338). The National Woman's Party, on the other hand, sought to end all legal disabilities against women with a new amendment to the Constitution. This Equal Rights Amendment was initiated in 1923 and, as is well known, still awaits full ratification by several states (Cott 1984: 43-68).

Lobbying was not an effective option in Austrian politics. In assessing the success of women's parliamentary work, the Social Democrat Adelheid Popp revealed cautious optimism:

> Women were not summoned to legislation in a period in which prosperity flourished and production was in full swing, but when boundless misery, utmost need assailed the people. These features had to influence decisively the efficacy of women in legislation. The wings were crippled by these harsh facts; if there nevertheless was success in obtaining so much recognition for women, this best refutes the imagined and formerly repeatedly quoted idea of the inferiority of woman (Popp 1927: 106).

In provincial diets and municipal councils, Social Democratic women usually agreed that women's special sphere in political work

---

15. For examples of lobbying at the state level see Gordon 1986.

was social welfare and social administration. The old argument that the municipality was nothing more than an enlarged household reappeared within their rhetoric. Women were able to achieve more than men in social administration, where they could expand their "inherent motherliness." Their method was not to make frequent speeches, but to work quietly in council commissions (*Handbuch der Frauenarbeit* 1930: 651-54, 658-59; *Die Frau*, 1 February 1929: 8).

The Catholic women's movement regarded active political work in the legislatures as very important, and encouraged women to enter Parliament, provincial diets and municipal councils (Schlösinger 1920: 1). Yet, as intimated by Christian Social municipal council member and, later, Parliamentary deputy Hildegard Burjan just after the first elections of the new Republic, Christian women were not to interest themselves in "actual politics." Rather, women were needed in the fields of social welfare, educational and economic reconstruction, and promoting women's interests.[16] For the special qualities this work required, women were uniquely endowed. They possessed a motherly heart "that loves to help when need is worst, that bestows its most ardent love on the weakest," and a healthy common sense "that tackles things in a real and practical way, that does not lose itself in abstract sophistry and is often capable of overcoming difficulties from which the mind of the most intelligent man shrinks back." Women should thus protect their feminine nature in order to do their best for society by complementing men's capabilities. Emotions and sudden impressions were not welcome. Instead, woman, with her clear-working mind, must introduce a finer tone into politics. Aggressiveness and hatred were to be ousted from Parliament, peace and reconciliation were to enter (Burjan 1919; Walter 1920). Christian Social politicians, such as Ignaz Seipel, twice Austrian chancellor in the 1920s, supported this attitude (Paul-Sajowitz 1987: 59).

After a decade of parliamentary work, Catholic women also reflected upon their achievements. Alma Motzko-Seitz, president of the Catholic women's organization of Vienna and Christian Social municipal council member in Vienna, found the results unsatisfactory. She explained that the reason was "not only the unfamiliarity

---

16. Catholic women's goals included, for example, prenatal maternity care, measures against abortion and alcoholism, family insurance and other laws especially helpful to large families, religious education in schools, marriage laws reflecting Catholic views, the recognition of homemaking as a profession, better professional training for women (preferably conforming to their "womanly nature"), and improved conditions regarding working hours, pay, and Sunday rest for gainfully employed women (Paul-Sajowitz 1987: 45-48).

with some matters that often made a quick orientation impossible, not only awe of what was novel, where one ought not to show any dilettantism," but also the lack of interest of male politicians in the way women worked, in the subjects women liked best (for example, culture and welfare). As well, men and women employed different tactics (Motzko-Seitz 1927: 147). In the eyes of the Catholic women's movement, women were practical and abhorred theory, while men not only favored analysis and abstraction, but were inclined to be opportunistic and seemed to enjoy the struggle for political power. Berta Pichl, a member of the Upper House of Parliament (*Bundesrat*), emphasized that women, on the other hand, chose the path of quiet preliminary work in the making of laws, and sought to fulfill the wishes of all parties through their preparations behind the scenes (Pichl 1929: 2).

### Party Integration or Autonomous Organization?

Their failure to achieve power inside parties or in the legislatures led women, especially in the liberal movement, to consider the idea of an independent women's party. As in other countries, the idea had been a subject of discussion from the beginning of the postwar era. In the United States, women could choose between the options of party integration or separate interest group organizations such as the League of Women Voters, the Women's Trade Union League, or the National Woman's Party. Interest groups there did not compete for votes with existing parties, but lobbied instead for certain laws.

In Austria, Social Democrats had always opposed a separate women's party. In 1919, they also refused to allow Social Democratic women to continue to organize themselves in their own political organizations. The ensuing full incorporation of the female party members into the party structure induced fears among women that male comrades would look down on them, that no satisfying cooperation would develop, and that their initiatives would be blocked (*Arbeiterinnen-Zeitung*, 2 November 1920: 1).[17] Such views, however, remained isolated: the majority of the Social Democratic women's movement was glad to flee the ghettoization of their pre-1919 independent organization (Bandhauer-Schöffmann 1989: 401). Furthermore, the Social Democrats organized women's committees that gave women an opportunity to discuss women's matters among themselves.

Financial dependence upon male comrades, however, caused dissatisfaction (*Arbeiterinnen-Zeitung*, 16 November 1920: 1; *Protokoll Parteitag 1921*: 129-30, 134-35). Some local women's committees

17. See especially the ambivalent opinion of Cilly Nemec in *Protokoll Parteitag 1919*: 195.

rebuked the men for their stinginess. The party conference of 1921 agreed to fund the women's committees with five percent of total membership dues, and some male discussants even protested that this was too little. However, this form of funding was not realized everywhere (Bandhauer-Schöffmann 1989: 403).

Social Democratic women also had difficulties in rallying male party members behind their goals. Calls for the abolition of all social and legal inequities in the treatment of women did not become a feature of the party program until 1926.

While the majority of the liberal women's movement did not believe in the value of a separate women's party, a minority followed the example of the American National Woman's Party and founded the *Österreichische Frauenpartei* (Austrian Women's Party) on 11 December 1929. A veteran of the moderate women's movement, Marianne Hainisch, served as its president.[18] The party identified "internal and external peace for the material well-being and the intellectual development of the people" as its first goal (*Neues Wiener Tagblatt*, 12 December 1929). Accordingly, the platform advocated international disarmament (*Das Wort der Frau*, 14 June 1931). A second aim was to attempt to bridge the gulf between the two major parties (the Christian Socials and the Social Democrats) that had grown continuously deeper since the fateful events of 1927. Liberal women sought to bring an end to "rampant party excesses" in this respect, and to work toward an understanding between all parties. Additional goals included equal rights for all citizens and the general purification of society. These were to be realized by women leading simple lives, coupled with the exemplary lifestyles of their political leaders. On the personal level, women were exhorted to participate more in public life in order to further their influence. Pressure was to be brought to bear on the candidates and platforms of other parties but, if necessary, the *Frauenpartei* would also nominate its own candidates.

Somewhat later, as liberal women took on the cause of Austria's housewives, the *Frauenpartei* added several planks to its platform. Most notably, it now called for the legalization of homemaking as a profession, in tandem with the introduction of illness and old-age insurance for homemakers and the reduction of pension taxes for poor women unable to work (Pint 1988: 81). Moreover, housewives were to be represented by their own board. Other demands of the *Frauenpartei*, including a reversal in shrinking female employment, the overhaul of celibacy laws for women in government administra-

18. For the party's history, see Pint (1988).

tion, abortion rights and marriage law reform, did not greatly differ from those of Social Democratic women.

Finally, economic issues dominated *Das Wort der Frau* (The Voice of Women), the journalistic organ of the *Frauenpartei*. To counter growing social misery, price increases, and rising unemployment, liberal women proposed lower taxes and shorter working hours. The shorter working day was to give workers time to cultivate small strips of land, thus increasing the food supply, a strategy named "inner colonization." Liberal women also advocated free trade, and promoted administrative reform aimed at reducing expenses and cutting the salaries of politicians and high officials.

The *Frauenpartei* was not to realize its expectations. Its strategy of supporting an established political party, and its attempt to launch an independent candidacy, were both unsuccessful. At the elections of 1930 it supported a small liberal group, the *Nationaler Wirtschaftsblock* (National Economic Bloc). Led by Johannes Schober this was a coalition of the *Landbund* (Farmers' Union) and the Pan-German People's party. Schober was the former head of the Viennese police who had been responsible for the severe police action at the *Justizpalast*-burning of July 1927, and had served as chancellor in 1929 and 1930. His aversion to "too much politics" and his sympathy for a government of "Beamten" (the Austrian version of civil servants) appealed to the *Frauenpartei* (Pint 1988: 105). To them, he represented the liberal ideal of a state free of conflicting parties. Furthermore, he had promised to support equal rights, and to nominate female candidates (*Neue Freie Presse*, 29 October 1930).

In the end, only one woman, the Pan-German party member Maria Schneider, won one of the eleven seats of the bloc in the National Assembly (Pint 1988: 106-109). After this disappointment, the Innsbruck branch of the *Frauenpartei* participated independently in the municipal elections of Innsbruck in 1931. Its ticket hinged upon a protest against mismanagement in the community, which it believed only able homemakers could remedy (Pint 1988: 119-20). Despite its promise to work in the municipal council without payment, this branch of the *Frauenpartei* collected only a few more votes than those of its own seven hundred members.

The vice-president of the *Frauenpartei*, Helene Granitsch, continued to believe in a feminine political order as the panacea for all problems. Politics as practiced by males had, in her opinion, brought chaos to the world with its spirit of conquest and seizure, love for war and violence, and lust for ego gratification (Granitsch 1933a). In response, female politics should strike out with their goal to

*save the world from hatred* – to put *in* the place of the *business-politician* the
arguments of *humanity* and to let the management of *idealism* take the
place of the regency of *materialism,* as it complies with the principle of
*motherly love* and *justice* (Granitsch 1932a; emphasis in the original).

Granitsch, however, was forced to realize that women did not
always lend their "natural" motherly love to good ends. The results of
the municipal elections of 1932, in which the National Socialists
gained support among women,[19] prompted her to seek explanations.
Ultimately, she was convinced that those women who had voted for
extreme parties were gullible and thoughtless (Granitsch 1932b, c).
They wished to shower adoration upon a political hero, just as they
sought a personal hero in their love lives. Carrying the metaphor further, Granitsch compared the public perversity of the vote to an
equally perverse personal relationship, in which a woman tends to
attach herself more to a man the worse he treats her.

Granitsch's assessment of women's political efficacy later grew
more pessimistic. Women had not been able to realize their powers
of the *Muttergeist* (motherly spirit), she wrote (Granitsch 1933b). They
had thoughtlessly joined the existing male party structure, and taken
up its battles over race, class, and nationalism, instead of furthering
the interests of women and humankind. Women had failed because
of their immaturity (Granitsch 1933c). Gloomily, she concluded that,
had women only been given the passive vote and not the active, the
world would be in a different – and better – state.

### The End of Democracy and of Women's Dreams

Disillusionment with women's achievements in politics, especially
within the liberal women's movement, was a cardinal factor in the
conviction increasingly held by many bourgeois women that only an
elite of capable people should govern. The upshot of such sentiments
was the triumph of Engelbert Dollfuß' authoritarian regime in 1933-
34. Dollfuß dissolved Parliament, forbade political parties, and, subsequently, outlawed the Social Democratic movement. The Catholic
women's movement believed that the new regime's plan for a corporative state representing all professions provided the ideal political
system. Based on a scheme advocated by Catholic theorist Ignaz
Seipel near the end of World War I, they supported a system of professional corporations elected by separate male and female electoral
bodies, in order to allow room for alleged gender differences in physical and psychic capacities and interests (Schöffmann 1986b: 228).

19. In Vienna, 16.2 percent of enfranchised women voted for the National Socialists
(Seliger and Ucakar 1984: 140-41).

The *Frauenpartei* supported Dollfuß' concept of concentrated government, as it seemed to promise internal peace and an end to party strife in Austria. Moreover, his emphasis on Austrian statehood was deemed a suitable reaction to the pan-German propaganda of the National Socialists. Finally, democratic elections had clearly not brought about the desired results for women. At the very least, the *Frauenpartei* saw the opportunity for a board of homemakers representing women's interests within the echelons of the new corporative state (*Das Wort der Frau*, 23 July 1933; Pint 1988: 132-33). They were to be disappointed. Women's wishes were not taken into consideration in the new state. During the regimes of both Dollfuß and his successor, Schuschnigg, women had no mechanism for decisive political influence (Schöffmann 1986b).

## Conclusion

The concept of gender difference, of women possessing a different nature from men but being at the same time equal to them, shaped expectations of women's impact on politics before and after their enfranchisement. The failure to realize the vision of a new society, shaped through female values of motherliness and a higher morality, contributed to the disillusionment and weakening of women's movements. It also led to the contention on the part of some contemporary male critics that women had not changed politics at all in exercising their right to vote. They maintained that women voted just like men and that women's suffrage was therefore ultimately superfluous (Kaiser 1986: 134).

Although some goals of the women's movements in the fields of social legislation and women's legal emancipation were realized after enfranchisement, far-reaching visions of a just and peaceful society were unsuccessful in both Austria and the United States. In Austria, vast plans for social changes were doomed in the growing conservative climate, and in the face of grave economic problems. While, in America, the 1920s were a period of economic upswing, conservative retrenchment characterized its political and social landscape as well.

A second element that prevented the realization of the dreams of the women's movements was the existence of male-dominated political parties. Here, conditions in the United States paralleled the Austrian case. While the established parties did woo women as potential voters, they saw no need to give priority to the demands of the women's movements, because no dynamic women's bloc appeared at elections. For traditional politicians, the core values of the women's movements (morality, harmony, and motherliness) had little resonance in the public sphere. They were largely associated with the home, not politics (Sapiro 1983: 31). Therefore, women's integration into parties often meant that women's issues were sacrificed to party loyalty (Gordon 1986: 87). Constant struggles against male unwillingness to cede power to women further characterized women's relationship to political parties.

Finally, separate female organizations were only successful if mechanisms for pressure, such as lobbying, existed. Yet these were weak vis-à-vis constellations of traditional political power. The Austrian liberal women's movement was unprepared for the sudden introduction of suffrage after World War I. It had not devised any clear-cut strategies, prior to enfranchisement, for realizing its goals and visions. The same can be said of the American suffrage movement (Cott 1987: 100).

With hindsight, we can observe that the non-partisan Austrian middle-class women's movements were caught up in their concepts of gender difference, and continued to advocate femininity as a panacea for all ills, instead of focusing on political structures and the question of political power (Elshtain 1981: 236). Indeed, no extensive discussions by women on the decision-making processes of the state are, to my knowledge, on record. Moreover, decision making usually did not take place inside legislatures or parliamentary committees, but within men's networks to which women had no access. In the First Republic of Austria, with its lack of democratic traditions, the failures and disillusionment associated with the women's movements could – and did – contribute to anti-democratic political resolutions. Tragically, the political changes of 1933/34 submerged women's visions of political influence on the state.

# References

## Newspapers and Women's Journals

*Arbeiterinnen-Zeitung.*
*Arbeiter-Zeitung.*
*Die Frau.*
*Frauen-Briefe.*
*Neue Freie Presse.*
*Neues Frauenleben.*
*Neues Wiener Tagblatt.*
*Die Unzufriedene.*
*Das Wort der Frau.*

## Government Publications:

*Beiträge zur Statistik der Republik Österreich.*
*Congressional Record, United States.*
*Protokolle der Sitzungen des Gemeinderathes der k.k. Reichshaupt- und Residenzstadt Wien.*
*Statistisches Handbuch für die Republik Österreich.*
*Stenographische Protokolle über die Sitzungen des Hauses der Abgeordneten des österreichischen Reichsrates.*

## Other Published Primary Sources:

Allgemeiner Österreichischer Frauenverein. 1894. *Zum Frauenstimmrecht in Österreich.* Vienna.

Braun, A. 1912. "Der Anspruch der Frauen auf politisches Recht." *Arbeiterinnen-Zeitung* May 7:2-3.

Brockett, L.P. 1869. *Woman: Her Rights, Wrongs, Privileges, and Responsibilities.* Hartford, Conn.

Burjan, H. 1919. "Die Frauen und die Nationalversammlung." *Reichspost* February 20.

Chittenden, A.H. 1914. "Why New York State Opposes Federal Amendment?" *The Woman's Protest* 4/3:5-6.

Danneberg, R. 1927. *Die politischen Parteien in Deutschösterreich: Die Wahlen im ersten Jahrzehnt der Republik.* Vienna.

Eberhard, E.F.W. 1927. *Feminismus und Kulturuntergang: Die erotischen Grundlagen der Frauenemanzipation.* 2d ed. Vienna.

Ettel, K. 1890. *Die Frau und die Gesellschaft: Ein Wort zur Frauenfrage.* Vienna.

Fickert, A. 1898. "Sollten die Frauen einer politischen Partei angehören?" *Frauenleben* 9:1.

*Das Frauenstimmrecht: Festschrift.* 1913. Ed. Österreichisches Frauenstimmrechtskomitee anläßlich der Internationalen Frauenstimmrechtskonferenz in Wien, 11. und 12. Juni 1913. Vienna.

*Frauenwahlrecht und Arbeiterinnenschutz: Verhandlungen der dritten sozialdemokratischen Frauenkonferenz in Österreich.* 1908. Vienna.

Freundlich, E. 1908. "Das Gemeindewahlrecht und die Frauen." *Arbeiterinnen-Zeitung* August 4:2.

Gerber, A. 1912. "Frauenarbeit und kommunales Frauenwahlrecht." *Neues Frauenleben* 24/4:1-3.

Granitsch, H. 1932a. "Politische Übersicht." *Das Wort der Frau* 2/9:1-2.

___. 1932b. "Die Bundespräsidentenwahl in Deutschland: Hitler und die Frauen." *Das Wort der Frau* 2/12:1-2.

___. 1932c. "Frauengedanken zu den Wahlen." *Das Wort der Frau* 2/14:1-2.

___. 1933a. "Das Chaos in der Welt: Politik – Technik -Wirtschaft – Ethik." *Das Wort der Frau* 3/4:1-2.

___. 1933b. "Erkenntnisgeist und Muttergeist." *Das Wort der Frau* 3/10:1-2.

___. 1933c. "Die Frau und der Staat." *Das Wort der Frau* 3/12:1-2.

*Handbuch der Frauenarbeit in Österreich.* 1930. ed. Kammer für Arbeiter und Angestellte in Wien. Vienna.

Katscher, L. 1905. "Erfahrungen mit dem Frauenstimmrecht." *Der Weg* 1/13:3-4.

Klausberger, M. 1917. "Politische Frauenpflichten." *Der Bund* 12/10:1-4.

Leatherbee, Mrs. A.T. 1915. *Anti-Suffrage Campaign Manual.* Boston.

Malkiel, T.S. [n.d.] *Woman and Freedom.* New York.

Motzko-Seitz, A. 1927. "Die katholische Frauenbewegung in Österreich." *Frauenkalender 1927*: 147-148.

*Parteitag 1930: Protokoll des sozialdemokratischen Parteitages, abgehalten vom 6. bis 8. Dezember 1930 im Arbeiterheim in Ottakring in Wien.* 1931. Vienna.

Pichl, B. 1929. "10 Jahre Frauenwahlrecht in Österreich." *Frauen-Briefe* 41:1-2.

Pollak, M. 1927. "Politik, die die Frauen verstehen – Politik, die die Frauen machen." *Arbeiter-Zeitung* August 14.

___. 1931. "Die Frau in der Partei." *Die Frau* 40/1:11-12.

Popp, A. 1918. "Das Frauenwahlrecht in der Gemeinde." *Arbeiterinnen-Zeitung* March 12:2-4.

___. 1927. "Die Frau als Gesetzgeber." In Granitsch, H. *Das Buch der Frau: Eine Zeitkritik.* Ed. H. Granitsch, 101-6. Vienna.

Popper-Lynkeus, J. 1913. "Die politische Gleichberechtigung der Frauen und ihre wahrscheinlichen Folgen." *Neues Frauenleben* 15/6: 154-58.

*Protokoll über die Verhandlungen des Gesamtparteitages der Sozialdemokratischen Arbeiterpartei in Österreich, abgehalten zu Wien vom 9. bis zum 13. November 1903.* 1903. Vienna.

*Protokoll der Verhandlungen des Parteitages der sozialdemokratischen Arbeiterpartei Deutschösterreichs, abgehalten in Wien vom 31. Oktober bis zum 3. November 1919.* 1920. Vienna.

*Protokoll der Verhandlungen des Parteitages der sozialdemokratischen Arbeiterpartei Deutschösterreichs, abgehalten in Wien vom 25. bis 27. November 1921.* 1922. Vienna.

Renner, K. n.d. "Der Staatsrat beschließt das Frauenstimmrecht." In *Arbeiterinnen kämpfen um ihr Recht: Autobiographische Texte zum Kampf rechtloser und entrechteter "Frauenspersonen" in Deutschland, Österreich und der Schweiz des 19. und 20. Jahrhunderts.* Ed. R. Klucsarits and F.G. Kürbisch, 307-11. Wuppertal.

Schindler, F.M. 1906. *Die soziale Frage der Gegenwart vom Standpunkt des Christentums.* 2d ed. Vienna.

Schlesinger, T. 1910. *Was wollen die Frauen in der Politik?* 2d ed. Vienna.

Schlösinger, M. 1920. "Brauchen wir Frauen im Parlament?" *Frauenarbeit und Frauenrecht* 2/11:1.

Schuler, S. 1930. "Gehört die Frau in die Politik?" *Arbeiter-Zeitung,* 29 September.

Seipel, I. 1930. *Der Kampf um die österreichische Verfassung.* Vienna.

Stanton, E.C., Anthony, S.B., and Gage, M.J., eds. 1881. *The History of Woman Suffrage.* Vol. 1. Rochester.

Troll-Borostyáni, I.v. 1886. "Eduard von Hartmanns Offenbarung über die Frauenfrage." *Allgemeine Frauenzeitung* 1/1:2-4.

_____. 1902. "Wege und Ziele der Frauenbewegung." *Neues Frauenleben* 14/6:5.

Urban, G. 1919. "Wahlvorbereitung der Frauen." *Die Frau* 1/2:1.

*Verhandlungen des Gesamtparteitages der Sozialdemokratie in Österreich abgehalten zu Brünn vom 24. bis 29. September 1899 im "Arbeiterheim."* 1899. Vienna.

Walter, G. 1920. "Die Aufgaben der Mandatarin." *Neues Montagblatt,* 20 September.

**Secondary Sources:**

Aptheker, B. 1982. *Woman's Legacy: Essays on Race, Sex, and Class in American History.* Amherst.

Baker, P. 1984. "The Domestication of Politics: Women and American Political Society, 1780-1920." *The American Historical Review* 89:620-47.

Bandhauer-Schöffmann, I. 1989. "Parteidisziplin." *Zeitgeschichte* 16:396-409.

Bussemer, H.E. 1988. "Bürgerliche Frauenbewegung und männliches Bildungsbürgertum 1860-1880." In *Bürgerinnen und Bürger: Geschlechterverhältnisse im 19. Jahrhundert.* Ed. U. Frevert, 190-205. Göttingen.

Chafe, W.H. 1972. *The American Woman: Her Changing Social, Economic, and Political Roles, 1920-1970.* New York.

Chamberlin, H. 1973. *Minority of Members: Women in the U.S. Congress.* New York.

Clemens, B. 1988. *"Menschenrechte haben kein Geschlecht!" Zum Politikverständnis der bürgerlichen Frauenbewegung.* Pfaffenweiler.

Cott, N.F. 1984. "Feminist Politics in the 1920's: The National Woman's Party." *Journal of American History* 71:43-68.

Elshtain, J.B. 1981. *Public Man, Private Woman: Women in Social and Political Thought.* Princeton.

_____. 1987. *The Grounding of Modern Feminism.* 2d ed. New Haven.

Evans, S.M. and Boyte, H.C. 1986. *Free Spaces: The Sources of Democratic Change in America.* New York.

Fallmann, A. 1989. "Zur Rolle der Frau im österreichischen Parlamentarismus (1848-1934)." M.A. thesis, University of Vienna.

Flexner, E. 1975. *Century of Struggle: The Woman's Rights Movement in the United States.* Cambridge, Mass.

Freismuth, E. 1984. "Die Frau im öffentlichen Recht." In *Die Frau im Korsett: Wiener Frauenalltag zwischen Klischee und Wirklichkeit 1848-1920.* Katalog der 88. Sonderausstellung des Historischen Museums der Stadt Wien, 30-40. Vienna.

Gellott, L. 1991. "Mobilizing Conservative Women: The Viennese *Katholische Frauenorganisation* in the 1920s." *Austrian History Yearbook* 22: 110-30.

Gordon, F.D. 1986. *After Winning: The Legacy of the New Jersey Suffragists, 1920-1947.* New Brunswick, N.J.

Guschlbauer, E. 1974. "Der Beginn der politischen Emanzipation der Frau in Österreich (1848-1919)." Ph.D. dissertation, University of Salzburg.

Hauch, G. 1995. *Vom Frauenstandpunktaus. Frauen im Parlament 1919-1933.* Vienna.

Hawlik, J. 1971. "Die politischen Parteien Deutsch-Österreichs bei der Wahl zur konstituierenden Nationalversammlung 1919." Ph.D. dissertation, University of Vienna.

Hinding, A. , ed. 1986. *Feminism: Opposing Viewpoints.* St. Paul, Minn.

Hönigschmied, H. 1952. "Der Einfluß des Frauenwahlrechtes auf das politische Geschehen Österreichs unter besonderer Berücksichtigung der Gesetzgebung." Ph.D. dissertation, University of Graz.

Hofmann-Göttig, J. 1986. *Emanzipation mit dem Stimmzettel: 70 Jahre Frauenwahlrecht in Deutschland.* Bonn.

Kaiser, V. 1986. "Österreichs Frauen 1918-1938. Studien zu Alltag und Rollenverständnis in politischen Frauenblättern." Ph.D. dissertation, University of Vienna.

Koonz, C. 1976. "Conflicting Allegiances: Political Ideology and Women Legislators in Weimar Germany." *Signs* 1:663-683.

Kraditor, A.S. 1971. *The Ideas of the Woman Suffrage Movement 1890-1920.* Garden City, N.Y.

Offen, K. 1988. "Defining Feminism: A Comparative Historical Approach." *Signs* 14:119-57.

Paul-Sajowitz, D. 1987. "Die christliche Welt der Frau in der Zwischenkriegszeit. Die christlichsozialen und katholischen Frauenzeitschriften in den Jahren 1918 bis 1934." Ph.D. dissertation, University of Vienna.

Pint, J. 1988. "Die Österreichische Frauenpartei 1929-1934: Ein Versuch bürgerlich-liberaler Frauen, gesellschaftspolitischen Einfluß zu nehmen." M.A. thesis, University of Vienna.

Sapiro, V. 1983. *The Political Integration of Women: Roles, Socialization, and Politics.* Chicago.

Schöffmann, I. 1986a. "Mütterliche Mythen. Marginalien zum politischen Diskurs des Bundes Österreichischer Frauenvereine." *Mitteilungen des Instituts für Wissenschaft und Kunst* 41/1:9-12.

____. 1986b. "Die bürgerliche Frauenbewegung im Austrofaschismus. Eine Studie zur Krise des Geschlechterverhältnisses am Beispiel des Bundes Österreichischer Frauenvereine und der Katholischen Frauenorganisation für die Erzdiözese Wien." Ph.D. dissertation, University of Vienna.

Scott, A.F. and Scott, A.M. 1982. *One Half the People: The Fight for Woman's Suffrage.* Chicago.

Seliger, M. and Ucakar, K. 1984. *Wahlrecht und Wählerverhalten in Wien 1848-1932: Privilegien, Partizipationsdruck und Sozialstruktur.* Vienna.

Slapnicka, H. and Marckhgott, G. 1987. *Aufbau der Demokratie: Politik und Verwaltung Oberösterreichs.* Vol. 1. *1861-1918.* Linz.

Strecker, G. and Lenz, M. 1984. *Der Weg der Frau in die Politik.* 5th ed. Melle.

Tax, M. 1980. *The Rising of the Women: Feminist Solidarity and Class Conflict 1880-1917.* New York.

Ucakar, K. 1985. *Demokratie und Wahlrecht in Österreich.* Vienna.

Weiland, D. 1983. *Geschichte der Frauenemanzipation in Deutschland und Österreich: Biographien, Programme, Organisationen.* Düsseldorf.

Zaar, B. 1984. "Die Einführung des parlamentarischen Frauenstimmrechts in Großbritannien, den Vereinigten Staaten von Amerika, Deutschland, Österreich und Belgien, 1917-1920: Ein Vergleich." M.A. thesis, University of Vienna.

___. 1987. "Dem Mann die Politik, der Frau die Familie – die Gegner des politischen Frauenstimmrechts in Österreich (1848-1918)." *Österreichische Zeitschrift für Politikwissenschaft* 16/4:351-62.

___. 1994. "Vergleichende Aspekte der Geschichte des Frauenstimmrechts in Großbritannien, den Vereinigten Staaten von Amerika, Österreich, Deutschland und Belgien, 1860-1920." Ph.D. dissertation, University of Vienna.

*Chapter 5*

⊲≫⊳

# WOMEN IN THE AUSTRIAN PARLIAMENT
## Opportunities and Barriers

...........................

*Gerda Neyer*

I n Austria, as in other countries, universal suffrage has not provided women with the same political opportunities as men. Women have gained only nominal entry to the spheres of political power and seldom, if at all, attain high political positions. My chapter examines some of the underlying causes, especially the structures and rules in the Austrian parliamentary system that lead to, and perpetuate, gender differences in the political participation of women and men.[1]

## The Austrian Parliamentary System

The Austrian federal parliament has two chambers, the Lower House *(Nationalrat)* and the Upper House *(Bundesrat)*. The Lower House consists of 183 members who are elected every four years in

---

1. This chapter is a revised and updated version of my contribution in Dachs, et al. (1991). It is based largely on two research projects that deal with women in political institutions and decision-making positions that I carried out in 1984/85 and 1988/89. Here, I restrict my exposition largely to the Austrian Lower House, with some attention to extra-parliamentary institutions. Moreover, I do not differentiate among the parties. The terms "Parliament" and "Lower House" are used synonymously.

general elections on the basis of a proportional electoral system. The Upper House is the representative body of the nine regional parliaments on the national level. It currently has 63 members who are not elected in general elections, but delegated to the Upper House by the provincial parliaments *(Landtage)* for the period of the respective provincial legislature.[2]

According to the constitution (Art. 24), legislative power is exercised by both the Lower House and the Upper House. In reality, the Upper House is of far less importance. It cannot pass bills, but only veto bills passed by the Lower House. The Upper House, however, hardly ever exercises its power of veto.[3] Its function is confined primarily to the constitutional requirement of voting on bills passed by the Lower House. Because of the minor political position held by the Upper House, legislative functions lie mainly with the Lower House. The Lower House receives the most public attention and is therefore the focus of efforts to increase the parliamentary representation of women.

## The Representation of Women in the Austrian Lower House

When women first entered parliament (then named the *Konstituierende Nationalversammlung*) in 1919, they accounted for eight out of 170 elected members or 4.7 percent. Later elections increased the total number of women to ten, or 5.9 percent. Eight were Social Democrats, one was a member of the Christian Social party, and another one belonged to the Pan-German party (see Table 5-1). Over the subsequent half century, the percentage of women in parliament remained relatively fixed. Until 1975, women won no more than 6 percent of the seats, so that their numerical representation remained as it was during the initial legislative periods of the First Republic.

Significant change first began to occur after the emergence of the autonomous women's movement in the 1970s. In 1983, for the first time in parliamentary history, and sixty-five years after women had achieved equal voting rights with men, the percentage of women in the

---

2. Representatives of the Upper House need not be members of the provincial parliaments, but they must be eligible for membership.
3. If the Upper House rejects a bill passed by the Lower House, the latter can override this veto. Between 1971 and 1990, 2,333 bills were passed. The Upper House exercised its right of veto in 79 cases; 73 of these vetoes were overridden by the Lower House.

Lower House exceeded 10 percent. The result, however, was not due to the elections, but to the nomination of women to replace men who had been appointed to the government.[4] Despite the introduction of a quota rule in the Austrian Socialist party (SPÖ),[5] the successful candidacy of the Green Alternative Party (GAL), and the promises of all parties to support increased female representation in the Lower House, the result of the 1986 general election was disappointing: women attained only twenty-one (or 11.5 percent) of the total 183 seats.

Protests by women of all parties against their meager representation, and against the disregard of women when vacated seats were filled, had some effect. By the end of 1990, the number of women in the Lower House had increased to twenty-seven or 14.8 percent. Following the general election of October 1990, women received an additional nine seats, and thus held nearly a fifth of the total number. Seventeen of the women elected belonged to the SPÖ (21.3 percent of that party's seats), seven each were members of the Austrian People's Party (ÖVP) and the Freedom Party (FPÖ), which amounted to 11.7 percent and 21.1 percent, respectively of their total seats; and five women came from the GAL or 50 percent of its seats (see Table 5-1). Following the formation of the government in December 1990, the SPÖ, under pressure from its women's caucus, nominated three women to replace men who had been appointed ministers; and another woman became a member of the Lower House in March 1991. In 1995, women held more than a quarter of the party's total of eighty seats, which is in line with the goal of the 1985 Party Conference. The total number of women in the Lower House in that year stood at forty, or 21.3 percent.[6]

Since the mid-1970s, the number of women in the Lower House has thus almost tripled in absolute and relative terms. Having ranked

4. Parliamentarians who are appointed ministers renounce their mandates for their period of office. Candidates who are sworn in to replace them as Lower House deputies hold this mandate only for a limited length of time ("fixed-time mandate"); that is, they must return the mandate to a minister if he or she leaves the ministerial post.

5. In 1995, the following parties were represented in the Lower House: SPÖ – the Social Democratic party; ÖVP – People's party (Christian-conservative); FPÖ – the Freedom Party (nationalist, sees itself partly as liberal); GAL – the Green Alternative party (ecological-social, represented in the Lower House since 1986).

6. In the past, the percentage of women in the Upper House was always higher than in the Lower House. Between 1970 and 1990 women comprised from 15.9 percent to 28.6 percent of members in the Upper House, compared with from 4.8 percent to 11.5 percent in the Lower House. However, in the Upper House elected in March 1991, the percentage of women was smaller (19.0 percent) than in the Lower House (21.9 percent).

only tenth among the twenty-one countries of the European Council in 1987 (Sineau 1990, 13), Austria moved up to sixth place in 1991, just behind the Nordic countries (Finland, 38.5 percent, Sweden, 38.1 percent, Norway, 35.8 percent, Denmark, 33.0 percent, and Iceland, 23.8 percent) and ahead of the Netherlands (21.3 percent) and Germany (20.4 percent). In a global perspective, Austria ranks in eighth place among 143 countries (Inter-Parliamentary Union, 31 June 1991). From a national perspective, however, and especially in the eyes of an Austrian female voter, the international standing is somewhat overshadowed by the fact that women form the majority (54 percent) of those entitled to vote, yet hold only 22 percent of the seats, and thus continue to constitute an obvious minority within the Lower House.

The question arises whether the increase in the number of female representatives in the Lower House has led to an increase in women's power and influence in the legislature. To provide an answer, we need to look more closely at the distribution of power among those political institutions that govern the legislative process in Austria.

## The Position of Parliament within the Political Decision-making Process

According to the Constitution, the central decision-making power in the Austrian political system lies with Parliament. In practice, however, substantial powers reside in extra-parliamentary institutions – the executive branch, the civil service, and the neo-corporatist organizations, chiefly trade unions and employers' associations of the social partnership. These institutions play a far more important role in the legislative process than the parliament; the main decisions on legislation are reached within the extra-parliamentary realm.

In general, the government initiates a bill. On its behalf, the relevant ministerial bureaucracy drafts a bill that is submitted for evaluation to other ministries, the provincial governments, and the neo-corporatist organizations. The final draft is approved by the cabinet, and then presented to Parliament for passage. About three-quarters of the legislation passed between 1971 and 1990 was based on this procedure.[7] Since all governments of the Second Republic,

---

7. In fact, the percentage of laws initiated by government is even higher, because bills initiated by members of parliament are also often based on government proposals. (Fischer 1991: 105f.)

with the exception of the first cabinet of Bruno Kreisky (1970/71), have held a majority of seats in the Lower House, most bills initiated by governments (about 40-45 percent) were approved without amendment (Fischer 1991: 105f.). This pattern is made possible by the strong ties between the political parties and the main political institutions in Austria.

The federal bureaucracy and the neo-corporatist organizations also enjoy considerable influence on legislation. The reason in part is that both the Parliament and the government must stand for election every four years, while the civil service and the neo-corporatist organizations are not effected by the results of the general elections.

Compared with other countries, extra-parliamentary institutions in Austria thus play an important role in political decision making. Especially influential is the "social partnership," a characteristically Austrian form of cooperation between the interest groups representing employers, farmers, and employees. The overall political significance of the social partnership lies, however, not in this cooperation but in the power that it holds over political decision making.[8] Some observers of the Austrian political scene even call the social partnership the "secret government." In most matters relating to employment and other economic and social questions, the social partnership holds a near monopoly in policy formulation that must be respected by governments.[9]

Moreover, the influence of the social partnership extends far beyond these specific areas to almost all areas of politics. Its influence and dominance in political life is further secured by the numerous formal and informal relations that bind it to the central decision-making bodies – the government, the bureaucracy, the parliament, and the political parties. Officials of social partnership institutions are often members of ministerial committees, commissions, and advisory bodies, as well as of those bodies that deliver expert opinions on pending bills. Social partner members also hold a considerable number of seats in both chambers of the legislature.

8. The historical origins of the social partnership lie in the programs initiated after the war to solve existing economic problems. During the Second Republic, the social partnership has gained considerably in power. Its influence in Austrian politics is even more astonishing if one considers that the social partnership lacks any grounding in the constitution.

9. In many policy areas, the social partnership monopolizes policy formation with almost no governmental interference. The powers exercised by the social partnership over political decision making have prevented the enactment of legislative initiatives in favor of women (for example, equal rights acts and parental leave for fathers), and, at the same time, have enabled passage of bills containing provisions that discriminate against women.

The transfer of substantial legislative functions from the parliamentary to the extra-parliamentary sphere, the practice of reaching agreement on legislation outside Parliament, and the positions that bureaucracy and the social partners hold in extra-parliamentary negotiation, have considerable disadvantages for women. Because major political power resides within social partnership organizations, the interests of those in the labor force, the majority of whom are men (58.4 percent), are granted more political weight than the interests of those who are not in the labor force, the majority of whom are women (53.1 percent). Yet, the hierarchical structure, and the formalized regulations for nominating officials that characterize the bureaucracies and neo-corporatist organizations, prevent women from reaching top positions in these institutions.

The following figures give an indication of the male dominance within these spheres. In the thirteen ministries of the 17th legislative period (1986-90) (see Table 5-3), there were two female and eleven male ministers, and only two women served among the eighty top civil servants in the highest echelons. On the second highest level of the ministerial bureaucracy, there were only two women as compared with ninety-five men. In only 100 (35 percent) of the 286 ministerial boards, commissions and advisory bodies – eight of them specifically for women – were women drafted as experts; they provided 202, or 6.6 percent, of the 3086 members of these groups. In December 1988, only one woman was to be found in the top positions of the social partnership: she served on the nine-member executive body of the Trades Union Federation, and that only because of statutory provisions (see also Neyer 1989). By the end of 1991, three members of the government were women, compared with fourteen men; two women held ministerial office, although one was without portfolio.[10] There was one female state secretary compared with three males. In the top ranks of social partnership institutions, there were three women representatives; two belonged to the executive body of the Trades Union Federation (compared with seven men),

10. The "State Secretariat for Women's Affairs" was converted into a ministry of the Federal Chancellery during the formation of the new government, and the former Secretary for Women's Affairs was given ministerial status. As minister of the Chancellery, however, the minister herself does not head a regular department. She is thus not equipped with enough budgetary resources to pursue independent policies on equal terms with the other ministers. Unlike a minister, even a minister without portfolio, a state secretary does not have the right to vote in the cabinet. Despite the creation of a Ministry for Women's Affairs attached to the Federal Chancellery, the jurisdiction and decision-making powers of the minister remain limited.

and one to the executive committee of the Federal Economic Chamber (compared with four men).

The extra-parliamentary sphere is clearly the place where men can directly formulate and negotiate their interests. Women, however, are forced to rely on Parliament, which, as far as the distribution of power is concerned, acts more like a rubber stamp than like a true final decision-making body. Parliament thus offers no counterbalance to the power dominance of the extra-parliamentary sector. In fact, by nominating candidates for parliamentary elections and seats, the dominant political institutions can assert their influence, and thereby also maintain strong representation of their interests within Parliament.

## Selection Procedures for the Lower House

Austrian electoral law, in both the First and Second Republics, is based on the party list principle. The electors do not vote primarily for individual candidates, but for a list drawn up by a party, that names the candidates it proposes in each constituency. Each list comprises, at most, twice the number of names as there are seats available in the constituency concerned. Since there are 183 seats in the Lower House, a maximum of 366 candidates can be nominated.

How many basic seats *(Grundmandate)* a party manages to obtain in a constituency, and therefore how many candidates of the party's list are elected in the first stage, depends on the number of votes cast for a party in a constituency. Thus, the placing of the candidates' names on the election lists is decisive for entry to the Lower House. Until the mid-1980s, the parties could reckon with relatively stable voter behavior in the individual constituencies. To a large extent, then, it was possible for the parties to identify, before an election, those places on the list that could be counted as safe, unsafe, or hopeless. On the basis of this knowledge, the parties decided whom they wanted to place in a safe position on the list, thus guaranteeing that person's entry to the Lower House. Austrian electoral reality was, and still is, well summed up by a statement made over seventy years ago by Karl Renner, the First Republic's first Chancellor: "The party itself places the candidates in rank order depending on how important they are to the party" (Ucakar 1985: 395).

While the parties still place their candidates on the list in the manner described above, it has become less easy to predict the number of seats each party will receive. Research into voting patterns since 1983 confirms that party loyalty among voters is increasingly breaking down (Plasser et al. 1987: 242f.), thus making it more difficult for the parties to predict election results. Researchers point to a weakening of party loyalty: voters are increasingly influenced by issues when they cast their votes (Plasser et al.: 243). This has opened up better chances for women to find appropriate recognition when the lists of party candidates are drawn up. Since women's issues have become accepted as subjects fit for public discussion, the parties can no longer ignore women's demands for stronger representation in Parliament without increasing the risk of losing their votes. This development had already begun to show in the mid-1970s,[11] but only since the mid-1980s, under increasing pressure from the Green parties formed from their corresponding social movements, have the traditional parties accorded women wider opportunities to assert their claims to seats. Consequently, the number of women appearing on electoral lists has increased noticeably. While in 1971 only 9.0 percent of all those nominated were women, the share rose to 15.1 percent by 1983, and as high as 28.3 percent in 1990 (see Table 5-2).

However, the number of women in favorable positions on the electoral lists did not increase to the same extent. The chances for men to be placed in eligible positions are still noticeably higher than for women. In 1990, only 9.7 percent of all women nominated gained a seat in Parliament, compared with 15.6 percent of all male candidates. In 1971 the respective percentages amounted to 11.1 percent for women and 17.2 percent for men (Table 5-2). Thus, not only do women have a lower chance of being placed on a party list; even when they are nominated, they tend to appear in "ornamental places" near the bottom. The increase in the number of women on the electoral lists represents, therefore, a new form of functional accommodation to women's demands. The parties use the larger representation of women on their lists to attract more women voters. They thus signal a growing openness towards parliamentary representation for women. Yet, in reality, they do not deliver what they seem to promise.

What accounts for the unequal placement of women and men on electoral lists? According to political scientists, the answer lies in the principles used to draw up party lists (Fischer 1974: 120ff.; Stirnemann 1988: 608ff.):

– the safe-seat principle
– the principle of territorial representation

---

11. Based on the election results in 1975 and 1979, the ÖVP argued that the SPÖ owed its election successes to the women-oriented policies it put into practice at that time.

- the principle of recruiting technocratic experts
- the principle of seat quotas for party organizations or organizations close to the parties.

In contrast to these alleged gender-neutral criteria, two of the parties have adopted gender-specific criteria. Since 1985, the SPÖ has had as a target figure a "25 percent-quota" rule for women; the GAL, at its first national congress in 1987, laid down in its statutes "a quota of at least 50 percent for women."[12]

With the safe-seat principle for members of Parliament, the established parties virtually guarantee their deputies in the Lower House successful re-election, provided (apart from personal or professional reasons) that they did not hold a so-called "limited-time seat," as a replacement candidate for deputies appointed to government posts. Due to the safe-seat principle, the Lower House is recruited largely from deputies who have already been members of the previous parliament. In the past, the proportion reelected varied between 75 percent and 80 percent. In 1990, the figure was 64.5 percent, with 64.7 percent of all men (101 out of 156 male representatives) compared with 63 percent of all women (17 out of 27) being reelected. The prevailing male dominance of the Lower House is thus perpetuated by the safe-seat principle, even when the principle is applied in a gender-neutral manner to both women and men. This was largely the case until the end of the 1970s.

In 1983, when the major parties began to lose seats, the safe-seat principle was relaxed for women. To maintain the proportion of women in Parliament, female candidates were regularly nominated as deputies to replace men appointed to the government. Safe reelection was not made possible for all these female "limited-time seat" holders in the 1986 general election, or to female deputies who had entered the Lower House during the legislative period to replace men who had retired. Thus, following the general election of 1986, only six out of eleven women who had been members of the Lower House for the first time in the previous parliament (1983-86) could retain their seats.

Despite the fact that later nominations have increased the number of women in Parliament, this method of recruiting has disadvantages for women. Instead of being granted eligible positions on electoral lists, women are offered the hope of later nomination. Moreover, as

12. The "50 percent minimum" ruling only applies at the federal level. The individual provincial organizations enjoy total autonomy in drafting their lists and are not required to keep to the 50 percent rule.

a result of reelection quotas for the 1990 general election, less than a third of all male deputies (31.3 percent) were elected to parliament for the first time compared with more than half (52.8 percent) of the female deputies. In contrast to the male deputies, representation by females lacks continuity.

Lack of continuity strengthens gender disparities in access to office and influence in the Lower House. Although the parties are being forced to assign more parliamentary seats to women, the political strength of women can be undermined by frequently replacing female representatives. There are two reasons for this. The first is that no permanent alliance can develop among women in the Lower House, because each new entrant must first adjust to (female and male) colleagues and structures. The second reason, for which there is evidence in the past, is that female parliamentarians who actively push women's issues in opposition to men and to the party line, are replaced by women who are less committed to such positions. Even when women are more strongly represented in the Lower House, the undermining of the safe-seat principle in their case limits their personal, ideological, and political power.

The criteria that guide the filling of vacant places on the party lists do not appear to counterbalance the safe-seat principle. Between 1971 and 1986, about 80 to 90 percent of the places on electoral lists were allocated to men. In most cases, women entering Parliament for the first time through election replaced retiring female deputies, and only in a few cases were vacant seats used to increase the proportion of women in Parliament. In the 1990 election, too, men received preferential treatment with respect to candidacy for mandates. Only nineteen, or 29.2 percent, of the 65 vacant seats were filled by women; the overwhelming majority of vacant seats – forty-six or 70.8 percent – were given to men.

The relative neglect of women in filling vacant places on the party lists raises the question of how these are allocated. There are no regulations for a linear advancement of candidates on the party lists. Other internal party or electoral criteria superimpose themselves on the linear principle. One of these criteria is the principle of territorial representation. In general, district and provincial level organizations decide on the composition of the constituency lists, and thus on the territorial representation of the nominees and deputies. When a Lower House deputy retires, the district organization he or she represented usually has a good chance of obtaining a mandate place on the party list for one of its candidates, provided that important internal party considerations do not require a change (Fischer 1974: 123;

Stirnemann 198: 624ff.). In the case of women, however, matters prove more difficult. Gender becomes a central criterion that ranks above others in the allocation of places on party lists. In the competition over who will fill a vacant seat, women normally only have a chance to be nominated if:

1. the vacant seat had long been occupied by a woman.
2. women and their organizations campaign forcefully, not only for women in general but also for particular female candidates.
3. the demands of party politics require, for example, that the number of women in Parliament be increased, or that the party image be improved by selecting a woman. (Neyer 1985: 23ff.).
4. women insist that party regulations be adhered to, for example, the quota-rules in the SPÖ and the GAL.

Until 1975, female deputies were usually recruited from those constituencies that had long been represented by a woman in Parliament. This meant that, as in the First Republic, almost two-thirds of all female deputies came from Vienna. Since then, pressure from the regional women's organizations led to a larger representation of women from the regional constituencies – at first, however, at the expense of Viennese women, who were given fewer seats in Parliament.[13]

While arguing for adequate regional representation has become an important way for women's organizations to promote female candidates, territorial interests are now generally less important to the parties. In recent years, the parties have expanded their possibilities for placing important candidates on the list in those constituencies where they can count on winning enough seats. The parties increasingly recognize technocratic experts as important candidates, that is, persons who because of their professional career or their institutional experience are considered essential to a party's parliamentary work. So far, the parties have detected expert knowledge and experience almost exclusively in men.

Gender-specific judgments are also applied in choosing the top party positions or party officials. The top positions of party organizations are often combined with a mandatory seat in the Lower House. Similarly, men in leading positions of party organizations are frequently given a safe seat in the Lower House. These principles of seat allocation do not apply to the leading positions in the

13. As of April 1991, there was at least one female representative from each constituency in the Lower House. Nevertheless, none of the parties that had won seats in all constituencies (that is, SPÖ, ÖVP, FPÖ) had complete regional representation for women.

women's party organizations or to women in leading party positions. Female party officials are more often honored with a seat in the Upper House, if they receive any seat preference at all.

Particularly disadvantageous for women is the system the parties use to allocate a fixed quota of places on their lists to party organizations and to those close to the parties, so as to guarantee a certain number of deputies.[14] This principle amounts, more or less, to fixed quotas for male-dominated interest groups and party organizations, and to the exclusion of women. The quota system within the parties is a further obstacle to the successful candidacy of women, because women are insufficiently represented in top positions, and the organizations are relatively autonomous in deciding whom to nominate to fill their quotas. Unlike the parties, they do not need to justify the way they allocate seats to the wider public, or to discuss the discrimination against women that results from this. The quota seats are thus largely distributed by, and shared among, men, which strengthens on a parliamentary level the male dominance found in the extra-parliamentary institutions.[15]

Yet, there are some women in the Lower House who hold top positions in the male-dominated interest groups and party organizations. In contrast to male representatives of the interest groups, however, these women were given access to the Lower House primarily on gender grounds, not because of their extra-parliamentary functions. Often, too, it is the parties, not the organizations, that nominate women for the Lower House. Having to justify themselves to female voters or faced with pressure from women at the grassroots level, the parties have given women mandates, sometimes despite the resistance of the organizations concerned. Only in exceptional cases have women gained access to a parliamentary career because they held top positions in extra-parliamentary organizations.

The arrangements governing seat quotas that enable men to maintain the status quo in the Lower House contrast with the absolute or proportional system that applies to women, and varies from party to party. In the older "absolute seat arrangement," women were granted a certain number of mandates ("women's

14. These rules apply chiefly to the two main parties. Within the SPÖ, the Socialist section of the Austrian Trade Union Federation receives a fixed number of seats in the Lower House. Similarly, each interest group affiliated with the ÖVP – the Chambers of Industry and Agriculture and the Employees' Federation – receives a quota of seats in line with its strength in a particular constituency.

15. The system of seat quotas means that 55.8 percent of Lower House seats are taken by officials attached to the social partnership (see de Goederen 1989: 426). The large majority of these are male.

seats"). The number, however, bore no relation to the number of women who were party members, as either officials or activists, but instead was based on the respective "party traditions." Depending on the party, this number varied in the course of the Second Republic from zero to eight seats. Since the middle of the 1980s, proportional seat quotas have been in force within both the SPÖ and the Green party. Until 1990, however, these arrangements had no more than symbolic significance. At the beginning of the 17th legislative period (1986), the proportion of female deputies in the Lower House in both the SPÖ and the Green party stood at only 12.5 percent, far below the quotas declared, or laid down, in their statutes. Nor were the resolutions on quotas uniformly fulfilled in the 1990 election. Following that election, only 21.3 percent of the Socialist deputies were women; only the later nomination of women to replace men who were appointed ministers brought the proportion of women up to the requisite 25 percent. The GAL did manage to achieve its aim of a 50 percent proportion of women in the Lower House, but this is partly explained by electoral arithmetic. In contravention of party resolutions, women held top place on the GAL party list in only four of nine provinces, while in two constituencies they were listed no higher than third place, and in two others no higher than fourth place. The equal allocation of seats between women and men in the GAL is thus not primarily attributable to the basic seats the party won, but rather to the additional votes it gained. Three of the party's five female deputies owe their entry into parliament to this.

The conclusion to be drawn is that the seat quota arrangements for men and male-dominated organizations, together with the parliamentary presence of men, still carry most weight within the parties. The operation of the quota arrangements shows that the transition from an absolute to a proportional quota system for women has not fundamentally increased participation or access to power. The practice of admitting a limited number of women into political decision-making positions has merely been replaced by the practice of gender-specific admission arrangements. In spite of resolutions embedded in the party statutes, women are forced to fight for representation in Parliament.

In summary, the principles guiding the construction of party lists encompass several gender-segregating effects. Differences between men and women are produced by:

1. the gender-neutral application of principles in a gendered context, for example, the safe-seat principle;

2. the gender-differentiating application of principles, for example, the recruitment of technocratic experts; and

3. the granting of seats to extra-parliamentary institutions that are male dominated on their higher levels, and discriminate against women when it comes to seat allocation.

Together, these three principles not only work against an increase in the number of women in the Lower House, but also affect the composition of the parliamentary committees and restrict women's influence in the Parliament.

## Gender-specific Features of Parliamentary Committees

Since women have only limited opportunities to participate in extra-parliamentary decision making, they are forced to make efficient use of parliamentary committees, which discuss legislation and prepare it for the plenary sessions. At the committee level, however, interventions concerning the content of legislation are rare, and only possible to a limited degree. In most cases, only minor amendments to the draft legislation can be achieved. Yet, there are examples – from the reform of family law to the amendments to social security legislation – in which even the few female members in Parliament have managed to use their committee work to block or weaken substantial legislative provisions detrimental to women. The increase in women's representation in Parliament might, then, serve to enlarge the possibility of influencing committee work; but this requires that women are nominated to committees in adequate numbers.

The number of committees, their members and replacement members, together with the political parity of committees, are decided by the Lower House at the beginning of each legislative period. In the past, this restricted women's chances of influencing legislative decisions. Thus, at the beginning of the 17th legislative period (1986-90) there were twenty-one women deputies, but twenty-five committees, each with 27, 25, or 22 members. In previous legislative periods, the relative numbers were even more unfavorable (Neyer 1989: 25 ff.). Only since 1990 have there been more female deputies than committees and committee members. For the first time in Austria's history, women even have a majority on one of the committees - the Family Committee! In the past two decades, women provided about a quarter of committee members; in about 30 percent of the committees, there were no women at all. As late as

1995 there were not enough women in the Lower House to assure them an adequate representation on all committees.

Women's chances of participating in parliamentary committees are not only limited by the number of female representatives in the Lower House, but also by the allocation of deputies to committees.[16] The composition of the committees is the responsibility of the parliamentary parties. According to Fischer (1982: 140f.), the following criteria are decisive:

- the importance of the committee
- social partnership interests
- the expert knowledge and personal interests of deputies
- the personal wishes of deputies
- demands on time through committee work
- appointment.

These criteria apply differently to men and women. An overview of the committee membership of women from the 13th to the 16th legislative periods (1971-86) shows that – independently of the legislative measures planned for a parliament – women are found in greater numbers on committees whose fields of activity are considered to be "women's issues": education (11.4 percent of all committee memberships), health and environment (11.4 percent), and family (33.3 percent). The percentages for the other committees are all below 8 percent. One exception is the Justice Committee, where women comprised 19.3 percent of total members. An above-average number of women were represented in this committee in the 1970s because the reform of family and criminal law, in the context of legal abortion, was under consideration at the time.

Women were overrepresented, compared to their numbers, on committees that dealt with women's issues. At the start of the 18th legislative period (1990), 14 of 23 members of the Family Committee were women. In the Committee for Petitions and Citizens' Initiatives, which deals with forms of political participation that have a high proportion of female activists and have long been considered "female preserves," women provided nine out of twenty-three members. The committees for health, justice, and education each have

16. For an adequate analysis of women's chances of participating in the parliamentary process, it would be necessary to investigate the bills discussed in committee and the influence of women in this debate. Apart from individual studies on specific topics, no systematic research has been conducted on the participation of women over several periods of Parliament. For this reason, I discuss some aspects of parliamentary life and the composition of committees.

eight female members out of approximately twenty-five members. With the exception of the Justice Committee, then, women tend to be assigned to committees that deal with "women's issues."

Such a situation is not desirable because it divides politics into a part that is relevant for women and one that is not, and thereby perpetuates the traditional historical exclusion of women from politics. This leaves politics as a predominantly male sphere in which female participation reflects the traditional role of women in society. In recent years, women have protested vehemently against this state of affairs.

Viewed over several legislative periods, it becomes evident that the number of women on a committee depends on its political importance, and that women are seldom represented on highly important committees, such as those that deal with finance, budget, and social affairs (Neyer 1985: 49). The further removed the content and relevance of the committee is from central political concerns, the more often women are represented on it.

The unusually high proportion of female parliamentarians on the Justice Committee during its deliberations on the restructuring of family law, marriage law, and criminal law appears to provide evidence to the contrary. It could be concluded from this that women are indeed strongly represented in parliamentary negotiations on key legislative proposals. Some points, however, argue against this. First, during the 18th legislative period (1971-75) when the most important parliamentary decisions were made on the reform of family law and abortion, two-thirds of the members of the Justice Committee were still men. Second, a reshuffling of personnel reduced the number of women when the planned ruling concerning the partition of marital assets and maintenance support after divorce ran into massive resistance from women on the committee (Köpl/Neyer 1985: 45). Third, the high proportion of women on the Justice Committees of the 1970s was a rare exception in parliamentary tradition. Never before or after were women granted such extensive participation in committee work,[17] even when the legislation under consideration had fundamental consequences for women's welfare and economic security, or for gender relations in society. From this it can be concluded that women are only accorded greater participation in legislative negotiations when it does not affect those gender-specific power and deci-

---

17. The large number of women in the Committee on Family Affairs does not contradict this statement. In Austria, family policy has never constituted a political area of its own. In fact, major areas of family policy lie not with the Ministry of Family Affairs, but with the Ministry of Justice and the Ministry of Social Affairs and Employment.

sion-making relations in the social and political spheres that determine the extent to which women exercise self-determination and control over their economic resources. It follows that the political importance of a committee is also measured by specific features of gender relations. As long as the legislative proposals of a committee affect gender relations in a formal, legal way, women are accorded strong representation on the committee. Where favorable economic consequences for women can be expected, men are overrepresented.

This pattern is also confirmed by the relatively low proportion of women on the Social Affairs Committee, which before 1986 was known as the Committee for Employment and Social Affairs (Neyer 1985: 49). Many women believe that this committee plays a key role in affecting the social context of gender politics, especially because it is here that all legislation on social and employment policy is dealt with.[18] Yet women have not been adequately represented on this committee.

The relatively small number of women on the Social Affairs Committee is partly explained by the way it is composed. Committees that are concerned with legislation that has already gone through negotiations within the social partnership are composed largely of parliamentary representatives from social partnership institutions. The number of female committee members from the parties that constitute the leading bodies of the social partnership (the SPÖ and the ÖVP) is correspondingly small. These parties provide twenty-one of the twenty-seven members of the Social Affairs Committee, but there are only two women from each party. The exclusion of women from the leading bodies of the social partnership guarantees their omission from the corresponding working groups at the parliamentary level. The consequences are far-reaching, because legislation that is based on agreements between the social partners gets preferential treatment in Parliament. Such legislation is rarely assigned to a sub-committee, and a more thorough treatment in committee is often waived. At the committee stage itself, discussion in many cases involves only formalities. This means that women play little role in formulating legislation, and also have little possibility to change the content of legislation in the very areas that determine the distribution of work,

18. For example, the parental leave provisions and amendments to both pension regulations and unemployment laws are all dealt with in the Committee of Social Affairs and Employment. In the current legislative period, for which major reforms of the pension laws have been proposed, there are only seven women in the Committee of Social Affairs, while there are fourteen women in the Committee of Family Affairs.

power, and resources along gender lines in the labor market and in socio-political areas.[19]

The small representation of women in the Committee for Employment and Social Affairs does not necessarily result from the insufficient number of women parliamentarians in established positions within the social partnership. Of the twenty-one female deputies in the 1986 Lower House, six were active in social partnership institutions, but only one was on the Social Affairs Committee. Even specialized professional knowledge and an established institutional base do not guarantee women representation on a committee that is crucial for gender relations.

Some argue that the professional competence of women is indeed taken into account when committees are formed. In fact, the relatively high numbers of women in the committees for education (six), budget (four), finance (three), and justice (three), compared with most committees at the start of the 17th legislative period, corresponded to the professional training of the twenty-one female parliamentarians. Five women held a degree in teaching, four in law, and another four in finance and economics. However, if the breakdown is based not on professional training but on occupation and the degree of involvement in professional institutions, there is little correspondence between professional competence and political engagement. As noted above six of the twenty-one female deputies were active in social partnership institutions, but this professional experience was disregarded in their committee assignments. The parliamentary committees gladly use the professional expertise of women, except when assigning committees that deal heavily with social partnership issues. This supports the view that the limited representation of women in top positions of social partnership institutions leads to their under-representation in the parliamentary committees dominated by the social partners.

At the same time, the example also reveals how women are excluded. Professional background serves as an important criterion in making committee assignments. Yet gender segregation prevails inside Parliament through the same mechanism that produces the dichotomy between the professional training of women and their chances of access to different professions in the labor market. The gender-biased weighting accorded to professional training and to qualifications

---

19. In recent years, however, the greater number of females in the Lower House has enabled women to oppose the policy of the social partners. Coalitions of women, sometimes across party boundaries, eliminated or changed major parts of bills, and thus reduced negative consequences. Overall, however, the number of women in the Lower House has so far not been large enough to counterbalance the influence of the social partnership in Parliament.

obtained through experience leads to yet another point. Men are usually assigned to fields of specialization in politics, and gain power on account of their professional background, while gender is the main factor in the case of women. Their specialized expertise comes into play in committee assignments only if the committees in question are concerned with "women's issues," or if they are concerned with issues on the political periphery. Peripheral issues are those that do not tap the key interests of extra-parliamentary institutions of the social partnership. This also explains why many female members of Parliament currently tend to sit mainly on the committees dealing with education, justice, health, family, and citizens' initiatives.

Some formal rules of appointment to committees are also gendered. The most recent example is the regulation adopted in 1990 that requires each committee to have at least one female member. This leads to the situation that women, on average, have to work on more committees, have to invest more time than men in committee work, and must gain expertise in a greater range of legislative issues.[20] Gender-specific models are also applied when it comes to "formal appointment" on the basis of expert knowledge. My 1984 study of female deputies in the 16th legislative period, showed that, in 18.2 percent of cases, the committee membership of women resulted from a formal appointment by the parliamentary parties based on the professional expertise of the deputies. But three-fourths of these appointments were to the Family Committee (Neyer 1985: 50ff.)!

Thus, committee appointments reflect gender-specific characteristics that reproduce the distribution of power in extra-parliamentary institutions at the parliamentary level. Although the increased female representation in the Lower House makes it more difficult to ignore women's issues, at the committee level men still dominate the political fields that determine gender relations in society.

## Concluding Remarks

My chapter has explored the gender-differentiating effects of Austria's political system. I have shown that the demand, now also voiced

20. Between 1970 and 1986, two-thirds of the women in Parliament, but only one-third of the men, were members of three or more committees. According to parliamentarians, membership in three or more committees amounts to a full-time job. Because of their small numbers, female representatives were forced to get on as many committees as possible and to acquire expert knowledge in several fields to represent their interests. Men, however, can limit themselves to a few fields and still preserve their status.

by men, for "more women in Parliament" will not change the situation very much. Greater representation of women in Parliament will not automatically mean that women will gain a greater share of power. Within the existing system, the demands for parliamentary parity for women may actually reinforce the gender bias. The stronger representation of women in the Lower House might lead the public to conclude that women have a considerable share in decision making, while, in reality, they have to carry political responsibility for decisions taken by men. In addition, the impression is given that female deputies compete in Parliament on an equal political footing with male deputies. The formally equal status among deputies veils the actual differences in power between male and female parliamentarians that arises from the entrenched positions of male deputies in the powerful extra-parliamentary institutions. The dual functions of decision-makers in both parliamentary and extra-parliamentary bodies ensure that male power cannot be breached by an increasing number of women in the Lower House, as long as women are largely excluded from the decision-making process in extra-parliamentary bodies. It will thus be necessary for women to concentrate even more than in the past on gaining representation in the extra-parliamentary sphere, in order to gain a greater share of power. Such a move would also challenge the traditional mechanisms through which power is distributed, and political decisions are reached.

**Table 5-1: Women in the Austrian National Assembly (Lower House)**

| 1st Republic* | Social Democrats | | Christian Social Party | | Other | | Total | |
|---|---|---|---|---|---|---|---|---|
| | no. | % | no. | % | no. | % | no. | % |
| 1919-1920 | 8 | 11.1 | 1 | 1.4 | 1 | 3.4 | 10 | 5.9 |
| 1920-1923 | 8 | 11.6 | 2 | 2.4 | 2 | 6.9 | 12 | 6.6 |
| 1923-1927 | 7 | 10.3 | 1 | 1.2 | 0 | - | 8 | 4.8 |
| 1927-1930 | 6 | 8.5 | 0 | | 0 | - | 6 | 3.8 |
| 1930-1934 | 9 | 12.5 | 1 | 1.5 | 1 | 3.7 | 11 | 6.7 |
| 2nd Republic | SPÖ | | ÖVP | | VDU/FPÖ | | GAL | Total |
| 1945-1949 | 8 | 10.5 | 2 | 2.4 | 0 | | | 10 | 6.3 |
| 1949-1953 | 8 | 11.9 | 2 | 2.6 | 0 | | | 10 | 6.3 |
| 1953-1956 | 9 | 12.3 | 2 | 2.7 | 0 | | | 11 | 6.7 |
| 1956-1959 | 7 | 9.5 | 3 | 3.7 | 0 | | | 10 | 6.3 |
| 1959-1962 | 8 | 10.3 | 3 | 3.8 | 0 | | | 11 | 6.7 |
| 1962-1966 | 8 | 10.5 | 3 | 3.7 | 0 | | | 11 | 6.7 |
| 1966-1970 | 8 | 10.8 | 3 | 3.5 | 0 | | | 11 | 6.7 |
| 1970-1971† | 6 | 7.4 | 2 | 2.6 | 0 | | | 8 | 4.8 |
| 1971-1975‡ | 8 | 8.6 | 3 | 3.8 | 0 | | | 11 | 6.0 |
| 1975-1979 | 9 | 9.7 | 5 | 6.3 | 0 | | | 14 | 7.7 |
| 1979-1983 | 11 | 11.6 | 7 | 9.1 | 0 | | | 18 | 9.8 |
| 1983-1986 | 11 | 12.2 | 8 | 9.9 | 1 | 8.3 | | 20 | 10.9 |
| 1986-1990 | 10 | 12.5 | 7 | 9.1 | 3 | 16.7 | 1 | 12.5 | 21 | 11.5 |
| 1990- | 17 | 21.3 | 7 | 11.7 | 7 | 21.1 | 5 | 50.0 | 36 | 19.7 |

Sources: Baumgartner (1981); Vogt (1977); Neyer (1985, 1989); ÖSTZ – The National Election (1970 and following)
* Maximum number of women in the Parliament.
† Women at the beginning of Parliament.
‡ Change in electoral law; increase in the number of deputies.

## Table 5-2: Austrian National Elections 1970-90: Female/ Male Candidacy and Election Results

| Year | Candidates[†] | | Female Candidates | | % of Females Elected | | % of Males Elected | |
|------|-------|------|------|------|------|------|------|------|
| | Party | no. | no. | in % | no. | in % | no. | in % |
| 1970 | SPÖ | 330 | 44 | 13.3 | 6 | 13.6 | 75 | 26.2 |
| | ÖVP | 330 | 27 | 8.2 | 2 | 7.4 | 76 | 25.1 |
| | FPÖ | 330 | 31 | 9.4 | - | - | 6 | 2.0 |
| | **Total** | 990 | 102 | 10.3 | 8 | 7.8 | 157 | 17.7 |
| 1971 | SPÖ | 366 | 47 | 12.8 | 8 | 17.0 | 85 | 26.2 |
| | ÖVP | 366 | 28 | 7.7 | 3 | 10.7 | 77 | 22.8 |
| | FPÖ | 366 | 24 | 6.6 | - | - | 10 | 2.9 |
| | **Total** | 1098 | 99 | 9.0 | 11 | 11.1 | 172 | 17.2 |
| 1975 | SPÖ | 366 | 55 | 15.0 | 9 | 16.4 | 84 | 27.0 |
| | ÖVP | 366 | 43 | 11.7 | 5 | 11.6 | 75 | 23.2 |
| | FPÖ | 366 | 36 | 9.8 | - | - | 10 | 3.0 |
| | **Total** | 1098 | 134 | 12.2 | 14 | 10.4 | 169 | 17.5 |
| 1979 | SPÖ | 366 | 59 | 16.1 | 11 | 18.6 | 84 | 27.4 |
| | ÖVP | 365 | 41 | 11.2 | 7 | 17.1 | 70 | 21.6 |
| | FPÖ | 366 | 47 | 12.8 | - | - | 11 | 3.4 |
| | **Total** | 1097 | 147 | 13.4 | 18 | 12.2 | 165 | 17.4 |
| 1983 | SPÖ | 366 | 65 | 17.8 | 8 | 12.3 | 82 | 27.2 |
| | ÖVP | 366 | 52 | 14.2 | 8 | 15.3 | 73 | 23.2 |
| | FPÖ | 364 | 48 | 13.2 | 1 | 2.1 | 11 | 3.5 |
| | **Total** | 1096 | 165 | 15.1 | 17 | 10.3 | 166 | 17.8 |
| 1986 | SPÖ | 366 | 98 | 26.8 | 10 | 10.2 | 70 | 26.1 |
| | ÖVP | 366 | 64 | 17.5 | 7 | 10.9 | 70 | 23.2 |
| | FPÖ | 365 | 47 | 12.9 | 3 | 6.4 | 15 | 4.7 |
| | GAL | 207 | 61 | 29.5 | 1 | 1.6 | 7 | 4.8 |
| | **Total** | 1304 | 207 | 20.7 | 21 | 7.8 | 162 | 15.7 |
| 1990 | SPÖ | 366 | 122 | 33.3 | 17 | 13.9 | 63 | 25.8 |
| | ÖVP | 366 | 94 | 25.7 | 7 | 7.4 | 53 | 19.5 |
| | FPÖ | 365 | 65 | 17.8 | 7 | 10.8 | 26 | 8.7 |
| | GAL | 221 | 92 | 41.6 | 5 | 5.4 | 5 | 3.8 |
| | **Total** | 1381 | 373 | 28.3 | 36 | 9.7 | 147 | 15.6 |

Source: ÖSTZ – The National Election 1970-90; Neyer (1985, 1989).
† Number of deputies in the National Assembly (Lower House): 165 to 1971; 183 since 1971.

## Table 5-3: Women in Government since 1966*

| Legislative Period | Ministers[†] | | | State Secretaries | | | Government Members | | |
|---|---|---|---|---|---|---|---|---|---|
| | Total | Women | % | Total | Women | % | Total | Women | % |
| 1966-1970 | 13[‡] | 1 | 7.7 | 6 | 0 | 0.0 | 19 | 1 | 5.3 |
| 1970-1971 | 13 | 1 | 7.7 | 2 | 1 | 50.0 | 15 | 2 | 13.3 |
| 1971-1975 | 14 | 2 | 14.3 | 4 | 1 | 25.0 | 18 | 3 | 16.7 |
| 1975-1979 | 14 | 2 | 14.3 | 4 | 1 | 25.0 | 18 | 3 | 16.7 |
| 1979-1983 | 14 | 1 | 7.1 | 9 | 5 | 55.6 | 23 | 6 | 26.1 |
| 1983-1986 | 15 | 1 | 6.7 | 8 | 2 | 25.0 | 23 | 3 | 13.0 |
| 1986-1990 | 15 | 2 | 13.3 | 2 | 1 | 50.0 | 17 | 3 | 17.6 |
| 1990- | 15[‡] | 2[‡] | 13.3 | 4 | 1 | 25.0 | 19[‡] | 3[‡] | 15.8 |

* Prior to 1966, there was only one woman in the government, namely a *Staatssekretär* (a Ministry-level position approximately equivalent to an Under Secretary in the Anglo-American tradition) during the provisional government (April 1945 – December 1945).
† Including the Chancellor.
‡ Including ministers without portfolio.

# References

Bourque, S. and Grossholtz, J. 1984. "Politics – an unnatural practice: political science looks at female participation." In *Women and the Public Sphere,*. Eds. J. Siltanen and M. Stanworth, 103-21. London.

Dachs, H. et al., eds. 1991. *Handbuch des politischen Systems Österreichs.* Vienna.

De Goederen, P. 1989. "Sozialpartnerschaft im Vergleich." In *Österreichisches Jahrbuch für Politik 1988* 423-45. Vienna.

Eisenstein, Z.R. 1988. *The Female Body and the Law.* Berkeley.

Evans, J., et al. 1986. *Feminism and Political Theory.* London.

Fischer, H. 1974. "Die parlamentarischen Fraktionen." In *Das politische System Österreichs.* Ed. H. Fischer, 111-50. Vienna.

____. 1991. "Das Parlament." In *Handbuch des Politischen Systems Österreichs.* Eds. H. Dachs et al., 96-117. Vienna.

Gerlich, P. 1974. "Funktionen im Parlament." In *Das politische System Österreichs.* Ed. H. Fischer, 77-109. Vienna.

Goot, M. and Reid, E. 1975. *Women and Voting Systems: Mindless Matrons or Sexist Scientism.* London.

Haavio-Mannila, E. et al. 1985. *Unfinished Democracy: Women in Nordic Politics.* Oxford.

Jones (Bulmash), K. 1989. "Der Tanz um den Lindenbaum. Eine feministische Kritik der traditionellen politischen Wissenschaft." In *Männer-Mythos-Wissenschaft: Grundlagentexte zur feministischen Wissenschaftskritik.* Ed. B. Schaeffer-Hegel and B. Watson-Franke, 99-116. Pfaffenweiler.

Jones, K.B. and Jonasdottir, A.G., eds. 1988. *The Political Interests of Gender. Developing Theory and Research with a Feminist Face.* London.

Köpl, R. and Neyer, G. 1985. *Politik von, für und gegen Frauen. Vol. 2: Gesetze.* Vienna.

Lovenduski, J. 1986. *Women and European Politics. Contemporary Feminism and Public Policy.* Brighton.

Mueller, C.M. ed. 1988. *The Politics of the Gender Gap. The Social Construction of Political Influence.* London.

Müller, W.C. 1983. "Direktwahl und Parteiensystem." *Österreichisches Jahrbuch für Politik*: 83-112. Vienna.

Neyer, G. 1985. *Politik von, für und gegen Frauen, Vol. 1: Parlamente und Regierungen.* In *Forschungsbericht des Instituts für höhere Studien.* Vienna.

____. 1989. "Geschlechtsspezifischer Zugang zu Entscheidungspositionen." In *Forschungsbericht im Auftrag des Bundesministeriums für Arbeit und Soziales.* Vienna.

____. 1991. "Frauen in der Politik. Am Beispiel der Repräsentation von Frauen im Nationalrat." In *Handbuch des Politischen Systems Österreichs.* Ed. H. Dachs et al., 296-308. Vienna.

Pelinka, A. 1971. "Parlament." In *Demokratie und Verfassung in Österreich.* Ed. A. Pelinka and M. Welan. Vienna.

Plasser F. et al. 1987. "Vom Ende der Lagerparteien: Perspektiven in der österreichischen Parteien- und Wahlforschung." *Österreichische Zeitschrift für Politikwissenschaft* 3: 241-58.

Randall, V. 1987. *Women and Politics. An International Perspective.* Chicago.

Sapiro, V. 1984. *The Political Integration of Women: Roles, Socialization, and Politics.* Urbana, Ill.

____. 1987. "What Research on the Political Socialization of Women Can Tell Us about the Political Socialization of People." In *The Impact of Feminist Research in the Academy.* Ed. Ch. Farnham, 148-73. Bloomington, Ind.

Siltanen, J. and Stanworth, M., eds. *Women and the Public Sphere: A Critique of Sociology and Politics.* London.

Sineau, M. 1990. *Mittel und Wege zur Verbesserung der politischen Mitwirkung der Frau.* Vienna.

Stirnemann, A. 1988. "Rekrutierung und Rekrutierungsstrategien." In *Das österreichische Parteiensystem.* Ed. A. Pelinka and F. Plasser, 599-643. Vienna.

Ucakar, Karl. 1985. *Demokratie und Wahlrecht in Österreich: Zur Entwicklung von politischer Partizipation und staatlicher Legitimationspolitik.* Vienna.

*Chapter 6*

≈≈≈

# THE GENDERING OF THE SERVICE SECTOR IN LATE NINETEENTH-CENTURY AUSTRIA

................................

*Erna Appelt*

F rom its emergence at the end of the nineteenth century until today, the service sector has been a sexually segregated, gendered
labor market (Appelt 1984, 1993; Nienhaus 1981; Gottschall 1990;
Willms 1982). My chapter examines the gendering of the service
sector in late nineteenth-century Austria and points to some very
specific strategies by which men defended their privileged status and
their domination of women.

## The Emergence of the Modern Service Sector

The sociological literature typically treats both capitalist modernization and the rise of the modern as processes of differentiation
(Habermas 1985; Münch 1984, 1988). An important result of this
socioeconomic differentiation was the formation of the service sector, which was closely connected to a permanent transformation in
patriarchal structures.

What were the most important factors that led to the growth of a
separate service sector in Central Europe? I would highlight three:

1. The liquidation of the *Grundherrschaft* (feudal controls over land and labor) as the final dissolution of feudal and explicitly patriarchal political structures in favor of a modern capitalist state organization after the Revolution of 1848.
2. The abolition in 1858 of the guild system (the organization of the economy through units of craft production that were also patriarchal in their assumptions) in favor of a capitalistically organized industrial economy (Matis 1972).
3. The disintegration of "das ganze Haus," that is, an older household form characterized by a unity between production and reproduction and, thus, an economically and socially autarkic household (Brunner 1968; see also the critical remarks in Ulbrich 1994).

The service sector, therefore, has its roots in the dissolution of patriarchal control in favor of modern state administration, and in the liquidation of patriarchally organized economic units in favor of capitalistically organized enterprises. This description is, of course, a simplification. Nevertheless, it is helpful as a framework for tracing differentiation as it affected the history of the service sector in Austria.

## Economic and Political Modernization

The neo-absolutist regime that came into power in the Habsburg Empire after 1848, and the liberal regime of the 1860s, effectively established the legal and administrative framework for economic development. The expansion of railroads, the founding of large-scale corporate banks, and the erection of a common Austro-Hungarian trading area, soon followed.

In most European countries, the industrial revolution was preceded by an agrarian revolution. In Austria, the patent concerning the liquidation of the *Grundherrschaft* and the restructuring of landholding patterns was proclaimed relatively late – on 7 September 1848. The timing of agrarian reform – in particular, the end of serfdom – in the various European nations (France 1789, Prussia 1810, Austria 1848, Russia 1861) provides a clear indicator of uneven socioeconomic development on the European continent (Matis and Bachinger 1973).

Uneven socioeconomic development is also significant because it influenced the relationship between the state and the economy. According to Gerschenkron's well-known thesis (1962) a country's degree of backwardness determines the typical features of its industrial development and its institutional foundations: the more backward the economy, the more important the role of the state. The Austrian part of the Austro-Hungarian monarchy lagged in comparison to Germany, but was more highly developed than the Hungarian half. In Austria, the banks were especially successful in presenting themselves as promoters of industrial development; in Hungary the government followed a conscious policy of industrialization (Gerschenkron 1977).

The extent to which the year 1848 marked a turning point in Austrian economic history has been challenged (Good 1984; Komlos 1983; Rudolph 1980), but there is no question that some dramatic changes followed in the revolution's wake, and that the state played a major role in them. The abolition of the judicial and administrative rights of the *Grundherren* was a crucial step in the liquidation of the traditional feudal and patriarchal system. These legal reforms reflected the political concerns of the liberal bourgeoisie. Reformers were mainly interested in liberating the individual from the bonds of obsolete power structures, by abolishing the *Grundherrschaft* and censorship, and by introducing trial by jury.

Although, subsequently, banks and railroads promoted trade within Austria, freedom of trade was first promulgated by law in Austria only in 1858. With this milestone, the patriarchal guild system gradually disappeared. The economic situation of families in the handicraft and small trade sectors was permanently changed, although elements of guild organization remained well into the twentieth century (Brusatti 1965).

The tie between political and economic change is illustrated especially well in the area of transport and communication. Walter Goldinger's research suggests that the Ministry of War and the general staff of the army were naturally very interested in railways, because they could be of decisive significance in case of mobilization. The first signs that the railway workers might organize also appeared to persuade the military establishment to have a stronger influence on the railway system (Goldinger 1973: 145). The expansion of the infrastructure through government policy was of vital interest for the military, but at the same time of utmost economic importance (März 1968).

The changing nature of government functions can also be clearly traced in the realm of social insurance in Austria, beginning with the obligatory accident insurance of 1887. Obligatory health insurance followed in 1888, for all workers and company officials employed in commercial, industrial, and trade enterprises. In the beginning, the legally mandated health insurance covered approximately 9 percent of the population of the Austrian part of the Habsburg Monarchy. This legal regulation of obligatory insurance represented a milestone in the evolution toward a welfare state (Bolognese-Leuchtenmüller 1978: 328).

The state also became involved in economic development in other ways. Generally speaking, there was a sharp increase in government spending throughout Europe between 1848 and 1914. The major source of this phenomenon in Austria prior to 1866 was the increase in military spending. After 1866, however, the spending for infrastructure (nationalization of railways and expansion of the postal, telegraph, and telephone networks) increased and accounted for 33 percent of total government spending by 1910 (Wysocki 1973: 92).

## The Service Sector in the Late Nineteenth Century

The modern service sector arose in the later phases of Austria's industrialization. The period between 1867 and 1873, the *Gründerzeit* (or founding era), was characterized by sharp rises in production, in the size of the railroad network, and in the number of corporations. In the last third of the nineteenth century, the more developed areas of the Habsburg Monarchy witnessed a rapidly rising accumulation of capital (März 1968; Matis 1973). The use of modern technology, as well as new organizational structures, favored the creation of larger plants. This affected not only the labor force and the extent of capital funds needed for the companies' own production, but also the necessary infrastructure. Industrial development required greater efficiency in the agrarian sector, new transport and communication facilities, and other services to produce at full capacity and benefit from cost-reducing competitive advantages. In addition, investments in education and child-rearing were essential conditions for training disciplined, skilled workers for industry.

In the 1880s these requirements became so well established that it seems justifiable to speak of a new phase of industrialization (Brusatti 1967; Mosser 1981). The same period saw a consolidation of the infrastructure that involved a dramatic expansion of the railroad and postal networks (see Tables 6-1 and 6-2). In 1848 there were ten telegraph stations in Austria; by 1913 there were 7,282. Eighteen eighty-one marked the beginning of telephone service, which was taken over by the state in 1895. Still, in 1910, 53 percent of the employed population remained in agriculture and barely 23 percent in trades and industry (Table 6-3). It is also important to

**Table 6-1: Expansion of the Railway System in Cisleithania (Imperial Austria)**

| Year | Number of Passengers in millions | Goods Transported in 1000s of tons |
|------|----------------------------------|-------------------------------------|
| 1882 | 37.35 | 52.07 |
| 1892 | 90.30 | 83.92 |
| 1902 | 173.62 | 119.36 |
| 1912 | 290.85 | 159.21 |

Source: *Österreichisches Staatswörterbuch. Handbuch des gesamten österreichischen öffentlichen Rechts*, Vienna 1905; *Österreichisches Statistisches Handbuch* 31, Vienna 1912.

**Table 6-2: Development of the Postal System in Cisleithania**

| Year | Number of Post Offices | Number of Letters Transported |
|------|------------------------|-------------------------------|
| 1848 | 1,094 | 20,737 |
| 1857 | 1,548 | 50,011 |
| 1867 | 2,225 | 106,904 |
| 1877 | 4,006 | 263,008 |
| 1887 | 4,434 | 449,410 |
| 1897 | 5,754 | 922,807 |
| 1907 | 8,823 | 1,517,816 |
| 1913 | 9,985 | 2,049,923 |

Source: *Statistische Rückblicke* 56. *Österreichisches Statistisches Handbuch* 32, Vienna 1913.

**Table 6-3: Employment in Cisleithania from 1869 to 1910**

| Year | Agriculture | Industry and Trades | Services |
|------|-------------|---------------------|----------|
| 1869 | 67.18 | 19.68 | 5.16 |
| 1890 | 62.41 | 21.23 | 6.23 |
| 1900 | 58.16 | 22.25 | 7.34 |
| 1910 | 53.00 | 23.13 | 9.87 |

Source: *Statistische Monatsschrift* 29, 30, and 40; 1894, 1904, and 1914.

remember that the socioeconomic modernization of the Austro-Hungarian Monarchy occurred quite unevenly (Good 1984; Matis 1972). Whereas large parts of Austria maintained their agrarian character, linked with a small business structure, industrial centers and agglomerations sprang up in other parts of the Habsburg Monarchy, above all in Bohemia, Moravia, Silesia, Lower Austria, Styria, and Vorarlberg. The expansion of the infrastructure was both the consequence of, and a pre-condition for, the general push toward industrialization.

The trend toward large-scale enterprises, and the growth of transportation and telecommunications, forged new employment opportunities in the administrative structures of large enterprises. Within firms, the administrative side began to function independently and in parallel to the manufacturing side. More and more positions were created to handle planning, technical development, administration, and marketing. This development created an increasing demand for employees in middle and higher management positions (Kocka 1981; Baryli 1972). However, a differentiation among the white-collar workers also occurred. The new white collar class that arose from the growth and restructuring of enterprises had very little in common with the former shop assistants of the eighteenth century (Braverman 1977). Employees in earlier periods had been subject to domestic employment regulations *(Dienstbotenordnung),* which in 1811 had been set down in a modified form in the General Civil Code *(Allgemeines Bürgerliches Gesetzbuch).* Under these laws, clerks had a personally subservient relationship with their employers and, under optimum conditions, passed through the stages from apprentice to assistant and, finally, to independent employer.

The first new regulation that controlled the legal status of the modern shop assistants is to be found in the Commercial Law Book *(Handelsgesetzbuch)* of 1862. During the phase of mature industrialization, the office manager could rise from the ranks and be among a firm's most important employees, even reaching higher management levels. At the same time, administrative work was clearly organized according to a hierarchy: bookkeepers, cashiers, shopkeepers, female clerks, secretaries, and merchant's assistants were all designated as lower-level employees. Within this hierarchy, all efforts were synchronized in order to control, analyze, and rationalize the flow of work. The explosion of personnel costs accompanying this organizational restructuring was slowed increasingly by employing women, especially in the civil service (Pechtl 1874; Nawiaski 1914).

## The Growth of Female White-Collar Workers

Traditionally, the Austrian civil service had been a kind of state-run fiefdom, with government officials often referred to as "little emperors." By the last decades of the nineteenth century, increasing numbers of women entered their domain. The first women were employed in the private postal service in 1869; in 1872, the Austrian government employed the first forty women in probationary positions as telegraph operators. In 1874, the first female postal officials appeared on the job. In this same year, the first women were employed in telegraph services and in general administrative positions of the Kaiser Ferdinand Nordbahn. In 1883, the postal savings bank system admitted its first female employees. By 1904, all governmental departments had begun to employ women. In 1900, 8,950 women were employed in the Austrian civil service; the majority of them (90 percent) worked in the postal and telegraph services (*Handbuch der Frauenarbeit* 1930).

What was the reason for this development? Why was there a sudden increase in the numbers of female employees in the civil service, which had been male-dominated up to that time? The technical revolution in telecommunications, as well as the expanded functions of public administration, caused an explosion of personnel costs, and created a new demand for cheap labor. As new positions and career possibilities opened up for male clerks, many of the new low-paid jobs were occupied by women. The government economized not only by paying low entry-level salaries to the mostly young and well-educated women, but also by excluding women from permanent positions. The fact that female civil servants were always employed on the basis of private law was decisive for their socioeconomic situation; they could not be placed on the permanent staff and did not enjoy the pension rights of permanent civil servants (Appelt 1985; Fehrer 1989).

A look at Table 6-4 shows the rapidly growing numbers of male and female employees in industry and trade, transport, and commerce, as well as in the public sector. Table 6-5 shows the increasing percentage of women among employees in various sectors. By 1910, one-fourth of all civil service employees were women. Expanding employment in large companies, together with the advent of department stores, also created a continually expanding demand for cheap female workers in the private sector. In private enterprises, the invention of the typewriter played a considerable role. Whereas clerks had traditionally been male, the first female clerks were employed at the same time the first typewriters were introduced. Companies that manufactured typewriters frequently trained young women, and furnished them to firms requesting them.

It is necessary to discuss not only the increasing demand for female employees, but also the increasing supply of women who applied for jobs as white-collar workers. For example, more than 800 women

**Table 6-4: Male and Female Salaried Employees According to Economic Sectors in Cisleithania in 1890, 1900, and 1910.**

| Economic Sector | 1890 | | 1900 | | 1910 | |
|---|---|---|---|---|---|---|
| | Male | Female | Male | Female | Male | Female |
| Industry and Trade | 36,328 | 1,827 | 69,149 | 4,247 | 95,501 | 14,676 |
| Transport and Commerce | 99,099 | 8,405 | 100,050 | 13,562 | 113,621 | 36,811 |
| Public Sector and Professionals† | 151,187 | 30,926 | 169,838 | 49,615 | 291,355 | 79,187 |

† Doctors, lawyers and other independent, self-employed persons, but not members of the military.

Source: *Berufsstatistiken nach den Ergebnissen der Volkszählung* 1890, 1900, and 1910.

**Table 6-5: Percentage of Female Employees in Various Economic Sectors in 1890, 1900, and 1910**

| Economic Sectors | 1890 | 1900 | 1910 |
|---|---|---|---|
| Industry and Trade | 4.8 | 5.8 | 13.3 |
| Trade and Commerce | 7.8 | 11.9 | 21.8 |
| Public Sector | 17.0 | 22.6 | 26.5 |

Source: *Berufsstatistiken nach Ergebnissen der Volkszählungen* 1890, 1900, and 1910.

applied for the first thirty jobs open to them on the Kaiser Ferdinand Nordbahn. There were three mains reasons for the expanding supply of female workers in white-collar jobs. First, as traditional economic units disappeared (and industrial concentration increased) more and more young middle-class men and women found it necessary to look for work outside the family. Second, the growth of administrative apparatuses expanded the number of low-paid officials and civil servants who held middle-class status but were unable to support their daughters. Third, the middle-class women's movement increasingly encouraged educated women from the middle class and the aristocracy to pursue careers.

Louise Otto-Peters, one of the leaders of the German women's movement, emphasized as early as 1847 that office work would serve as a future source of income for single women (Otto-Peters 1847). Beside teaching, office work appeared to be the female occupation most compatible with middle-class norms and values, even if it did challenge the image of the domestic woman. In Austria, Marianne Hainisch maintained a viewpoint similar to that of Otto-Peters. Hainisch fought to establish public secondary schools for girls, and to give them access to universities as a way of improving their career possibilities (Hainisch 1930: 13). The financial situation of unmarried women from the middle class, especially the lower middle class, was often quite uncertain. If their parents were unable to provide for them, the women had either to earn their living by sewing – which, according to the customs of their class, would have to be kept secret – or to depend on the sympathy of relatives.

Female employment did not expand at the expense of male employment. Between 1880 and 1910, the number of employed men rose sharply as a percentage of the total male population (*Volkszählungsergebnisse* 1880, 1890, 1910; Banik-Schweitzer 1979). Therefore, during this period of a rapidly increasing female labor force, the demand for gainfully employed workers grew faster than the supply of male workers. So women filled, for the most part, newly created positions. Still, men systematically resisted the employment of females in the service sector. I now turn to an assessment of the mechanisms used to integrate the first women into the service sector, and to the strategies used by white-collar males to defend their jobs and their privileged status.

## Paternalistic Mechanisms of Integration

The inclusion of women in the workforce contradicted certain middle-class conceptions of femininity, ideas that were also held by some activists in the women's movement as well. One way of reconciling the contradictory ideologies was to "adopt" working women in the firm or office as "daughters." Not considered to be independent members of their *Berufsstand* (vocational group), women belonged only by virtue of their connection to male family members. The almost familial link to the shop or office was also closely tied to residence with a family appropriate to one's rank. Only when these two protections were installed, was there a basis for admitting middle-class women to the ranks of the professional civil service.

In small stores, salesgirls usually lived in the household of the employer, "belonged" to the family that employed them, and ate at its table. There was often little distinction between them and maid-servants. The young women often stood behind the counter during the day, and were used for domestic duties in the evenings and on weekends (Gronemann 1900; Nienhaus 1981; Appelt 1985).

The inclusion of women, primarily of daughters of professionals of the same rank, in the public sector took place in a similarly paternalistic way. Here, too, family bonds were strong. For example, when the Austrian railways began to employ women, the Kaiser Ferdinand Nordbahn employed only wives, daughters, and widows of male Nordbahn employees. The *Beamten-Zeitung* wrote:

> The board of the Ferdinand Nordbahn has decided to use women in telegraph and administrative services for a daily wage of 1.50 florins. This decision was welcomed by the civil servants of the Ferdinand Nordbahn, even more so because only wives, daughters, or widows of Nordbahn employees may claim these jobs. Three widows of Nordbahn officials, who, because of their husbands' abnormal period of service, did not receive a pension, but only severance pay, are already clerks of the society (BZ 1874).

From the beginning, the postal savings bank employed female bookkeepers (although on a temporary basis and without established terms of employment). The precondition for employment was that the women came from the family of a civil servant or official. Married women were not admitted.

These patterns are certainly consistent with the efforts of civil servants to regulate access to their ranks, what Max Weber early on termed "closing" the ranks *(Schließung)*. Contrary to the notion of the freeplay of supply and demand in labor markets, closing mechanisms operated along familial lines; professional class consciousness could, on occasion, overwhelm gender solidarity (Appelt 1993, 1994).

These forms of integrating women had important consequences. The recruitment of women from civil service and white collar families guaranteed that they would be relatively well-educated and familiar with the traditions of public service. It also made possible intensive supervision of women's social behavior. Finally wage discrimination could be legitimized, because it was presumed that employed women were taken care of as part of white collar and civil servants' families.

## The Evolution of Gender-specific Job Profiles

The labor force status of women in late nineteenth-century Austria was also shaped by the institutionalization of gender-biased job profiles for occupational categories (Nienhaus 1981; Appelt 1985; Gottschall 1990). As in other industrializing countries, "female" occupations in Austria began to cluster in areas where the service sector took on healing, helping, and serving functions that were previously performed by women in private households, such as nursing and childcare. In effect, skills acquired by women in the household became professionalized in the labor market. Other occupational categories, especially in the area of social work, emerged from charitable and church activities. The middle-class women's movement played a significant role in the professionalization of private and voluntary social services for the aged, for the ill, and for children (Gottschall 1990).

"Female" qualities were also in demand for jobs in the growing clerical staffs of large-scale bureaucratic enterprises. The emerging profile of the perfect secretary, for example, implied not only subordination to authority, but also the personal qualities of sensitivity, empathy, and modesty. Advertisements in daily newspapers just after World War I illustrate well how qualifications for "female" jobs had more to do with personal conduct and behavior than with specialized job skills. "Wanted: perfect lady typist. Educated young woman from good family" (*Die Presse*, 1 October 1919). "Wanted immediately: experienced lady typist from a good family who prefers a modest income to unemployment" (*Neues Wiener Tagblatt*, 18 December 1925). "Wanted: private secretary for responsible personage in Vienna. Only distinguished, tactful ladies with some business training and refined comportment need apply" (*Die Presse*, 3 November 1918).

## Strategies of Exclusion

Government and male-dominated institutions played a significant role in creating a gendered labor market. Especially among low skilled employees and civil servants, there was fear that women would "invade" and compete for "men's" positions. Several factors were decisive in excluding women from better jobs. The most important was their limited access to higher education. Beyond this, the employee and public service labor unions acted in the interests of men by playing upon the anxieties of male employees who feared demotion as well as competition from women. Finally, women were excluded by statute from key organizations that exerted a preponderant influence on professional and political careers, for example, the Conservative Christian Federation and the Free Masons, both of which still bar women from membership (Schauffler 1930).

At the end of the nineteenth century, it was mainly lower paid, less skilled white-collar males who protested against employing women. In 1883, the minutes of the commercial clerks' meeting stated that the hiring of women was to be rejected vigorously as "a threat to the entire body of assistants." They warned that the low wages of the saleswomen would lower their own wages (*Protokoll* 1883). In 1904, the "Conference of White-Collar Workers" announced on "German Shop Assistant Day" that "it has never been considered cultural progress but rather a product of necessity for women to earn their livelihood; it is a sign of a disease in the social body." And with regard to the particular position of shop assistant, it stated that "female traits are not suited to this occupation; on the contrary, it goes against both the physical and mental attributes of the female nature" (*Nachtrag* 1904).

Employment practices in the postal service presented especially large stumbling blocks for women. On 3 March 1901, the members of the Viennese Postal Clerks Union decided at their general assembly no longer to admit female employees as supporting members. In 1902, the postal clerks demanded that women not be admitted as clerks in first and second class post offices, and took their grievances to the postal management (BP 1902, no. 2). On "Postal Subclerks' Day" (*Allgemeiner Posthilfsbeamtentag*, 6 December 1906) in Vienna, this matter was discussed in detail. A postal clerk from Graz remarked:

> A factor vitally affecting our interests is the status of women in the postal service. Although emancipation is attempting to spread in all directions, the basic principle remains the same – that the man should feed his wife and his family and not the opposite. We men must strive to procure greater sources of income in order to cover mounting expenses, which is not the case for women. For this reason it is inexplicable that jobs in the civil service should be created to secure a higher income for women while men and their families must starve (BP 4. No. 2).

In 1905, the postal employees union passed a resolution that put forth the following demands: the exclusion of married women from the postal service, the exclusion of all women from skilled jobs at the post office, and the complete separation of male and female careers at the post office (BP 1905, no. 4). These demands were also brought before the Austrian Parliament, where only a few Social Democratic deputies opposed them (BP 1905, no. 5).

To understand this attitude, it is important to remember that some occupational groups such as postal subclerks were threatened by proletarianization (Lackenbacher 1930). The employment of wives was held to be demeaning to their already questionable status. In contrast, the "intact" patriarchal family model signified membership in the middle class. Thus male postal employees were defending not only their occupational status, but also their gendered position as breadwinners of the family. Within this context it is interesting to note that middle- or high-ranking civil servants, who did not need to fear any setback in their social or professional status, welcomed the new career opportunities for the female relatives of minor officials (BZ 1874, no. 13).

In other sectors, too, female employees had to struggle against discrimination and exclusion. In 1901 the "Civil Servants' Section of the Austrian Women's Association" (*Beamtensektion des Allgemeinen Österreichischen Frauenvereins*) introduced a petition in Parliament calling for uniform treatment of female personnel with respect to retirement and pay conditions, for official status (*Beamtenstatus*) for female employees, and for the inclusion of females in the tenure of service system (*Dokumente* 1902).

At the 35th anniversary celebration of female employment in the public service, the speaker, Caroline Barth, reminded her audience:

> In 1892 we turned to the Parliament in order to secure retirement pensions and tenure. The Parliament showed an interest in our cause and provided us with an old age pension scheme that unfortunately did not correspond to our wishes and needs, because after 21 years of service we were forcibly referred to a private pension association without accounting for our period of service. We were forced to ask for a state advance, which we received but had to pay extra for the years of service that were not counted (*Dokumente* 1902).

In 1907, at the urging of female government employees from the "The Public Association of Government Employees under Contract" (*Reichsverein der staatlichen Vertragsbeamten*) a draft of a law "eliminating unbearable hardships for female civil servants under contract" was introduced before the Parliament. Female civil servants were upset mainly about pay discrimination. Male assistants received the same pay after three years of service that women received after fifteen to seventeen years (Schauffler 1930).

## Summary

In the second half of the nineteenth century, radical changes occurred in the social structure of Austria. The foundations for traditional patriarchal control were being eliminated along with traditional economic structures. The feudal patriarchal system of *Grundherrschaft* was abolished, and freedom of trade was introduced. These innovations laid the groundwork for capitalist economic development.

These penetrating changes also affected the microcosm of social life: the household. Urban households became tied increasingly to the labor market, and as incomes grew, consumption became a central feature of household life. The result was a rapidly changing occupational structure. In the last third of the nineteenth century, the service sector grew in both the private and public spheres, a trend which has persisted until today. The newly created administrative structures in private firms and in the public sector were hierarchically organized, especially along gender lines.

The demand for white-collar workers grew with the expansion of the service sector and outstripped the supply of males. Men felt doubly threatened by the growing number of women in private sector firms and in the public sector. They not only feared female competition at the workplace, but they also saw the erosion of the middle-class family as an institution that had, up to that point, ensured their role as providers.

It is therefore not surprising that male white-collar workers and officials sought to defend their interests with all possible means. Many would have preferred to have women completely excluded from white-collar jobs. But since it soon became evident that this was impossible, they did their utmost to control and regulate the employment of women within the hierarchical system.

The paternalistic integration of women into the service sector, the evolution of gender-specific profiles in professional occupations, and, finally, the exclusion of women from male organizations and associations, played decisive roles in this process. They provided male white-collar workers with considerable advantages over their female counterparts. Thus, at the end of the nineteenth century, the way was already paved for a segregation of the service sector labor market that secured privileged positions for men and relegated women to the lower strata of the hierarchy. This hierarchical construction institutionalized pay discrimination, and perpetuated the notion that women were primarily destined for work within the household.

**Table 6-6: Industrial Employees in the Habsburg Monarchy by Province**

| Provinces | 1869 | 1890 | 1900 | 1910 |
|---|---|---|---|---|
| Lower Austria | 5,198 | 11,491 | 24,675 | 38,070 |
| Bohemia | 7,052 | 12,185 | 23,283 | 35,496 |
| Moravia | 2,667 | 4,219 | 8,109 | 11,334 |
| Styria | 1,302 | 2,203 | 3,113 | 4,149 |
| All Industrial White Collar Workers | 25,511 | 38,155 | 73,396 | 110,117 |
| Percentage of Industrial White Collar Workers | 63% | 79% | 80.6% | 80.8% |

Source: *Berufsstatistiken nach Ergebnissen der Volkszählungen* 1869, 1890, 1900, and 1910.

# Abbreviations

BP – Der Beamte der Postanstalt
BZ – Beamten-Zeitung

# References

Appelt E. 1985. *Von Ladenmädchen, Schreibfräulein und Gouvernanten: Die weiblichen Angestellten Wiens 1900 – 1934.* Vienna.
___. 1993. "'Denn das Gesetz unserer Zeit heißt Ökonomie ...' Weibliche Angestellte in Prozeß sozioökonomischer Modernisierung." *Frauen-Arbeitswelten. Zur historischen Genese gegenwärtiger Probleme.* Ed. B. Bolognese-Leuchtemüller and M. Mitterauer. Vienna.
___. 1994. *Staatsbürgerschaft und soziales Geschlecht: Zur politischen Transformation des Geschlechterverhältnisses. Studien an ausgewählten europäischen Ländern.* Habilitations dissertation, University of Innsbruck.
___. 1984. "Weibliche Angestellte vor dem Ersten Weltkrieg." *Aufrisse* 5(3): 17-19.
Banik-Schweitzer R. 1979. "Zur Entwicklung der Berufs- und Betriebsstruktur in Wien 1879-1934." *Summa Wirtschaftsberichte* 6.
Baryli, A. 1972. "Die Sonder-Sozialversicherung der Angestellten." In *Österreich bis 1938.* Vienna.

*Der Beamte der Postanstalt. Zentralorgan, Fach- und Interesseblatt der Posthilfsbeamten Österreichs.* 1902-6. Vienna.

*Beamten-Zeitung. Zeitschrift des Ersten Allgemeinen Beamten-Vereins.* 1874.

Bolognese-Leuchtenmüller B. 1978. *Bevölkerungsentwicklung und Berufsstruktur: Gesundheits- und Fürsorgewesen in Österreich 1750-1918.* Vienna.

Braverman, H. 1977. *Die Arbeit im modernen Produktionsprozeß.* Frankfurt am Main.

Brunner, O. 1968. *Neue Wege der Verfassungs- und Sozialgeschichte.* Göttingen.

Brusatti, A. 1965. *Österreichische Wirtschaftspolitik vom Josefinismus zum Ständestaat.* Vienna.

Croner, F. 1962. *Soziologie der Angestellten.* Cologne.

*Dokumente der Frauen* 1902. No. 24, 24 March.

Ehmer, J. 1980. *Familienstruktur und Arbeitsorganisation im frühindustriellen Wien.* Vienna.

Fehrer, R. 1989. *Die Frau als Angestellte in Wirtschaft und Verwaltung Österreichs.* Linz.

*Frauenbewegung, Frauenbildung, Frauenarbeit.* 1930. Ed. Bund österreichischer Frauenvereine. Vienna.

Gerschenkron, A. (1962). *Economic Backwardness in Historical Perspective.* Cambridge, Mass.

____. (1977). *An Economic Spurt that Failed.* Princeton, N.J.

Goldinger, W. 1973. "Die Zentralverwaltung in Cisleithanien – die zivile gemeinsame Zentralverwaltung." In *Die Habsburgmonarchie.* Vol. 2 Ed. A. Wandruszka and P. Urbanitsch. Vienna.

Good, D. 1984. *The Economic Rise of the Habsburg Empire, 1750-1914.* Berkeley.

Gottschall, K. 1990. "Frauenerwerbsarbeit und Tertiarisierung: Zur Erosion und Rekonstruktion geschlechtsspezifischer Arbeitsteilung in der Dienstleistungsgesellschaft." In *Grenzen der Gleichheit. Frauenarbeit zwischen Tradition und Aufbruch.* Ed. E. Vogelheim. Marburg.

Gronemann, C. 1900 "Weibliche Handelsangestellte." *Dokumente der Frauen:* 2/22 (February).

Gross, N.T. 1966. "Industrialization in Austria in the Nineteenth Century." Ph.D. dissertation, University of California. Berkeley.

Habermas, J. 1985. *Theorie des kommunikativen Handelns.* 2 vols. Frankfurt am Main.

Kocka, J. 1981. *Angestellte im europäischen Vergleich: Die Herausbildung angestellter Mittelschichten seit dem späten 19. Jahrhundert.* Göttingen.

Komlos, J. 1983. *The Habsburg Monarchy as a Customs Union: Economic Development in Austria-Hungary in the Nineteenth Century.* Princeton.

Lackenbacher, E. 1930. "Die Erschütterung des Angestelltentums." *Der Kampf* 23 (November).

März, E. 1968. *Österreichische Industrie-und Bankpolitik in der Zeit Franz Josephs I.* Vienna.

Matis, H. 1972. *Österreichische Wirtschaft 1848 – 1913: Konjunktureller und gesellschaftlicher Wandel im Zeitalter Franz Josephs I.* Vienna.

Matis, H. and Bachinger, K. 1973. "Österreichs industrielle Entwicklung." In *Die Habsburgmonarchie.* Vol. 2. Ed. A. Wandruszka and P. Urbanitsch. Vienna.

Mosser, A. 1980. *Die Industrieaktiengesellschaft in Österreich 1880-1913.* Vienna.

Münch, R. 1984. *Die Struktur der Moderne: Grundmuster und differentielle Gestaltung des institutionellen Aufbaus der modernen Gesellschaften.* Frankfurt am Main.

___. 1988. *Theorie des Handelns: Zur Rekonstruktion der Beiträge von Talcott Parsons, Emile Durkheim und Max Weber.* Frankfurt am Main.

*Nachtrag zur Verhandlungsschrift des Deutschen Handlungsgehilfentages über die Ausschußsitzung vom 25. bis 28. Mai 1904.* 1904.

Nawiaski, H. 1914. *Die Post und ihr Personal.* Vienna.

*Neues Wiener Tagblatt,* 18 December 1925.

Nienhaus, U. 1981. "Von Töchtern und Schwestern: Zur Geschichte der weiblichen Angestellten im Deutschen Kaiserreich." In *Angestellte im europäischen Vergleich.* Ed. J. Kocka. Göttingen.

Otruba, G. 1977. "Zur Geschichte der Angestellten und ihrer wachsenden Bedeutung in Österreich bis 1918 (im Vergleich zu Deutschland)." *Österreich in Geschichte und Literatur* 21(2): 74-102.

Otto-Peters, L. 1972. "Die Theilnahme der Frauen an den Interessen des Staates." In *Die deutsche Frauenbewegung: Ihre Anfänge und erste Entwicklung, 1843-1889.* Vol. 2: *Quellen.* Ed. M. Twellmann. Meisenheim.

Pechtl, H. 1874. "Staatsdiener und Staatsdienst in Österreich." *Beamten-Zeitung* 5/16.

*Die Presse,* 3 November 1918; 1 October 1919.

*Protokoll der ersten Tagung der österreichischen Handelsangestellten.* 1883 (7-8 September). Vienna.

Rudolph, R. 1980. "Social Structure and the Beginning of Austrian Economic Growth." *East Central Europe* 7/2: 207-24.

Schauffler, R. 1930. "Die Kanzlei- und Verwaltungsbeamtin." In *Frauenbewegung, Frauenbildung und Frauenarbeit in Österreich.* Ed. M.S. Braun. Vienna.

Ulbricht, C. 1994. *Frauen im Dorf. Handlungsspielräume und Erfahrungswelten von Frauen im 18. Jahrhundert aus der Perspektive einer lokalen Gesellschaft.* Frankfurt am Main.

Willms, A., 1982. "Modernisierung durch Frauenarbeit? Zum Zusammenhang von wirtschaftlichem Strukturwandel und weiblicher Arbeitsmarktlage in Deutschland, 1882 – 1939." In *Historische Arbeitsmarktforschung.* Ed. T. Pierenkemp and R. Tilly. Göttingen.

Wysocki, J., 1973. "Die österreichische Finanzpolitik." In *Die Habsburgmonarchie: 1848 – 1918.* Ed. A. Wandruszka and P. Urbanitsch. Vienna.

*Chapter 7*

❦

# WOMEN AND THEIR WORK IN THE LABOR MARKET AND IN THE HOUSEHOLD

..............................

*Gudrun Biffl*

The participation of women in the labor force has increased significantly in the developed industrialized world over the last thirty years. The basic trend also holds for Austria, but it has not been as pronounced as in the Northern European countries or in the Anglo-Saxon world. The reason is that the labor force participation of women in Austria was already high by international standards before the 1960s, due to special features of the country's economic structure. My chapter examines the labor supply development of women in Austria from the turn of the century, with special focus on the last three decades.

## The Labor Force Participation of Austrian Women in International Perspective

In 1990, 1,470,000 women were in the labor force in Austria, representing 43.6 percent of the female population over 15 years of age and 56.4 percent of the 15 to 65-year-olds, the more commonly used definition of participation rate. These labor force participation rates are smaller than at the beginning of the century. In 1910, 1,329,400 women were in the labor force, about 56 percent of the population over 15. After World War I, the activity rate of women was similar to that before the war (54.6 percent in the census year 1923). During the great depression, the labor force participation of women declined at a rate faster than for men, and, by 1934 it stood at 47.4 percent. As the economy recovered and particularly during World War II, women came into the labor market in larger numbers. Already by 1939, 1,429,500 women (52.2 percent of the female population over 15 years of age) worked in the Ostmark, the territory of Austria that was incorporated into the German Reich.

**Table 7-1: Female Labor Force Participation, 1910-1990: Austria and the United States**

| Austria | | | | U.S.A. | |
|---|---|---|---|---|---|
| Year | Labor Force | % of pop. 15+ | % of pop. 15-65 | Year | % of pop. 14+ |
| 1910 | 1329.4 | 56.0 | 61.8 | 1910 | 22.8 |
| 1923 | 1405.3 | 54.6 | 59.9 | 1920 | 23.3 |
| 1934 | 1289.2 | 47.4 | 53.2 | 1930 | 24.3 |
| 1939 | 1429.5 | 52.2 | 59.3 | 1940 | 25.4 |
| 1951 | 1299.3 | 44.2 | 51.8 | 1950 | 28.6 |
| 1961 | 1359.9 | 45.3 | 55.2 | 1960 | 35.4 |
| 1971[†] | 1202.8 | 39.2 | 49.9 | 1970 | 39.9 |
| 1981[†] | 1376.8 | 42.4 | 54.8 | | |
| 1990[†] | 1470.4 | 43.6 | 56.4 | | |

Source: Austrian Central Statistical Office. Census data and adjustments by Austrian Institute of Economic Research. For USA: Ehrenberg and Smith (1985: 15).
† Wives of farmers, who declared themselves as housewives are not included in the labor force. This classification did not exist earlier.

Table 7-1 also shows that labor force participation of women was higher in Austria than in the United States until the late 1960s. It was higher also than in Great Britain, where the labor force participation rate of women was around 35 percent from the turn of the century until the 1930s (Long 1958). From the 1960s on, however, female participation in the labor force grew relatively slowly in Austria. As Figure 7-1 shows, female labor force participation grew more dramatically in Sweden, the United States, Great Britain, and France than in Austria. Among the industrialized European countries, only Germany experienced equally slow growth in the labor supply of women, and the current level of the female activity rate in Germany continues to be somewhat lower than in Austria. Female labor force participation rates are also lower in Southern Europe, Switzerland, and the Netherlands than in Austria.

**Figure 7-1: International Comparison of Total Female Activity Rates***

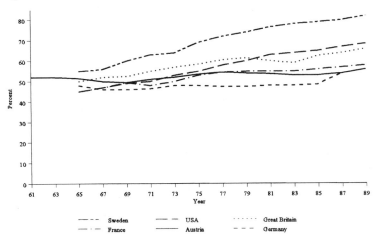

| | | |
|---|---|---|
| − − − Sweden | − − USA | · · · · · · Great Britain |
| − · − France | ———— Austria | − − − Germany |

*Shown as percentage of total female population 15-65 years old

As elsewhere, labor force participation in Austria differs over the life cycle of women. It peaks in the 20-24 age bracket, and then gradually falls off. Austrian women from 25 to 34 years old currently have a participation rate of 66 percent, which is below the average for the industrialized western world. For example, the level for 1989 was 73.4 percent in the United States, 74.7 percent in France, and 89.4 percent in Sweden. Looked at from a long-term perspective, however, one can see that the labor force participation of 25- to 34-year-old women was higher for a long time in Austria than in other countries. Sweden only surpassed the Austrian level in 1968, France in 1974, the United States in 1979, and Great Britain as recently as 1987 (OECD 1990).

Labor force participation of 35- to 44-year-old Austrian women corresponded to the average in the mid-1960s when international differences were rather smaller than now. This age bracket experienced the strongest expansion of any age group in Austria in the 1970s and 1980s. Yet, growth in labor force participation was even more pronounced in the other industrialized countries (except Germany) so that a gap between Austria and other countries opened up. The difference in the activity rate between Austria (65.7 percent) at one end of the spectrum and Sweden (92.8 percent) at the other, amounted to 27.1 percentage points in 1989 (OECD 1990).

The labor force participation of young females has declined in Austria over the long run, and is significantly lower than in comparable industrialized countries.[1] In spite of an extensive apprenticeship schooling program, the labor force participation of female teenagers is lower in Austria (45 percent) than in the United States (55.9 percent), Great Britain (71.5 percent) and Sweden (51.3 percent). But the activity rate of teenagers in Austria is still higher than in Germany or France. In France, the educational reform of the mid-1960s eliminated the apprenticeship program, and this brought the activity rate down to 9.4 percent in 1989.

In contrast, international differences in the labor force participation of 20- to 24-year-old women have diminished over time. The activity rate of women in this age bracket is the highest of any age group in Austria, and is surpassed only by Germany (73.6 percent) and, of course, by Sweden (82 percent). At 72.8 percent, it is slightly higher than in United States (72.4 percent) and Great Britain (72.2 percent) and greatly exceeds that in France (59.7 percent).

The growth of labor force participation among 45- to 54-year-old Austrian women conforms rather well to international patterns. Both the level and the change over time are similar to France and the United States. In the 1980s, however, labor market opportunities for Austrian women were not favorable, so the growth in their labor force participation lagged behind that of France and the United States.

Activity rates of women older than 55 have generally been lower in Austria than in the majority of industrialized countries, with the exception of the relatively short period of economic boom from 1969 to 1975. In this phase, the labor force participation of 55- to 60-year-old women increased rapidly and approached that of the United States.[2] In spite of the substantial rise, there was still a strong

---

1. In Great Britain and the United States, the youth labor market is organized differently than in many continental European countries, because it allows the combination of part-time employment with full-time education. In Austria, as in Germany and France, institutional factors surrounding education explain the pattern of teenage labor force participation. The apprenticeship system and its relative importance in the educational structure play the most important role in determining the participation rate of 15- to 19-year-olds because apprentices are counted as employed.

2. This development has something to do with the extreme labor shortage in Austria at that time –unemployment rates were running around 1.5 percent. Supply factors have to be taken into consideration as well. This was the generation of the unusually small birth cohorts of World War I. The women of this generation were left single or widowed to a large extent, due to the heavy loss of males of equal age in World War II. They largely replaced men in production and lost their jobs only when the economy experienced a severe downturn in 1974/75. By then, they had reached the legal retirement age.

decline in the number of female workers in this age group, due to its small cohort size. Currently, the Austrian activity rate of 55- to 60-year-old women is around 25 percent which makes it the lowest in this international comparison.

Women older than 60 work to a very limited extent in the labor market. Their participation rate amounted to 6 percent in 1989, rather close to the German rate of 11.8 percent. As expected, Sweden, with 50.6 percent, lies at the other end of the spectrum.

This short, comparative overview of the age-specific labor force participation of females in Austria shows relatively high rates for Austrian women until the 1960s. After that, the integration of women into the labor market continued, but at a slow pace by international standards. The Austrian situation, however, should be viewed against the tendency toward long-term increases in female activity rates which are associated with a strong rise in part-time work. The share of part-time labor in total female employment is currently around 45 percent in Northern European countries and in Britain, 26 percent in the United States, and 23 percent in France. By comparison, only 17 percent of female employment in Austria is part-time (OECD 1989; Neubourg 1985). In Austria, part-time jobs for the young and for elderly persons hardly exist. Retirement regulations prohibit work of any substantial character by the elderly in Austria, while legal restrictions and the demands of schoolwork make part-time employment almost impossible for young people. Part-time work by females is thus concentrated in the middle-age bracket in Austria, and largely represents work with little career potential.

## Causal Factors behind the Labor Force Participation of Austrian Women

The participation of women in the labor market is influenced by three sets of forces. One set operates on the supply side of the labor market through such factors as age, family status, number of dependent children, health, educational attainment, and socio-economic status. The second set operates on the demand side through such factors as the business cycle, the seasonality of work, and the regional and sectoral composition of job opportunities. The third set of influences derives from institutional and socio-political forces, for example, the tax structure, labor and welfare legislation, and the availability of child care facilities.

Over and above these specific factors is the general trend towards increased participation as a result of ongoing changes in socio-cultural attitudes toward female work. The causality runs both ways. The change in attitudes, and the growing self-confidence of women, leads to increased labor force participation, which in its turn alters cultural norms.

### Supply Side of the Labor Market

Cohort-specific profiles show that there has been an increase in the labor force participation of women in Austria from one generation to the next (Zweimueller 1987), which is generally the case in the industrialized world. The typical labor force participation pattern over the life cycle has undergone significant change over time, however. In the 1950s and early 1960s, many women withdrew from the labor market upon arrival of the first child, and after a relatively short span of employment, so that the highest activity rate was around 20 years of age. Labor force participation declined slowly between 25 and 50 years of age, and abruptly after that. This was not the case in the Northern European countries, Great Britain, and the United States. Here, in the same period, the rate rose as women reentered the labor force after raising families. This produced a distinct second hump in the activity rate over the life cycle. In Austria, such a pattern was hardly discernible. Female labor supply started to increase for 35- to 45-year-olds (reentry age) only in the second half of the 1960s, so the second peak of female labor force participation that had appeared elsewhere in the industrialized world started to manifest itself in Austria only in the early 1970s. Beginning in the 1970s, middle-aged women also entered the labor force in increasing numbers, but here, too, they did so at slower rates in Austria than in other western industrialized countries. In the Northern European countries, for example, the labor force participation profile of women now looks much like that of men over the life cycle – peaking early, staying flat until middle age, and then declining. Figure 7-2 shows that Austria has moved in this direction, but that the more traditional pattern of an early peak and a gradual decline over time still persists.

In Austria, as elsewhere, the spread of higher education dampened the labor force participation of teenagers, but it became the main driving force behind the long-term rise of female labor force participation over the rest of the life cycle. The structural shift toward higher education among females is not enough, however, to account for the rise in female labor force participation. Table 7-2 shows that activity rates of women are higher today than in the 1960s and 1970s at all levels of educational attainment. The total activity rate of women rose between 1971 and 1981 from 49.9 percent to 54.8

**Figure 7-2: Labor Force Participation over the Life Cycle***

*Shown as percentage of the total population in the labor force

percent. Assuming a constant educational structure of the population between 1971 and 1981, the change in the education-specific labor force participation rates accounts for 20 percent of the rise in the total female participation rates. The increased educational attainment of women accounts for a further 30 percent of the total increase in female labor force participation. Thus, some 50 percent of the rise in female activity rates in that period are due to factors other than education. In international comparisons, the rise in the educational attainment of women in Austria was moderate compared to other industrialized countries.

Other key factors that drive female participation rates are the timing of first marriage, and the timing, spacing, and number of children borne by a woman. The median age of first marriage for women (approximately 22) was rather stable in Austria for a long time. In the mid-1970s, however, it began a steady rise to 25 (Central Statistical Office 1990) and the long-standing difference with respect to men was slightly reduced to 2.5 years. The postponement of first marriage could be due to demographic factors since it was concentrated in the baby-boom generation (the largest birth-cohort was that of 1963), a phenomenon that is observable abroad and well documented (Espenshade 1985; Davis 1982). The effect of this behavioral change upon female labor supply is positive although marginal, because single women have higher activity rates than married women.

**Table 7-2: Labor Force Participation of Women by Degree of Educational Attainment**

| Age Groups | University | Junior-College | Polytechnic | Vocational | High-School | Total |
|---|---|---|---|---|---|---|
| 1971 | | | | | | |
| 15 - 19 | — | 18.8 | 90.7 | 92.8 | 56.4 | 60.0 |
| 20 - 24 | 73.7 | 50.1 | 82.8 | 74.8 | 64.2 | 68.0 |
| 25 - 29 | 77.0 | 63.1 | 66.2 | 59.1 | 50.0 | 56.2 |
| 30 - 34 | 72.4 | 57.4 | 59.1 | 54.2 | 47.2 | 50.8 |
| 35 - 39 | 67.6 | 59.3 | 59.8 | 54.1 | 48.6 | 50.9 |
| 40 - 44 | 72.9 | 65.1 | 61.7 | 57.2 | 49.7 | 53.0 |
| . 45 - 49 | 75.0 | 63.4 | 63.2 | 60.6 | 50.2 | 53.7 |
| 50 - 54 | 76.2 | 60.9 | 60.6 | 56.5 | 44.6 | 48.5 |
| 55 - 59 | 67.2 | 52.9 | 47.8 | 43.7 | 32.6 | 35.8 |
| 60 - 64 | 45.9 | 30.1 | 21.8 | 14.3 | 11.7 | 13.2 |
| 65 and older | 16.5 | 7.1 | 7.4 | 4.5 | 2.7 | 3.2 |
| Total[†] | 66.9 | 50.0 | 55.6 | 52.3 | 33.8 | 39.1 |
| Working Age[‡] | 73.2 | 55.8 | 64.4 | 58.5 | 45.2 | 49.9 |
| 1981 | | | | | | |
| 15 - 19 | — | 19.8 | 86.7 | 96.6 | 47.1 | 53.7 |
| 20 - 24 | 83.7 | 44.6 | 89.3 | 84.3 | 69.5 | 74.0 |
| 25 - 29 | 88.5 | 63.0 | 75.7 | 63.8 | 58.4 | 65.5 |
| 30 - 34 | 83.2 | 68.6 | 67.8 | 60.7 | 55.0 | 61.0 |
| 35 - 39 | 77.3 | 67.2 | 67.2 | 64.3 | 55.9 | 61.7 |
| 40 - 44 | 78.0 | 66.5 | 66.7 | 65.3 | 55.6 | 60.3 |
| 45 - 49 | 76.1 | 67.2 | 66.4 | 62.3 | 53.7 | 57.3 |
| 50 - 54 | 74.5 | 66.7 | 62.4 | 58.0 | 49.4 | 53.5 |
| 55 - 59 | 63.3 | 45.2 | 36.9 | 32.3 | 29.9 | 32.4 |
| 60 - 64 | 33.3 | 17.0 | 14.0 | 9.5 | 7.7 | 9.5 |
| 65 and older | 9.9 | 5.3 | 4.7 | 1.8 | 1.3 | 1.8 |
| Total[†] | 73.8 | 48.0 | 58.2 | 56.3 | 33.6 | 42.4 |
| Working Age[‡] | 80.4 | 53.3 | 68.2 | 64.4 | 47.2 | 54.8 |

† Total labor-force as a percentage of population over 15 years of age.
‡ Total labor-force as a percentage of population between 15 and 65 years of age.

It is widely believed that the decline in fertility has been a precondition for increased entry into the labor market. In Austria, the number of live births per 1,000 women has declined since 1964. Only in 1969, however, did the labor force participation of women start to rise, that is, after a time lag of five years. Also, formal statistical analysis shows that fertility behavior does not explain the labor supply decisions of any age group between 15 and 45. It becomes obvious that the decision to have children, to work, and/or to continue schooling are simultaneous decisions. Fertility is not an exogenous variable but rather part of the endogenous process that we seek to understand (Biffl 1988).

Closer analysis of female labor force behavior shows that, more than any other group, women with small children changed their labor force behavior in the 1970s and 1980s. There is still a difference in the activity rate of women with dependent children compared to those with no children, but this difference is diminishing over time. According to census data for 1981, the activity rate of women with children under the age of six was about 85 percent of that of women without children (Österreichisches Statistisches Zentralamt 1985). In countries with a higher participation rate than in Austria, Great Britain, for example, there is hardly any difference in the participation rates of women with children under the age of six and of women with no children (Joshi, Layard, and Owen 1985). Also, the Swedish case makes very clear that there need not be a negative correlation between female labor supply and fertility. Sweden has experienced the largest rise in female labor supply, with hardly any reduction in fertility (Gustafsson and Jacobsson 1985).

More generally, the family status of women affects their labor supply decisions. Married women spend significantly less time in the labor market than single women, in part because they face less severe financial pressure. Over time, however, the labor force participation of married women has increased both in Austria and abroad. In 1961, census data showed that the labor force participation rate of 15 to 65 year old married women was 40 percent; it rose slightly by 1971 to 42.5 percent and by 1981 by 7.2 percentage points to 49.7 percent. Activity rates for single women are on a long-term decline, but the level (1981: 63 percent) is still significantly higher than for married women (ÖSZ 1974; 1985). The difference in activity rates by family status has narrowed over time, which may indicate a reduction in the sexual division of labor in household work.

The total rise in female labor supply in the 1970s has been fostered to a certain extent by the long-term rise in the number of single women. The share of married women in the female population declined from 55.4 percent in 1971 to 52.8 percent in 1981, while the share of single women rose from 21.9 percent to 24.5 percent, and that of divorced women from 4.9 percent to 5.1 percent (ÖSZ 1974; 1985). Unmarried and divorced women have similar activity rates;

the labor supply behavior of married women conforms to that of widowed women.[3] This structural shift towards a rising share of single women is mainly a consequence of the changing age structure toward more teenagers, who have a relatively high share of singles.

Wage differentials between men and women, according to international research, also strongly affect the labor supply decisions of married women by influencing the allocation of time between market and household work (Becker 1965). This hypothesis is hard to test in Austria, due to the lack of time-series data on hourly earnings by sex. We can use median gross earnings by sex[4] as an indicator for the development of wage differentials, because part-time work does not constitute a large part of female work in Austria and does not vary much over time. According to Table 7-3, the income differential between men and women did not narrow in the 1960s and 1970s, which – according to theory – should have had a dampening effect upon female labor supply. Only in the course of the 1980s did the income differential narrow, but not as much as in those countries that also experienced a strong rise in female labor force participation. In Sweden, hourly wages of women amounted to slightly more than 80 percent of male wages in the early 1980s. In Austria, Germany, and France the hourly wage gap was in the range of 70 to 75 percent at the beginning of the 1980s.[5]

There are two explanations for the relatively slow narrowing of the wage gap between women and men in Austria. Unions in Austria, unlike in Sweden, have never pursued the objective of reducing sectoral differentials in wages. Since women tend to be in low-wage branches to a greater extent than men, they are most affected by the absence of such a solidarity wage policy.[6] Also, the Austrian policy of using foreign workers as a supplementary labor supply had a significant impact on the Austrian wage structure. It worked against a reduction in wage differentials according to skill level, economic sector, and region (Pollan 1990). Foreign workers are to a great extent in competition with female workers for the same kind of jobs. The Austrian policy toward foreign workers increased labor market segmentation in Austria and negatively influenced the job prospects of women.

3. Disaggregated data on family status do not exist on a time-series basis.
4. For example, social security data from *Lohnstufenstatistik des Hauptverbands der österreichischen Sozialversicherungsträger.*
5. Analysis for Austria in Biffl (1988).
6. In Austria, macroeconomic wage flexibility seems to be more important than microeconomic flexibility. See Guger (1990).

**Table 7-3: The Female/Male Income Differential in International Perspective†**
(Female income as a percent of male income)

| Year: | Manufacturing | | | Total Economy | |
|---|---|---|---|---|---|
| | Germany | France | Sweden | Sweden | Austria |
| 1960 | 65.4 | 64.3 | | | |
| 1964 | 67.5 | 64.1 | 73.6 | | 64.2 |
| 1967 | 69.4 | 64.6 | 77.6 | | 65.4 |
| 1970 | 69.2 | 66.7 | 80.0 | | 65.6 |
| 1973 | 70.3 | 66.4 | 83.9 | 71.5 | 65.0 |
| 1976 | 72.3 | 69.1 | 86.6 | 74.8 | 64.8 |
| 1979 | 72.6 | | 89.1 | 79.7 | 62.8 |
| 1982 | | | | | 66.0 |
| 1985 | | | | | 66.2 |
| 1987 | | | | | 67.4 |
| 1989 | | | | | 67.4 |

Source: Austria: Wages based on social security data. Includes full- and part-time workers. Up to 1987, data from an end-of-July survey; data from 1987 based on annual income per head. † Austrian ratios calculated from data on median gross income. Ratios for other countries calculated from data on hourly wages. Other: Gustafsson and Jacobson. (1985).

## The Demand Side of the Labor Market

Several long-term structural employment factors affect the employment of women (Biffl 1988). In industrialized economies, one of the major reasons for the long-term rise in female labor force participation is the growing importance of clerical work and of the service sector. Countries with rapid growth in the clerical labor force and service sector experienced the fastest growth in female labor force participation rates. By contrast, Austria (and Germany) have had rather limited employment growth in these areas.

In the early 1960s, the share of Austrian women in total employment was rather high by international standards. This was due in part to the high share of employed females in Austria's relatively large agricultural sector (see Table 7-4), which declined in the 1960s when labor scarcity and better pay enticed agricultural workers into the industrial sector. In addition, after World War II the traditional consumer goods sector (textiles, clothing, leather, food) had a high share of female employment.[7] By contrast, Table 7-4 shows that only 43.1

7. Agriculture and traditional consumer good industries typically have a large female work force. These sectors have been pillars of the Austrian employment structure

percent of all women found employment in the services sector, a much smaller share than in other western industrialized economies.

**Table 7-4: The Sectoral Distribution of Female Employment in International Comparison** (Percent shares)

| Year: | 1963[†] | 1971 | 1981 | 1985 | 1989 |
|---|---|---|---|---|---|
| Agriculture | | | | | |
| Austria | 27.8 | 16.7 | 10.4 | 9.5 | 8.1 |
| Sweden | 8.8 | 4.5 | 3.2 | 2.7 | 2.0 |
| USA | 3.9 | 2.0 | 1.6 | 1.4 | 1.4 |
| Great Britain | 2.1 | 1.6 | 1.2 | 1.1 | 1.0 |
| Germany | 17.8 | 11.6 | 7.0 | 6.6 | — |
| Manufacturing | | | | | |
| Austria | 29.1 | 30.2 | 26.0 | 23.7 | 22.0 |
| Sweden | 23.8 | 18.9 | 15.3 | 14.2 | 14.4 |
| USA | 21.4 | 19.5 | 18.2 | 16.4 | 15.7 |
| Great Britain | 33.7 | 29.4 | 20.8 | 18.0 | 16.6 |
| Germany | 33.4 | 33.6 | 28.2 | 26.3 | — |
| Services | | | | | |
| Austria | 43.1 | 53.2 | 63.5 | 66.8 | 69.9 |
| Sweden | 67.4 | 76.6 | 81.6 | 83.0 | 83.6 |
| USA | 74.7 | 78.5 | 80.2 | 82.1 | 82.9 |
| Great Britain | 64.2 | 69.1 | 78.0 | 80.9 | 82.4 |
| Germany | 48.8 | 54.8 | 64.9 | 67.0 | — |

Source: OECD, Labor Force Statistics, Austrian Institute of Economic Research.
† 1961 for Austria.

The manufacturing sector remained an important source of jobs for women until the mid-1970s when it came under severe competitive pressure, particularly in those branches where women formed a major part of the work force. Between 1975 and 1989, females lost 79,000 jobs (a drop of 23 percent) in the secondary sector. This job loss was, however, more than compensated by job creation in the services sector.

---

dating back to the turn of the century, which helps explain the high degree of integration of women into the formal labor market at an early stage.

Between 1975 to 1989, female employment grew 245,000 or 36 percent. In 1989, 70 percent of all women worked in the services sector, 22 percent in the secondary sector and 8 percent in the primary sector.[8] In the Anglo-Saxon countries and in Northern Europe some 80 percent of all women now work in the services sector. In Austria, as in the United States and Great Britain, the share of sales personnel in female employment is high (25 percent in 1989), while the share of the public, social, and personal service sectors is relatively small (34 percent in 1989). By contrast, in Sweden almost 60 percent of all women work in public, social, and personal services.

Disaggregating employment into 26 separate branches shows which ones filled their growing labor demand in the 1970s and 1980s primarily with women. Did the rise of female employment in Austria lead to a greater concentration of women in certain economic branches (as was the case in Sweden where a clear segregation of male and female work can be discerned), or were women spread more evenly over the branches? The pattern over time of the coefficient of variation in Table 7-5 indicates that female employment became more equally spread over economic branches in the 1960s and 1970s; beginning in the mid-1980s, however, the trend reversed.

The data suggest that women in Austria are increasingly in direct competition with male workers in the labor market. The unions and the representatives of female workers have never tried to promote part-time work for women, even though it would tend to increase the labor force participation of women. They argue that such a policy would keep women in positions that have little career potential, which would mean that over the life cycle, and over generations, women could not improve their relative position with respect to men, but would instead remain segregated as a more or less non-competing group. The policy stance against part-time work, together with the foreign worker policy and the comparatively small structural shift toward service work, all served to dampen the growth of female labor force participation in Austria.

From the 1960s, female employment expanded most in sectors with a low degree of unionization and low wages (trade, tourism, catering, personal services, cleaning). In these sectors, the organization of work has adapted to the female life cycle of labor force participation (Davies and Rosser 1986). Alternative forms of work are particularly prominent in these spheres, for example, part-time work,

---

8. Agriculture in Austria still consists chiefly of small scale farms that are labor intensive, with a rather limited degree of mass production techniques.

**Table 7-5: The Sectoral Distribution of Female Employment in Austria, 1961-1989**

| Sector: | 1961 | 1971 | 1981 | 1985 | 1989 |
|---|---|---|---|---|---|
| Agriculture | 50.3 | 47.6 | 48.2 | 48.2 | 48.2 |
| Utilities | 13.2 | 14.2 | 15.6 | 15.4 | 15.5 |
| Mining | 6.1 | 8.3 | 10.4 | 10.6 | 9.8 |
| Food | 36.9 | 37.3 | 40.0 | 38.9 | 40.1 |
| Textiles | 67.3 | 61.2 | 60.2 | 59.4 | 58.2 |
| Clothing | 67.6 | 73.6 | 77.6 | 78.7 | 79.5 |
| Leather | 40.9 | 39.7 | 51.7 | 49.4 | 55.7 |
| Wood-processing | 16.3 | 17.8 | 19.5 | 20.3 | 20.4 |
| Paper | 33.5 | 31.6 | 29.8 | 27.4 | 24.2 |
| Graphics | 37.6 | 37.6 | 37.7 | 37.9 | 38.3 |
| Chemicals | 35.9 | 36.6 | 33.2 | 31.2 | 30.6 |
| Stone and Glass | 29.0 | 24.3 | 22.8 | 22.5 | 22.6 |
| Metals | 23.7 | 22.9 | 22.6 | 22.0 | 22.3 |
| Construction | 5.9 | 8.0 | 10.8 | 12.0 | 12.2 |
| Trade | 49.9 | 50.7 | 52.3 | 53.0 | 52.7 |
| Restaurants | 73.8 | 74.1 | 70.4 | 69.0 | 60.1 |
| Transport | 10.4 | 12.4 | 17.0 | 17.8 | 18.3 |
| Money | 37.7 | 44.8 | 47.0 | 46.1 | 45.0 |
| Business Services | 54.2 | 44.7 | 47.6 | 50.8 | 48.9 |
| Personal Services | 70.0 | 71.3 | 77.2 | 78.6 | 77.7 |
| Art, Sports | 32.4 | 33.2 | 32.7 | 35.9 | 37.0 |
| Health | 65.8 | 68.0 | 73.0 | 74.4 | 72.4 |
| Education | 20.5 | 22.5 | 52.9 | 53.9 | 56.3 |
| Public Institutions | 39.5 | 44.4 | 43.9 | 44.6 | 45.8 |
| House Rentals | 98.1 | 95.7 | 97.6 | 88.4 | 98.1 |
| Household Services | 93.1 | 88.5 | 82.7 | 84.1 | 83.7 |
| Mean | 42.7 | 42.7 | 45.2 | 45.0 | 45.1 |
| Variance | 25.3 | 24.4 | 24.0 | 23.4 | 24.0 |
| Coefficient of Variation | 59.3 | 57.2 | 53.1 | 52.1 | 53.1 |

Source: Austrian Institute of Economic Research.

time-sharing, and contracting out. This development follows not only from the gender-specific division of work in the family, but also from political factors, because unions have devoted little attention to controlling conditions of female work. Female labor plays an important role in the current restructuring of work processes, because these alternative forms of work are strategic components in promoting greater flexibility in the workplace.

### *The Role of Institutional Factors*

The introduction of individual taxation in Austria in 1973 strongly promoted the labor force participation of married women. The contribution to family income through the market work of the wife is higher in a system of taxation based on individual income rather than on household income, in which the additional income of the woman is taxed at the marginal rate of the main income earner, usually the man. This is particularly the case when male earnings are high. Countries with above-average female participation rates tend to have systems that tax individual income: Sweden, for example, made this kind of tax system compulsory in 1971 (Gustafsson 1985).

Further institutional arrangements that affect female labor force participation are regulations relating to maternity leave, child birth, and child care. In this respect, Sweden has perhaps the most generous regulations. Austria's regulations on maternity leave are favorable in international comparisons. But child care facilities in Austria are more-or-less limited to cities and are more costly than in Sweden. The high labor force participation of Swedish women suggests that the provision of child care and general care facilities is a key determinant of female labor supply.

## Work in the Household

The widening spread in labor force participation rates between Austrian women and women in other Western industrialized countries since the 1960s should also be viewed as a result of the differing productivity developments in the household production sector in the various countries, and of differences in the degree to which household work has been transferred into the labor market.

In countries with particularly high female activity rates, traditional household tasks have been transferred to a large extent into the formal labor market. Through the market mechanism, a price for these goods and services has been established. This has had a major impact on the status of women in society and in the family. A short overview of the division of female work between the household and the labor market should illuminate the constraints faced by women as they decide how to allocate their time between non-market and market work.

Work has a much larger dimension than is typically measured. Household production does not find its way into the system of national accounts because it involves unpaid work. Although work in the household does not have market value, it is clearly not worthless; it is important for the welfare and reproduction of a society, and is highly interrelated with the labor market and the market for goods. The economic system is influenced by changes in working hours, in traditional age- and sex-specific work-sharing, and by structural shifts in the population. Also, the function of government changes with new patterns of work-sharing between the household-sector and the market-sector. Over time, the state has had to take on functions that were formerly filled by the household. Because economic and labor market policies have to take into account the fact that the market and household sectors are interconnected, I analyze the structure of household production and evaluate the output of household production for Austria, well aware of all the caveats of such an undertaking (Biffl 1989). My data offer a preliminary picture of the sexual division of household work in 1981 based on the time budget survey by the Central Statistical Office in Austria.

### *Working Time in the Household and in the Labor Market*

When analyzing non-market work, it is necessary to spell out operational definitions and demarcation lines. Here I define housework as unpaid work of household members for their own consumption. This work comprises traditional household jobs such as cooking, washing, cleaning, caring for children and sick or elderly household members, as well as do-it-yourself activities such as repair work and gardening. The "third person criterion" is used for the evaluation of household production; that is, a job is taken to be a productive economic activity if a third person could do that job on a remunerative basis.[9] According to results from an Austrian time budget survey in 1981 (reported in Figures 7-4 and 7-5), slightly more than half of total working time, 51 percent, is spent on the production of goods and services for own consumption in the household sector, 49 percent on paid

---

9. This operational definition of the economic part of household activities has been introduced by Reid (1932).

work in the labor market. These results correspond rather well with other industrialized countries (Goldschmidt and Clermont 1982).

**Figure 7-3: Total Working Hours by Age and Sex**

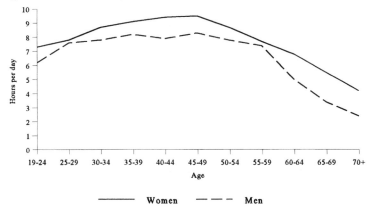

Taken together, the household- and market-work data reported in Figure 7-3 show that women tend to work on average longer hours than men over the whole life cycle. Paid and unpaid work, however, are not evenly distributed over age and sex. Men tend to spend little time on work in the household. Between the ages of 19 and 50, they devote on average $1\frac{1}{4}$ hours per day to unpaid work, and instead supply the bulk of their labor power in the form of paid work. After the age of 50, they tend to withdraw from the labor market and to put more time into household work.

**Figure 7-4: Paid and Unpaid Work over the Life Cycle – Men**

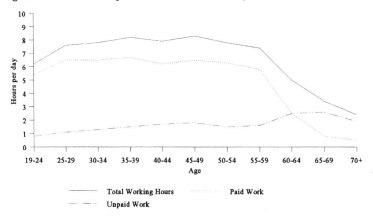

Figure 7-5 shows that women in any age group tend to spend more time on household work than men. In their main working years women devote half their total working hours to paid work and half to unpaid work.

**Figure 7-5: Paid and Unpaid Work over the Life Cycle – Women**

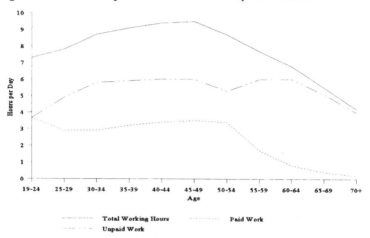

The total workload of women differs according to professional status (see Table 7-6). Housewives who are not in the labor market work on average 7.9 hours per day, which corresponds well with the total working hours of employed men. Women who have a job, however, tend to work longer hours than men in the same occupational category. Females in agriculture have the longest working hours, closely followed by those who are self-employed in the nonagricultural sector. Female wage and salary earners work longer hours, the less their educational attainment. This may be linked to the greater earning power of better-educated women. The higher wage income of better-educated women facilitates the substitution of household work for goods and services bought on the market. Low wage earners must work more in the household to supplement their work in the labor market and to make ends meet.[10] There is also a marked difference in working hours by family status. Total working hours are much the same for single men and women. Married persons and single parents, particularly if they are women, have the largest work load.

10. The capital stock in the household also differs according to family income, which has an effect upon the productivity of household labor.

**Table 7-6: Working Hours in the Household and on the Labor Market by Sex and Professional Status** (Hours and minutes per day)[†]

| Professional Status | Men's Work | | | Women's Work | | |
|---|---|---|---|---|---|---|
| | Paid | Unpaid | Total | Paid | Unpaid | Total |
| Employed | 6'51 | 1'18 | 8'09 | 5'29 | 3'59 | 9'28 |
| Unemployed | 0'14 | 2'02 | 2'16 | 0'17 | 6'44 | 7'01 |
| Retired | 0'33 | 2'26 | 2'59 | 0'13 | 4'48 | 5'01 |
| Students | 0'52 | 0'53 | 1'45 | 0'35 | 1'27 | 2'02 |
| Housewives | — | — | — | 0'21 | 7'32 | 7'53 |
| Other Dependents | 1'11 | 1'34 | 2'45 | 0'20 | 3'41 | 4'01 |
| Self Employed | | | | | | |
|   Agricultural | 9'32 | 0'45 | 10'17 | 6'04 | 5'25 | 11'29 |
|   Non-agricultural | 7'55 | 0'38 | 8'33 | 6'47 | 3'41 | 10'28 |
| Wage and Salary Earners | 6'29 | 1'26 | 7'55 | 5'15 | 3'46 | 9'01 |
|   Blue Collar | 6'37 | 1'26 | 8'03 | 5'25 | 4'23 | 9'48 |
|   Skilled | 6'19 | 1'25 | 7'44 | 6'10 | 3'06 | 9'16 |
|   Unskilled[‡] | 6'59 | 1'28 | 8'27 | 5'18 | 4'34 | 9'52 |
|   White Collar | 6'21 | 1'25 | 7'46 | 5'09 | 3'27 | 8'36 |
|   High School | 6'38 | 1'19 | 7'57 | 5'17 | 3'49 | 9'06 |
|   Vocational | 6'19 | 1'30 | 7'49 | 5'45 | 3'24 | 9'09 |
|   Polytechnic | 7'10 | 1'03 | 8'13 | 5'19 | 3'12 | 8'31 |
|   Junior College | 5'48 | 1'40 | 7'28 | 4'01 | 3'40 | 7'41 |
|   University | 6'09 | 1'15 | 7'24 | 4'23 | 2'16 | 6'39 |

Source: Austrian Central Statistical Office, Time Budget Survey, 1981.
† Average over the week (Monday through Sunday).   ‡ Includes semi-skilled workers.

The Austrian data are similar to existing international evidence on working hours; on average a person works between three and four hours in the household and four to six hours on the labor market (Szalai et al. 1972). The gender distribution between work in the household and on the market is more egalitarian, the higher the labor force activity rate of women. According to studies for the United States, women with more education spend less time on general household tasks and more on child care over the life cycle than women with a lower educational attainment (Leibowitz 1974).

## *Evaluation of Household Production*

There are two methods for evaluating the production of households: the input approach and the output approach. The input approach uses the market values (wages) of comparable market activities to evaluate working time. The output approach measures the cost of substituting household production with goods and services of the open market. Here I use the input approach, because evaluating output, although preferable from an analytical point of view, is impossible due to lack of data. Working time is evaluated by using the minimum wage of a household helper in Graz (on the lower end of the regional wage scale) and Vorarlberg (on the upper end of the regional wage scale). Wages of professionals for the various household functions, for example cook, nurse, and teacher, were not used, since the productivity level of a spouse in these separate functions tends to be lower than that of specialists in the market. The professional usually has access to better capital equipment, a different work organization, and economies of scale, which lead to higher labor productivity. The quality of the product is also not always comparable, because much household work involves joint production, for example, cooking and watching the children at the same time.

The principle of evaluating with opportunity costs, for example, the average wages of women according to educational attainment, has not been used; the decision on splitting total working hours between market work and household work is to a great extent determined by the potential wages for market work. Women with higher education tend to work more frequently in the labor market, thus substituting household work with goods and services bought in the market. Wage differentials, which should to a certain extent mirror productivity differences, are determined in the formal labor market. Due to lack of information on the level of productivity of housework, I assume that the productivity per person is equal in all households.

Based on two estimates using the data for 1981, the value of household production ranged between 318 billion AS, or 30 percent of GDP, and 402 billion AS, or 38 percent of GDP (see Table 7-7). Eighty percent of the total value of household production was due to female work, 20 percent due to male work. A large part of female household work (48.6 percent) falls in the area of general household tasks (washing, ironing, cleaning, sewing). On average cooking accounts for 22.4 percent of all housework time, shopping 10.7 percent, gardening and repairs 9 percent and child care 8.4 percent. The contribution of men to household work is mainly in gardening and repairs, which together account for 60 percent of their household work.

International comparisons of unpaid housework have to take into consideration that the method of evaluation is crucial for the outcome. For Finland, Suviranta (1986) calculated a spread of estimated household output value between 30 percent of GDP when using the

**Table 7-7: The Value of Household Production by Economic Function and Sex**

| Function | Total | | Men | | Women | |
|---|---|---|---|---|---|---|
| | Graz | Vorarlberg | Graz | Vorarlberg | Graz | Vorarlberg |
| Cooking | 59,726 | 75,522 | 2,743 | 3,403 | 56,983 | 72,119 |
| Shopping | 37,783 | 47,819 | 10,083 | 12,761 | 27,700 | 35,058 |
| Housekeeping | 130,795 | 165,611 | 7,333 | 9,356 | 123,462 | 156,255 |
| Gardening/Repairs | 60,595 | 76,690 | 37,643 | 47,642 | 22,952 | 29,048 |
| Childcare | 26,747 | 33,851 | 5,378 | 6,806 | 21,369 | 27,045 |
| Care for the Sick | 2,374 | 3,005 | — | — | 2,374 | 3,005 |
| Housework Total | 318,020 | 402,498 | 63,180 | 79,968 | 254,840 | 322,530 |

Source: Austrian Statistical Office, Time Budget Survey, 1981; own calculations.

output approach, and 41.7 percent of GDP when using the input approach. For France, Chadeau-Fouquet came up with estimates that ranged between 32 percent and 77 percent of GDP. The lowest value is obtained when using the wage of a household helper as a weight in the input evaluation and the highest when using the skill structure of the female population and the associated wage rates for these skills, that is, the opportunity cost principle. Similar results are obtained by Murphy (1982) for the United States and Hawrylyshyn (1976) for Canada.

Evaluating the production of goods and services in the household sector is an important step towards recognizing the total economic contribution of women to society. An expanded gross domestic product concept that includes the household sector would make visible the complementarity between market and household production, and the sexual division of labor that characterizes these two spheres.

In my view, the relatively limited increase in female labor force participation in Austria can be interpreted in the light of a social choice model, which tends to preserve the traditional division of labor between men and women in the paid and unpaid production sectors. The limited investment growth in the human capital of women relative to men (the gender disparity of educational attainment in Austria by the end of the 80s is one of the highest of all OECD countries, see OECD 1993) implies a lower professional orientation of women. Therefore, women remained concentrated in lower skilled jobs with little career and income potential. The foreign worker system installed in the 1960s, which allocated foreign workers to certain firms and types of job, tended to reinforce the division of traditional production methods and labor segmentation along gender lines. In contrast to the Anglo-Saxon and Nordic countries, no significant labor market affirmative action programs, or equal opportunity legislation that would have enticed firms to reduce work segmentation by gender, were put into place in Austria. The limited supply of child-care facilities, an educational system that did not provide full day care for students, and the limited supply of public or private services for the care of handicapped, sick, weak, and old people, tended to preserve dependence on the household sector.

## Concluding Remarks

The above analysis presents some of the basic features of female work in Austria, and the division of work between the household and the labor market over the life cycle. It focuses on the high level of female labor force participation in Austria up to the 1960s, and the slow growth after that when viewed in an international perspective.

There are two distinct features of the slow rise of overall female activity rates in Austria. First, the labor force participation of older women (more than 55 years) declined in Austria, while it stagnated or even rose in most industrialized countries. Second, the labor force participation of middle-aged women rose considerably faster in the western industrialized world than in Austria. The decline in the activity rates of older women can be attributed to a large extent to the relatively generous retirement arrangements and pensions that were introduced in Austria in the 1960s. It is more difficult to find explanations for the comparatively slow growth of female labor supply among middle-aged women, but they clearly lie in supply and demand factors, as well as in general policy measures concerning such matters as child care, tax legislation, and foreign workers. The relatively moderate rise of educational attainment of Austrian women can help explain why the incentive to work has been weaker in Austria than in countries with more highly educated women. The same dampening effect on female labor supply arises from the comparatively limited rise of female wages, particularly the stagnation of pay relative to men. The limited structural shift of employment towards services in Austria has the same effect. A large share of goods and services is provided by the household sector in Austria. The shift of household work onto the labor market has been most pronounced in Sweden, the country with the highest participation rate of women. In the Northern European countries, the government has taken over functions which are to a large extent provided by the household sector in Austria, particularly in the area of child care and social services. The more generous the provision of child care and general care facilities, the higher the labor force participation of women.

# References

Becker, G. 1965. "A Theory of the Allocation of Time." *The Economic Journal* 75: 493-517.

Biffl, G. 1988. "Arbeitsmarkt 2000, Prospects for the development of the labor market until the year 2000." In *Forschungsbericht des Bundesministeriums für Arbeit und Soziales*, 21. Vienna.

___. 1989. "Der Haushaltssektor: The economic value of unpaid work." *Monatsberichte des Österreichischen Instituts für Wirtschaftsforschung*, 62(9):567-576.

Chadeau, A. and Fouquet, A. 1981. "Peut-on mesurer le travail domestique?" *Economie et Statistique*, no. 136.

Davies, C. and Rosser, J. 1986. "Gendered Jobs in the Health Service: A Problem for Labor Process Analysis." In *Gender and the Labor Process.* Ed. D. Knights and H. Willmott. Brookfield, Vt.

Davis, K. 1982. "Wives and Work: Consequences of the Sex Role Revolution." *Population and Development Review* 8(3):495-511.

Ehrenberg, R.G., and Smith, R.S. 1985. *Modern Labor Economics: Theory and Public Policy.* Glenview, Ill.

Espenshade, T.J. 1985. "Marriage Trends in America: Estimates, Implications and Causes." *Population and Development Review* 11(2):193-245.

Goldschmidt-Clermont, L. 1982. *Unpaid Work in the Household.* Geneva.

Guger, A. 1990. "Corporatism: Success or Failure? Austrian Experiences." Austrian Institute of Economic Research Working Paper 36.

Gustafsson, S. 1985. "Institutional Environment and the Economics of Female Labor Force Participation and Fertility: A Comparison between Sweden and West Germany, Science Center Berlin." Discussion Paper (IIM/LMP 85-9).

Gustafsson, S. and Jacobson, R. 1985. "Trends in Female Labor Force Participation in Sweden." *Journal of Labor Economics* 3(1): 256-74.

Hawrylyshyn, O. 1976. "The Value of Household Services: A Survey of Empirical Estimates." *The Review of Income and Wealth* 22(2):101-31.

Joshi, H., Layard, R., and Owen, S. 1985. "Why Are More Women Working in Britain?" *Journal of Labor Economics* 3(1): 147-76.

Leibowitz, A. 1974. "Education and Home Production." *American Economic Review* 64(2): 243-50.

Long, C.D. 1958. *The Labor Force under Changing Income and Employment.* Princeton.

Murphy, M. 1982. "Comparative Estimates of the Value of Household Work in the United States for 1976." *Review of Income and Wealth* 28(1):29-43.

Neubourg, C. de. 1985. "Part Time Work: An International Quantitative Comparison." *International Labor Review* 124(5):559-76.

OECD. 1989. *Employment Outlook 1988.* Paris.

OECD. 1990. *Labour Force.* Paris.

Österreichisches Statistisches Zentralamt (ÖSZ). 1990. *Demographisches Jahrbuch 1989.* Vienna.

Österreichisches Statistisches Zentralamt (ÖSZ) 1974. *Ergebnisse der Volkszählung: Beiträge zur österreichischen Statistik* 309(14).

Österreichisches Statistisches Zentralamt (ÖSZ) 1985. *Ergebnisse der Volkszählung: Beiträge zur österreichischen Statistik* 630(22).

Pollan, W. 1990."Lohnunterschiede in der Industrie." *Austrian Institute of Economic Research Monthly Report* 63(11): 616-22.

Reid, M.G. 1934. *Economics of Household Production.* New York.

Suviranta, A. 1986. "Determining the Value of Unpaid Housework, Method Comparison." *Housework Study part XIV.* Ed. Ministry of Social Affairs and Health. Helsinki.

Szalai, S. 1972. *The Use of Time: Daily Activities of Urban and Suburban Population in Twelve Countries.* Ed. A. Szalai et al. The Hague.

Zweimueller, J. 1987. *Development and Determinants of Female Labor Force Participation in Austria.* University of Linz, Research Memorandum No. 17.

*Chapter 8*

≈

# FEMININITY AND A PROFESSIONALISM
## A Psychoanalytic Study of Ambition in Female
## Academics and Managers in Austria

.............................

*Gertraud Diem-Wille*

## Introduction

In Europe, femininity is still equated with the middle-class view of women that arose in the eighteenth and nineteenth centuries.[1] The essence of woman is her role as mother. She is described as "the second sex."[2] A man gains his sense of self-worth through his career and his involvement in public life. The realm of the woman is the home and the family. The expansion of the range of opportunities open to women as they have gained access to higher education and to a wider range of careers is seen as an "invasion" of the male domain. For women, only those forms of career that correspond to the feminine mother image are publicly tolerated: caring, providing, nursing, teaching, or child care. The few women who break into man's

1. In a historical study, Badinter (1981) showed that the emphasis on maternal instincts makes its first appearance in the seventeenth century. It is only from this time on that the essence of woman is equated with maternal feelings.
2. Simone de Beauvoir (1971) describes woman's position in relation to man. "Man" is equated with the concept of mankind. Thus woman is relegated to the position of "second sex."

domain are dismissed as viragos and caricatured in the newspapers. Theweleit (1974) has clearly demonstrated that the polarization of female roles is a "male fantasy." When thus stereotyped, "woman" is credited with specific qualities and characteristics, such as passivity, sensitivity, indecisiveness, concrete thinking, insecurity, submission, and self-sacrifice. It makes no difference that everyone knows women who do not conform to this characterization. It is often pointed out that men have a vested interest in assigning women to these roles. When women behave otherwise, it earns disapproval, as Gold demonstrates:

> He is dynamic – She is aggressive.
> He is conscientious – She is pedantic.
> He looses his cool – She fumes.
> He is firm – She is stubborn.
> He is a man of the world – She's been around.
> He gives a considered opinion – She's biased.
> He shows his authority – She's domineering.
> He's discreet – She's secretive.
> He's got a hangover – She's moody. (Gold 1990: 56)

Clearly, there is a double standard in the way the same behavior is judged.

In sociological research, too, it is common to present femininity and masculinity as poles on a continuum, that is, in one-dimensional fashion. Personal qualities that are strongly pronounced in men are defined as masculine, and their opposite as feminine (Rustermeyer 1989).

On the other hand, the psychoanalytic model of personality is founded on the premise of bisexuality, that is, that all people have both masculine and feminine qualities. Alongside the conscious realm, which is considered in sociological surveys, lies the realm of the unconscious, which influences behavior. Figuratively speaking, the conscious represents the tip of the iceberg, while the majority of the iceberg that is under water represents the unconscious. Feelings toward other people are also not one-dimensional when seen from the psychoanalytic point of view. Particularly in close relationships, love and affection are present, but so are contradictory emotions like aggression, jealousy, and hate. Another important contribution, made by Freud, is the suggestion that every adult also contains a child that, in part, controls or influences behavior. If we are to understand how successful career women relate to their femininity in their sexual identity, and what determines their ambition, it is not enough to observe external appearances or to examine their personal qualities in the light of the one-dimensional approach to masculinity and femininity. In a psychoanalytical study, it is important to gain access to both conscious and unconscious aspects of emotional development. My study uses the life histories of these successful career women to uncover their unique qualities and inner realities. In this way, it differs from sociological examinations. These focus on external reality, concentrate on stability and change in social systems, and stress the interrelationships of social sub-systems in which an individual's fate is seen as an element of the whole.

In changing the emphasis from external to inner reality, I am in no way playing down the importance of these external factors. Quite the reverse. I take as my starting point that external conditions, such as family background and personal abilities, play a major role. My goal, however, is to show how these conditions can be influenced by the inner reality. Thus, in a particular family, one brother can become a top manager while the other finds great difficulty in earning a living at all. Children can see the same people, for example, their parents, very differently, and parents can also develop different relationships with each child. How an individual perceives outer reality cannot be judged from the outside. What I aim to show here is how a woman's sense of identity and her motivation for a career are determined by her inner picture and perceptions of significant family members. I argue that it is not the objective qualities of the father that are important for a child's development, but the image of the father constructed by the child, the so-called father-image. Mitscherlich (1985: 87) makes this point:

> Pioneering work by Freud led him to discover that not only external events and experiences are laid down in the psyche. Fantasies can change the meaning of external events, so a new psychic reality is created, which in its turn has an effect on, and changes external reality.

I would also like to clarify another possible misconception. When talking of successful career women and men, I am not making any sort of value judgment. I am not implying that career success depends on having a mature personality, mental stability, or a successful upbringing. In fact I am trying to show that a variety of interpretations are possible in explaining career success. In the case of some of the subjects, involvement in a career can be seen as a form of hyperactivity that helps to ward off a threatening depression. With other "career women" and "career men," we find that personality development has remained at the emotional level of a child, but that they are able to apply their intellectual and emotional abilities to one particular area, namely to their careers. However, in both academia and business there are also emotionally mature people of both sexes who are able to sublimate their tension and aggression and exploit their abilities to the fullest.

## Methodology

My investigation aims to portray the internal reality of women and men who have been successful in multi-national companies and universities and who have attained top management positions. I have selected two different career areas. The idea was to compare business with academic careers, assuming that financial rewards would be the main incentive for the managers while prestige and interest in research would be the most significant factors for academics. I chose contrasting professional groups for my sample so that, alongside gender-related differences, I could show a second distinctive factor, namely the difference in professional socialization. The study examines in detail the life histories of a small number of successful people. Seven to eight representatives in each of the four groups, that is, female and male managers and male and female professors, were questioned. Detailed narrative interviews provided data on the self-image and self-esteem of the subjects, and on their life histories and personality development. The interviews were supported by an additional projective drawing test (the enchanted family developed by Kos/Biermann 1973) and a projective personality test for psycho-diagnostics (the Rorschach test developed by Bohm 1951 and 1975). The narrative interviews were taped and transcribed, and formed the basis of a qualitative text analysis.

## Historical Background of the Sample Group

At the time of the interviews, the individuals in the sample were between 40 and 52 years old. They were intentionally chosen from the generation born during or after World War II, the time between 1939 and 1945 when Europe was thrown into turmoil. For all of them, their education came in a relatively peaceful period of economic regeneration. In attempting to describe this group of thirty successful professionals in a historical context, a wide variety of political and social factors related to the differences in their backgrounds come to light.

Let us begin with the collapse of the Austro-Hungarian Empire after World War I, which strongly influenced the parents of my sample group. After the disintegration of the multi-national empire, Austria became a small state of about seven million inhabitants, which many doubted could survive. The grandfathers of the sample group were mainly craftsmen and small businessmen from Bohemia, Moravia, Slovakia, Hungary and Germany, who had settled in Vienna. At that time, Vienna was something of a melting pot, where more than two million people from all the former regions of the monarchy had made their homes. In an Austria now greatly reduced in size, considerable pressure built up in Vienna itself. It is not surprising, therefore, that some of the parents came from very large families of from eight to twelve children, some of whom died at an early age. The period between the wars saw an increasing level of tension between the Christian Socialist and the Social Democratic Parties that came to a head in the Civil War of 1934. The parents are mostly depicted as having little interest in politics. "It [politics] never played a big part in family life." The National Socialist Party, which had at first been banned by the Austrian fascist regime created in 1934, succeeded in forcing through the annexation of Austria to Germany in 1938. For various reasons, this was widely supported by the Austrian people.

Nazism and World War II touched and changed the lives of all the families. The Jewish parents of one subject were forced to flee from Austria. They met while in exile and returned to Austria after the war. Another subject had a Jewish father who lived in a German enclave in the east. He was taken in by the new German thinking at first, until he saw many of his socialist friends being taken away and imprisoned. He had to "disappear," and, by the end of the war, had lost everything and had to make a new beginning in Austria. The father of one of the top managers came to Vienna from the Balkans. He became a committed Nazi, volunteered for its special elite troop, and became involved in the cruel partisan struggle in Yugoslavia. At the end of the war, when Vienna was captured by the Russians, his five-year-old son witnessed a near-fatal incident. Some Russian soldiers found his father's railway uniform – it just happened that he was a railwayman as well as a member of the special elite troop – and threatened to shoot the mother and the three children. Only by imitating the sound of a train was the mother able to convince the soldiers that the uniform was not that of the special troop, thus saving herself and her children. The son tells of his memories of hunger in postwar Vienna when the death rate went up to three times the usual level, most of those who died being small children (Bandhauer-Schöffmann and Hornung 1990). His younger brother and sister died of illness and starvation. His father was a prisoner of war, but managed to escape after a few months and returned home to care for his sick wife. Three of the interviewees lost their fathers in the war. Their mothers were forced to bring the children up alone, and so had to live in severely strained circumstances. Another manager described how his parents helped people who were being persecuted on political or racial grounds to escape. He had to live through the accompanying tension and danger. Although he has an open-minded attitude, he feels angry that his parents had put all of their lives at risk. One manager's father was repatriated as a German national in 1945 and they did not see each other for twenty years. His mother did not want to abandon the life she had carefully built up, so they agreed to a separation that turned out to be permanent. Another university professor began the story of his career at primary school. As a child, he lived in a town now near the Hungarian border that was initially part of Hungary, for a time part of Austria, then part of Germany, and then part of Hungary again. This meant that the language of instruction in school often changed; to this day he can read aloud any Hungarian text with a perfect accent even though he cannot understand it.

These extracts from the stories of the thirty interviewees show how historical events can have an impact at many levels. A theme common to all is that the parents and grandparents survived many crises, including financial ruin, exile, and death in the family, but never gave up or resigned themselves to their fate. Regardless of how threatening the circumstances were, they seemed determined to overcome the difficulties on their own. We will see that having shared their parents' successful struggle for survival is a significant element in the psychic stability of these successful people.

The period of recovery in the 1950s brought opportunities that enabled the interviewees to improve their personal and financial situation. Houses destroyed in the war had to be rebuilt, so there was an enormous expansion in the construction sector. There was a move away from small firms to large companies, as a result of which many of the smaller, uncompetitive firms struggled or even failed. The parents urged their children to go to university and to pursue careers that were different from theirs. In the group of male managers, there are a few examples of small businesses which, in spite of enormous effort, barely supported the family; one father had an office supply store and a mother ran a tiny candle shop. By contrast, another mother succeeded in making enough from a wool and needlework shop to enable her to set up a second shop.

The sample group all completed their higher education in the 1960s, and began their careers at universities and in computing at a time when both were undergoing rapid expansion. One individual started work as a secretary in a department of six people. Ten years later she ran the department, which had grown to a staff of eighty. New departments responsible for education and training were set up, and new sister companies, especially in neighboring countries in Eastern Europe, led to further expansion. One personnel manager reported a one-third increase in staffing levels over the previous five years. In the universities, new teaching posts were created to cope with the increasing influx of students. This growth provided the favorable conditions that led, particularly in the case of the women, to career success stories almost like fairy tales. That is how one woman described her change in status from secretary to section head and then, just two years later, to manager and head of department. The firm needed people who could take responsibility and who knew what they were doing. As a secretary, she had organized overseas exhibitions in Eastern Europe, which she did so well that her boss promoted her to section head with particular responsibility for this type of work. The work expanded till she was running a whole department.

Another manager, who was hired by a company to act as a model at trade fairs, later became supervisor of all the hostesses. When she was offered a job in the public relations department, she jumped at it. Although she had only basic vocational qualifications for the post, she was rapidly promoted on the basis of her practical experience. The third manager who reached a top position without the benefit of a degree, emigrated to Canada. She was working as a bank trainee when, as a result of a reorganization, she was given some management responsibilities. She handled these in an unconventional but highly successful manner, and, as a result, was promoted to manager.[3]

## Background Information: External Reality

The people in the study, who are in top positions in international companies or in universities, have nearly all improved their social position (29 out of 30), and now earn more than their parents. With the exception of the group of male managers, the parents of the study group were all employed in middle-level jobs as civil servants,

---

3. It is important to realize that these unconventional career paths are more likely to occur in periods of expansion or change than in times of stability.

teachers, or journalists. The families of the male managers were self-employed in business or a trade.

The majority of the sample are firstborn (23 out of 30) and half of the women are only children. Only one of the female managers comes from a large family – she was the fifth of six children. First-born children generally receive unusual amounts of love and affection from their parents, which is actually an expression of the parents' insecurity and unconscious fears. They need to prove to themselves that they are qualified as parents, and so are under much greater pressure to succeed than with subsequent children. The fact that many of the women were only children explains why their upbringing was not strictly gender related. As only children, the daughters received every possible encouragement. In contrast to their parents' generation as a whole, where 40 percent of children were born out of wedlock, all the parents of the successful career men and women are either married or widowed.

As would be expected, there are differences between the men and the women in their own current family situations. The majority of the men in the sample are married (14 out of 16), while in the case of the women, only half are married (7 out of 14), the rest being either single or divorced. The men have twice the number of children (29) compared with the women (12). Half of all the women have no children and only two have more than one child. The wives of the men in the sample are mainly housewives (13 out of 16) who bear the main responsibility for running the household. A similar picture emerges in other studies. Gallese (1986) analyzed students at the Harvard Business School (n=82) and found that one-third of the women were married, one-third single, and one-third divorced. Only 29 percent of them had children. There were 38 children in all, i.e. an average of 0.4 children per family (Gallese 1986: 250). In a study of female university lecturers in Germany, Bimmer (1983) found that 58 percent were single, 31 percent married and 2 percent widowed (n=415), although the age range in this study was much wider than in mine (Bimmer 198: 163).

## The Dynamics of Career Success

The central issue of my study is the inner dynamics that lead to career success. First, I show the pattern of inner dynamics that promotes career success in both men and women. I was not able to identify any specific gender-related criteria that differentiated the men from the women in my sample. There was nothing special in the life histories of the women or in the differences among them that could be related back to their common gender. What is it that distinguishes those people who reach the top of the hierarchy? Are there specific constellations of factors that explain why so much energy and determination should be invested in a career? What experiences or perceptions engender such enormous ambition?

First of all, my assumption that the people in my sample did not lead a balanced life was confirmed; in all cases, there is excessive emphasis on their careers. Both men and women have, for many years, invested the majority of their time in their work. The issue of the costs or the sacrifice in their private lives is of no significance to these successful people. Although many mention spending almost every weekend at the office or at their desks, they do not perceive this as a sacrifice. The success they have achieved is a kind of gratification. From the psychological point of view, placing excessive emphasis on career can have a variety of inner origins. It can be a form of successful sublimation if other personal sources of gratification are not possible. It can be an expression of an inner conflict or an unconscious rivalry that can be worked through thus and satisfied in a concrete form. It can be a way of distracting from inner tensions or depressive inclinations in order to avoid having to face up to loneliness. From the data I collected, the four determining factors that seem to be relevant for these professionally successful men and women are: 1) strong oedipal conflict in the development of sexual identity; 2) acceptance by the parents; 3) parents as role models in overcoming problems in life; and 4) attitude to authority – adaptation versus rebellion.

The qualitative research methods I used provide not only personal descriptions of the interviewees' relationship with their parents, but also make it possible to draw inferences about unconscious inner conflicts that mainly relate to the oedipal phase. Oedipal conflicts are completely unconscious and find their expression in intense feelings of competitiveness, hate, and fear of castration. On the other hand, we know from the literature on the subject that intense oedipal conflicts are the root cause of maladaptation and neurotic behavior. Why is it that the people in my study are able to channel the explosive power of their oedipal conflicts in a constructive way? Typical pathological reactions involve self-destructive behaviors apparent in failure, inhibited aggression, delinquency, adopting the role of outsider, and in other forms of self-punishment. These self-staged disasters are intended to calm the feelings of guilt that arise from the forbidden desire for one parent and the wish to "steal" him or her from the other. According to Chasseguet-Smirgel (1974), women in particular feel intensely guilty towards their mothers and this inhibits their personal development and their achievement of recognition in their careers.

This conflict and rivalry is compounded when the parents are actually jealous of their children and do not allow them to develop independently. The men and women in my sample, however, feel accepted and valued emotionally by one or both of their parents. They feel closely bound up with them; indeed, through their own successes, they provide their parents with narcissistic gratification. In other words, the parents are proud of their children and can share in their professional success. The guilt felt by the individuals in my sample about doing better than their parents is lessened by the pleasure and narcissistic satisfaction that they give them. Some individuals in the sample who were less successful in achieving autonomy from the significant parent, feel that they are achieving success on behalf of this much-loved parent. What differentiates them from examples of pathologically symbiotic relationships, is that they genuinely have the ability to achieve the academic and career successes that their parents desire. There are records of abnormal development resulting from the discrepancy between parental expectations and the individual's actual abilities, for example, when parents place excessive pressure on their offspring to achieve in areas such as music or art.

A third element that has formed the inner reality of the individuals in my sample is the example of their parents in showing determination and staying power. Even in crises, they persevered and refused to give up. All the interviewees describe their parents' (and often their grandparents') attitude to work as austere. Work is the focal point of life. Honesty, decency, and reliability are important values.

The fourth relevant dimension concerns the attitude to authority. This takes two forms: rebellion or adaptation. In this dimension, there is a gender-related tendency that is the opposite of what one might expect. It is mainly the female academics and managers who, in different ways, have gone against the explicit wishes of their parents in important matters. The men in the sample describe themselves as accepting of authority and parental norms.

In describing the four key elements that shape the inner reality, and thus seem to determine career success, I have inevitably omitted other factors that are significant for the development of the self and the personality. I would like to point out again that a qualitative study of thirty people cannot allow generalizations to be made about the whole population. It is simply an analysis of patterns and trends from the biographical data collected that may or may not be representative, and not an ideal construction of a typical group.

## Biographical Examples

Some examples from the case histories are useful for illustrating the four dimensions described above.

### *Conflicts in the Development of Sexual Identity*

As one component of sexual identity, we must consider the physical appearance of the female academics and top managers. They come across as attractive women. Typically, they are slim, fashionably dressed in a suit or dress, nicely made-up, and wear tasteful jewelry. Their smart appearance and sex appeal are consciously employed to help them achieve their aims. This was later confirmed in the interviews. The style of the female professors is different. Their dress is more casual; they mainly wear flat shoes, for example. Among these professors there is a small group who consider appearance to be of little importance. However, this difference between the two professional groups in terms of dress and appearance is not necessarily gender related. Among managers, outer appearances are part of the professional image that is intended to impress. In the academic world, dress and formality are less important.

In their interviews, the women managers said they believed that being female was a significant factor in their success and actually conferred initial advantages. They denied experiencing discrimination. When asked if being a woman had been an advantage or a disadvantage in their career progression, they gave similar answers. "It makes no difference," said one. "It's all down to performance," said another. One manager, who had to work as a secretary in spite of having a degree, said she had not found the change of status difficult. "With a bit of effort and enjoyment of my work" it had been easy. Another one saw herself as a "colorful bird" standing out from the crowd with certain "privileges" that came from being a woman. "There are quite a few things that are more difficult to refuse a woman than a man" and "a request to a superior is more likely to be granted, if it comes from a woman" were comments from this group. These statements may well apply to all these women, but they still present a one-sided picture, because the disadvantages of being female are not taken into consideration.

The female professors present a more complex picture. They can see both advantages and disadvantages. They believe that it is much harder for them than for men to be acknowledged intellectually by their colleagues. In their dealings with students, they have no problems, in fact, quite the opposite. "Students prefer the women," said one interviewee. They explain that they devote a lot of time to the pastoral care of students and that this is important to them. "My relationship with my students is the most important one for me," said another. The pastoral care of students offers an opportunity for the sublimation of mothering abilities.

As I have mentioned earlier, feelings that are accessible to the conscious mind represent only one part of the psyche. So it is important to report the answers of the women to questions about their relationship with their mothers and fathers at the conscious level, and then to evaluate them on the unconscious aspects of these relationships.

The image of their mother among the women managers is, according to their statements, largely positive (in five out of seven cases). They talk of having a close relationship. They describe their mothers as capable and ambitious women whom they admire and respect. They are presented as good role models. Some of the admired mothers are housewives and some of them work. The "housewife-mothers" however, are not content with their lot and encourage their daughters to do otherwise.

In the case of the female professors, the situation is reversed. The majority describe conflict in their relationship with their mothers. They see their mothers as critical and characterize them as strict and cold, with strong principles and little understanding of their daughter's interests. They are not presented as good role models. Only one of them had a realistic, that is, partly positive and partly critical, view of her mother, while another had a wholly positive view.

In their relationships with their fathers, the opposite picture emerges. The majority of the female managers speak of their fathers as either failures or tyrants. Only one woman manager speaks tenderly of a father she much admired. The fathers of the female professors, however, serve as positive role models for their daughters. The women were greatly loved by their fathers and strove to emulate them. The fathers encouraged them and were proud of them. "We used to make things together," said one; "we used to discuss things for hours," said another. Even fathers lost in the war are seen positively in the imagination of two interviewees who believed that their fathers would have been pleased about their success and would have understood them had they still been alive.

A pattern emerges from these cases. In each, there seems to be one parent who understood and accepted the daughter. A negative relationship full of conflict seems to have developed toward the other parent. In only one case was there a good relationship with both parents.

If we bring in the unconscious dynamics, however, the situation becomes more complex. In the oedipal configuration, both sexes pass through phases during which they desire to possess the parent of the same sex (negative oedipal desire) and the parent of the opposite sex. Together with the oedipal impulse, feelings such as jealousy, rivalry, hate, and fear arise. To understand my analysis, it is important to remember that the feelings originating from this oedipal development are threatening, and so are always suppressed.

Let us look first at the group of successful women (five managers, and two professors) who describe their relationship with their mothers as completely positive, but who feel they had a negative and distant relationship with their fathers. Behind the picture of the good, much admired mother, two different patterns emerge at the unconscious level. One pattern shows rivalry against the mother and fear of her overwhelming power; the other pattern shows suppressed aggression against a restrictive mother.

One manager, let's call her Monika, is an example of suppressed rivalry towards the mother. Monkia spoke of her admiration for her mother. "My mother was … an incredibly capable woman. Really incredibly capable. She started with nothing, as everything was lost during the war as a result of ill-considered investments … ." (Monika: 16) Criticism of her mother is only expressed indirectly, and only emerged when she was asked to draw her family. She could not do this because she would have to have drawn her mother as an army officer or a head physician, and she did not want to do this. "Somebody once described my mother jokingly as 'Maria Theresa' [the powerful Empress of Austria from 1740-80]. I think that's absolutely true, though. She really is a dominant personality, who could make a success of anything … everyone else was more or less a lackey or a servant" (Monika: 22). Behind this statement lies an unspoken reproach of the mother for having everyone under her influence, especially the father. Monika shows the strength of her desire for her father's love throughout the interview. She constantly refers to him (he is mentioned on 17 out of 42 pages of the transcript). Her close intimate relationship with her father, who is a journalist and poet, has not diminished. She says: "He wrote lyrics, stories, radio plays and I loved his … his poems. And when I was 50 – had my 50th birthday party – everyone asked me what I wanted. And I said a poem from Daddy. So he wrote me a long poem" (Monika: 15). Here we can see that the oedipal drama is still alive. For twenty years, Monika has been in a relationship with a married man, which reflects the inaccessibility of her father. In this constellation, her great desire to have a child could not be fulfilled.

So what is the significance of suppressed oedipal rivalry in the development of a professional career? I believe that unconscious rivalry provides a strong stimulus toward career ambitions. Competition with the mother is transferred to a less threatening setting – the career. Here, these women can outdo all other women – especially their mothers. Any comparison with their own mother is hidden, in that they idealize her. The sexual dimension of professional success becomes clear when one of the women managers says that she has "eighty men under me" in her department – a fantasy of sexual omnipotence.

Comparison with the mother is also obvious in the interview with another manager, although she is not aware of it. First, she says that her mother was the "family banker" who carefully managed her father's small salary. She then immediately mentions in passing the scale of her own daily business: "over $10 million by phone" (Rosalia: 6). The fact that these women do not want to work with other women is another indication of their suppressed rivalry toward their mothers. That they only have male colleagues is mentioned with some pride. In this way, they avoid comparisons with other women. However, as these women had a lot of support from their mothers, they also express feelings of tenderness. This means their feelings of aggression are not so threatening and do not give rise to such a strong sense of guilt.

The phenomenon of the "Cinderella complex" is, from the psychoanalytical point of view, an example of how women hinder their own progress (Dowling 1987). If success is connected in their fantasies with thoughts of revenge against their mother, this means every success produces feelings of guilt and self-castigation.

We find a contrasting pattern among the women who describe their relationship to their mothers positively. In this case, the unconscious attempts to win over the mother are prominent. In what way is this apparent and how does this affect the child's development? The example of a university professor whom I have called Birgit shows this. Her father died in the war and Birgit is the eldest daughter. Her mother spent a lifetime mourning her father and did not form any subsequent relationships. The daughter tried to take the father's place, but the mother would not accept this. Her sorrow at this rejection shows through when Birgit says: "Mother was 40 when father was killed. She wore black for seven years. I don't know why she didn't realize what that meant to a child" (Birgit: 15).

Birgit felt rejected by her mother and could never show how much that had hurt her. She had to be a "big girl," did not cause any trouble, was never ill, and studied hard at school. But the mother never had any understanding for her daughter's studies. In this constellation, her professional success represents a symbolic gift to her mother. If the daughter sees herself as part of the mother, her success is just an extension of her – she becomes a sort of extra limb, enhancing the mother's value. At the same time, the daughter fantasizes that she is the most important part of the mother, who would be worthless without her. The price paid for this is an inadequate separation between mother and child.[4]

In the drawings of the women who were critical of their mothers, the strong desire for the father shows clearly. They often want to rescue him from the wicked mother. In this group, rivalry with other women is much more conscious and strongly differentiated. The women can see where they have experienced discrimination and so can develop a certain sense of solidarity with other women. In both managers and professors, it is a case of highly motivated women, who compensate for their inner conflicts by immersing themselves in their work. Closely interlinked with this first dimension, is the second – namely, the acceptance by the parents.

### Acceptance by the Parents

The second driving force for professional success is encouragement from one or both parents. It is striking that in my sample of both men and women, the majority are firstborn children. Out of 30 interviewees, 23 are firstborn and one-third are only children. Half of the 14 women interviewed had no brothers and sisters. Only children are at the center of attention of both parents, and firstborn children also tend to receive special attention from parents (Forer and Still 1982). Especially strong support from parents can lead to a solid sense of self-esteem. It can also place excessive demands on a child. Examples of both appear in our sample. Again there are two patterns, which are present in both sexes. In one, the child is given freedom to be independent; in the other, the child is seen as an extension of the parents. In both groups, parental support and encouragement are

---

4. I give a more detailed example of this in the next section, when I discuss the case of Sybille.

never associated with unclear boundaries or with being given too free a rein. On the contrary, daughters describe their parents' approach to upbringing as being strict, consistent, and inflexible. The parents instilled clear, middle-class norms – to be honest, punctual and thrifty, reliable, and responsible.

Now an example of each pattern:

A university professor, whom I call Simone, describes the support and encouragement she received from her father. He was her best friend because he often worked at night and was at home during the day. She is an only child. They often went for walks together and had long discussions. Her father was interested in handicrafts; they did all sorts of repair work together, and even made toys. She talks proudly of the things her father encouraged her to make: "Before I went to school, I'd already made some inventions, like ski poles with lamps attached, so you could ski at night. I'd also worked out exactly how you could convert a rocking horse into a toboggan, and I drew it up properly, with plans" (Simone: 22). This episode shows how her father believed in her abilities and let her develop plans on her own. She could gain confidence in her own ability to do these things, without being inhibited by ideas of "girls' work" or "boys' work." She knows she can do things if she plans carefully and has patience.

For children to orientate themselves successfully in the world, it is important that their upbringing is unambiguous. In pathological families, we often find contradictory norms, the "double-bind" situation. The parents of the females interviewed often had rigid standards, but there was still room for battles and arguments. None of the interviewees (male or female) were mentally broken by rigid rules. The struggle against external rules and demands functioned psychodynamically as a safety valve for feelings of aggression. These conflicts were necessary to help them become aware of their own abilities. They functioned as a regulator for the instinctive desires of the child.

Now let us look at the opposite pole, that is, encouragement within the framework of a symbiotic relationship (a negative oedipal constellation). This type of relationship is also present in both the male and female interviewees.

One of the professors, whom I call Sybille, describes her childhood as very special. When I asked her what career plans she had as a child, she focused on her relationship with her mother:

> S:"I had such a happy childhood, I was so close to my mother. It was not until I was 28 that my mother died, and up till then I'd just wanted to be with her. Delayed puberty, I suppose ..."
> I:"Mmm."

S:"I don't know what that means … as I said, my mother helped me in my studies, helped me with my homework, looked after me." (Sybille: 11)

It's clear that Sybille doesn't answer the question directly, because it was obviously never a question of *her* career plans, but her mother's. Her mother had always wanted to study, but couldn't afford it. She achieved this unfulfilled desire through her daughter. Even while she was at the university, there was no separation between mother and daughter. The mother studied with her daughter through all her exams right up to the end. The cost of this symbiotic relationship is that Sybille remains a child. She notes that "until I graduated, I didn't know where babies came from." It actually only became possible for her to enter into a sexual relationship with a man after her mother's death. Sybille was a much-wanted child. She was born when her mother was 24 and in her second marriage, and had thought she would not be able to have any children. Sybille sees herself as a product of her mother. All her achievements are for her. She is quite content with the strong narcissistic confirmation she receives from her attractive and intellectual mother. She is the most important part of the mother, the "phallus." At a conscious level, she has no desire for separation. In a classic fairy-tale manner, the negative aspects of her relationship with her mother are transferred to the wicked stepmother.

How has this sort of support and encouragement influenced the child's career ambitions? Children can only develop a sense of self-esteem when they can see that their parents believe in them and in their abilities. Even in family situations where there was conflict, the parents never completely rejected the child or her abilities. The parent's identification with the daughter (in spite of the presence of some jealousy, according to the interviews) makes it possible for her to achieve things and to develop confidence in her ability to achieve. Erikson (1974) called this first phase of acceptance the "acquisition of basic trust." The child has the feeling of being held.

As is already clear from the case studies, we are not dealing with "superparents" here, but simply with mothers who are "good enough" and who can communicate this sense of acceptance. A positive cycle results. Success gives the children confidence in their abilities, and this then increases the chance of further success. The parents (or one parent) fostered the growth and development of their daughters and had ambitions for them.

### Effect of Parents and Grandparents as Role Models

The parents' ambitions for a daughter, and the encouragement they give her, only engender a drive for success if the parents themselves have similar values. A successful career is the result of staying power and tenacity. It means one can cope with, and overcome, difficulties. Inspired by the "multi-generation family therapy" of Boszormeny-Nagy and Spark (1981) and Stierlin (1982) I looked into the family histories of the interviewees back to their grandparents. The common cliché that successful women and men came from well-off and stable families was completely disproved. Every multi-generation family history in my study has problematic or tragic elements. I will illustrate this with one example.

A female manager, whom I call Gudula, describes the grandfather on her father's side as the driving force of the family. He sacrificed a lot in order to build up a small business, which eventually employed a staff of seventy. Grandmother and grandfather worked as one – like "hammer and anvil." Her father took over the business and expanded it further. The idea of being a craftsman who earned an honest living was held up as a shining example in the family. All the money had to be re-invested in the firm. However, Gudula's mother "wasn't one of their sort" and was never fully accepted. After Gudula's mother's death, which was closely followed by the loss of her father in a car crash and her brother's suicide, her grandfather resumed control of the business at the age of sixty and continued until his death. Gudula learned to adopt high standards, for example "one had to strive to be better, to achieve more, and one had to take care how one behaved in public, like being modest … for example, we always just took bread and butter for our school lunch, not sandwiches, so that we weren't flaunting the fact that we perhaps had more money than the others" (Gudula, 19).

Even now, it would be inconceivable to Gudula to earn money quickly or dishonestly. The restricting influence of these family norms is apparent in her story. It took a personal crisis – the end of a long-term relationship – to make her begin to question whether work should remain the most important thing in her life. Doing something just for fun was forbidden, and she still finds it difficult.

The family histories of my sample are almost as exciting as novels. The central character is typically found in the grandparents' generation. In the case of the men I interviewed, they, too, often identify the grandmother as the one who built up the business – who was "the heart of the firm."

In all the case histories, work is central. It is the vehicle for keeping family members alive, or as a means of "getting-on." There are numerous examples in these families of disastrous changes of fortune, physical handicaps, death, persecution, and emigration. It is characteristic of the parents and grandparents that they have never given up or allowed themselves to be disheartened. None of the interviewees are ashamed of, or try to hide, their social background. The stories all reveal a deep respect for the achievements of the parents' and grandparents' generations. The interviewees respect their parents and grandparents, not for being better than their children, but for the way they have overcome often very difficult circumstances in their own lives.

### *Adaptation or Rebellion*

This is the one dimension where we find strong gender-related differences. In complete contrast to the male stereotype, we find among the career men a picture of the good, well-adapted child who does not question his parents' views and norms. With few exceptions the men report no conflicts or arguments with their parents, and have followed a straightforward career path. They respect authority and tend to conform. One top manager, whom I call Felix, gave the following answer to a question about his attitude to authority:

> I tended to accept authority, I still do, although I try and resist it ... you have a feeling of respect for anyone in charge, any shop assistant or stupid policeman. Why do you not do this or that? Because there's some rule or other about it (Felix: 34).

One might expect this sort of answer from females, the "passive sex" (Mitscherlich 1984). However, in the interviews with the women, there are stories of rebellion against parental norms and massive conflict with at least one of the parents. This is why I call the career women "rebels." They used many different tactics in their rows with their parents. One refused to go to the university; another, whose father was a school principal, refused to settle down in school and ran away. One of the women managers emigrated to Canada against her parents' wishes. The conflict was frequently related to sexuality – marrying the man their parents did not like, getting pregnant, or having sex before marriage. This often led to the sudden severance of a close bond with the father. Here is a brief example from the case of Gudula.

Gudula describes her relationship with her father as very close. Her rendering of the "enchanted family" is represented by a double line. "I have a very strong bond with my father," she says. This "umbilical cord" is then cut through with a line. Gudula rebelled against the conservative lifestyle of her parents by getting pregnant:

> That was a complete shock for my parents ... my father presented me with the alternatives. Either he would kill himself or I would have the

child or have an abortion. I'd already had one abortion and so I said, it's your problem (Gudula: 30).[5]

Even Gudula describes her hasty marriage as rebellion against her parents. The explosive nature of the conflict becomes clear in her father's threats, which are intended to prevent Gudula from breaking out of the parental framework.

Women who, as children, succeeded in breaking away from the family norms, find it easier as adults to overcome stereotypes and to be themselves. They do this by channelling their aggression positively and constructively. They aim directly for what they want to achieve. The current female stereotype suggests that women only try to gain power by indirect means: they become ill, feel unhappy, make others feel guilty, or manipulate them.

Among the men in top positions in my sample, I have found them to be well adapted and to have internalized the pressure to succeed that their parents put on them. International companies and educational institutions seem to need well-adapted leaders in top positions who are used to identifying with parental norms and do not challenge the basic rules. Their power and aggressive impulses are used against competitors; in this way they remain "good sons" who now identify with their firms and are successful in getting acknowledged.

## Conclusion

My paper has investigated the four dimensions of inner reality that drove the interviewees to pursue a professional career. The four dimensions are closely interconnected. The interviewees are all highly motivated people whose oedipal wishes result in inner conflicts. Their careers then offer them a safety valve for their aggressive impulses. Their sense of reality allows them to find ways of gaining social recognition, power, and money. At the same time, there is clear variation among individuals within each dimension. For all the women in the study, professional success has become a part of their identity that they could no longer do without. Regardless of whether they actively support feminist issues or not, they represent new role models for the next generation of women by combining perseverance and professional success with feminine qualities and values.

---

5. The English is an accurate rendering of the German. Based on the last sentence, she apparently meant that her father would kill himself if she had the child.

# References

Anderson, H. Ch. 1958. *Märchen und Erzählungen.* Odense.

Badinter, E. 1981. *Die Mutterliebe. Die Geschichte eines Gefühls vom 17. Jahrhundert bis heute.* Munich.

Bandhauer-Schöffmann, I. and Hornung, E. 1990. "Von Mythen und Trümmern." In *Mitteilungen des Instituts für Wissenschaft und Kunst* 45(4):11-18.

Beauvoir, S. 1972. *Das andere Geschlecht.* Frankfurt am Main.

Boszormeny-Nagy, I. and Spark, K. 1981. *Unsichtbare Bindungen: Die Dynamik familiärer Systeme.* Stuttgart.

Chasseguet-Smirgel, J. et al. 1974. *Psychoanalyse der weiblichen Sexualität.* Frankfurt am Main.

Chodorow, N. 1958. *Das Erbe der Mutter: Psychoanalyse und Soziologie der Geschlechter.* Munich.

Dowling, C. 1987. *Der Cindarella-Komplex.* Frankfurt am Main.

Erikson, E. 1974. *Identität und Lebenszyklus.* Frankfurt am Main.

Freud, A. 1937. *Das Ich und die Abwehrmechanismen.* Vienna.

Freud, S. [1923] 1971. "The Ego and the Id." In *Standard Edition.* Vol. 19. Ed. J. Strachey and A. Freud. London.

___. [1933] 1971. "The Introductory Lectures on Psycho-Analysis." In *Standard Edition.* Vol. 22. Ed. J. Strachey and A. Freud. London.

Forer, L. K. and Still, H. 1982. *Erstes, zweites, drittes Kind ...: Welche Bedeutung hat die Geschwisterfolge für Kinder, Eltern, Familie?* Reinbek bei Hamburg.

Fromm, E. 1971. *Analytische Sozialpsychologie und Gesellschaftstheorie.* Frankfurt am Main.

Gold, B. 1990. "Frauen und Führung: Die Last der Tradition." *Psychologie heute* 56(6): 8-11.

Horney, K. 1920. *Die Psychologie der Frau.* Frankfurt am Main.

Kos, M. and Biermann, G. 1973. *Die verzauberte Familie: Ein tiefenpsychologischer Zeichentest.* Munich.

Mitscherlich, M. 1985. *Die friedfertige Frau: Eine psychoanalytische Untersuchung zur Aggression der Geschlechter.* Frankfurt am Main.

Olivier, Ch. 1987. *Jokastes Kinder: Die Psyche der Frau im Schatten der Mutter.* Düsseldorf.

Parker, B. 1975. *Meine Sprache bin ich.* Frankfurt am Main.

Rustermeyer, R. and Thrien, S. 1989. *Die Managerin – der Manager: Wie weiblich dürfen sie sein, wie männlich müssen sie sein?* Paderborn.

Stierlin, H. 1982. *Delegation und Familie. Beiträge zum Heidelberger familiendynamischen Konzept.* Frankfurt am Main.

Theweleit, K. 1977. *Männerphantasien.* 2 vols. Frankfurt am Main.

Winnicott, D.W. 1983. *Von der Kinderheilkunde zur Psychoanalyse.* Munich.

*Chapter 9*

⟶

# THE DISCOURSE ON FEMALE SEXUALITY IN NINETEENTH-CENTURY AUSTRIA

............................

*Marie-Luise Angerer*

"What is woman? Disease, says Hippocrates" (Freyer 1991: 245).

## Introduction

Developments in gynecology in the nineteenth century were closely connected to changing images of women (Jordanova 1989; Ehrenreich and English 1989; Honegger 1981, 1989, 1990; Honegger and Heintz 1984; Fischer-Homberger 1981, 1984; Martin 1987; Mendus and Rendall 1989; Geyer-Kordesch and Kuhn 1986). My chapter focuses on the relation between notions of the female body and the female "soul" in scholarly and scientific writings of that period: how the latter derive from the former, and how they resemble or reinforce each other.[1] I will assess uniquely Austrian developments within the general shifts of the late eighteenth and the nineteenth century that were particularly important in the evolution of such well-known "pictures" of the woman as they appear in the works of Klimt, Freud, and Weininger.

1. In this respect a very important discourse is "pedagogish," which for reasons of space, I cannot treat here. See Angerer (1990).

The first part of my essay describes the development of medical practice with respect to females in Austria from the progressive institutions under Joseph II up to the establishment of a monopoly in the hands of male gynecologists in the first third of the nineteenth century. The second part concentrates on the psychological inner space: on the "discovery" of the unconscious by Sigmund Freud during his treatment of (primarily) female patients diagnosed with hysteria. I will argue that notions of the female body and psyche were developed to correspond with particular aspects of masculine psychic needs. It was not only that the female as the "other" was an ideal surface on which to project male anxieties, but also, that abstract generalizing about women as "female" promoted the concrete exclusion of women from social relations.

## A Short Sketch of Developments in the Nineteenth Century

Naturally, these developments took place within a more general cultural context that was also undergoing changes. In the second half of the eighteenth century the ideology of the Enlightenment took shape and began to be institutionalized. In his writings, Michel Foucault (1973, 1975, 1980) describes these processes: a new body of knowledge developed – the humanities – with "man," his language, his history, his being, as the subject. In the course of the nineteenth century, speaking, seeing, and controlling became recognized as scientific strategies. From the middle of the eighteenth century new institutions were created to put this new knowledge into practice: schools, the modern military, factories, prisons, and hospitals. According to some claims, it is in this era that the "citizen" was born. Foucault, however, argues that it is rather the "docile body," the object of these new institutions, that is really born. The docile body develops and is shaped by the disciplines practiced in these institutions.

However, as Bartky (1988: 63) has rightly pointed out, Foucault "describes the development of these docile bodies throughout, as if the bodily experiences of men and women did not differ, and as if men and women bore the same relationship to the characteristic institutions of modern life" (Bartky 1988: 63). But it is precisely in the second half of the eighteenth century – as hospitals and schools were being built for the populace – that the differentiation in the everyday life of women and men increased more and more clearly. The man's sphere was equated with the external world: the public and production. The woman's sphere became the physical and psychological inner world: house and home. Parallel to this physical separation of the sexes was an increasing intellectual differentiation between the male and the female body. At the same time, the emerging nation-states began to recognize women as important for securing the state, especially in the area of popular policy, and their bodies received increasing attention. This attention, in the form of medical, pedagogical, and hygienic intervention, was not initially accepted. Women had to be convinced of the advantages, in part with force.

In the sphere of medicine there were two decisive developments around 1800. Physicians discovered that conception occurs independently of the female orgasm. As a consequence, the earlier doctrine of the correspondence between the male and female sexual organs also lost its validity. This opened the way for recognizing and investigating the differences (physiological, anatomical, etc.) between male and female bodies (Laqueur 1987: 2).

Between 1730 and 1790, depictions of the female skeleton appeared in anatomy books for the first time in Germany, Italy, and France. Until then, only male skeletons had been used to depict the human skeleton. This shift attacked the medical-biological-anthropological worldview inherited from Aristotle and Galen. Jacques Moreau de la Sarthe, one of the founders of "moral anthropology" now argued: "Not only are the sexes different, they are different in every conceivable respect of body and soul, in every physical and moral aspect" (Laqueur 1987: 2).

Through the middle of the eighteenth century, then, gender-specific physiology was ignored, or elaborately explained away. We get an idea of this from the writings of an eighteenth-century Eisenach physician discussed by Barbara Duden (1987). In his case records, even menstruation was not treated as a specifically female physiological process, but as something that had to have a correspondence in the male body. The physician argued that men possess the "golden vein" (hemorrhoids). The only difference is that men do not bleed periodically or from a single place in the body. "In contrast, they lose blood, either regularly or occasionally, from various places: the nose, the golden vein, a wound, bloody expectorations ...; the golden vein and the menses were seen as spontaneous therapeutic emptyings of the body that were fully analogous and interchangeable" (Duden 1987: 136).

The idea of gender-specific physiology established itself in the course of the nineteenth century, just as medical opinion was becoming increasingly the arbiter of social questions (Schiebinger 1987: 70). The moral and physiological nature of the female were spoken of as a single indivisible entity (Schiebinger 1987: 69); that is, we see the development of the idea that physiology determines the "moral" state, or soul (Steinbrügge 1987: 31ff.).

Also, beginning in the middle of the eighteenth century, the medical profession took over the role of midwives, and, over the course of the next eighty years, the specialty of gynecology developed its present scope. During this period, "female diseases" began to be differentiated into organic (or bodily) diseases and "nervous diseases of the female." Two types of physician specialized in female diseases: early on, the gynecologist and the neurologist and, towards the end of the nineteenth century, the psychoanalyst (Lewin 1984; Masson 1986). In this evolution, the cause of the classic female disorder, hysteria, shifted "upstairs" (Braun 1985). The sensitive, highly strung nerves of the female, and not the female sexual organs (in this period meaning the uterus and ovaries) were made responsible for hysteria. The first "talking cures" of patients diagnosed with hysteria gave Josef Breuer and Sigmund Freud their first glimpse into the "dark continent" of the psychic inner space of the female.

## Women's Diseases and their Treatment in the Austrian "Biedermeier"

### *The Conquering of Feminine Interior Space*

The developments I describe here took place between 1780 and 1850 against the background of the late Enlightenment. Joseph II, the son of Maria Theresa, was a vigorous proponent of the Enlightenment in Austria. In his short reign (1780-1790), he initiated numerous social reforms and projects against considerable resistance. His social projects included the opening of the first General Hospital in Vienna in 1784, and the establishment there of the Vienna Maternity House, under the direction of Johann Lukas Boer, as a "general sanctuary for unwed mothers," which served about 1200 patients a year (Lesky 1981: 201). In 1785 came the establishment of the Military Surgical Academy. A Charitable Postnatal Station was added in 1789, along with practical instruction in obstetrics (Neuburger 1921: 1-2). Seventeen eighty-four marked the opening of the Vienna Lunatic Asylum – the first institution in Europe solely for the mentally ill (Kopetzki 1989: 321).

Vienna had attracted distinguished physicians from other parts of Europe during the reign of Maria Theresa, for example, Van Swieten, the Empress' Royal Physician. This trend continued under her son. Johann Peter Frank, Professor at the University Medical Clinic and Director of the General Hospital, wrote his voluminous *The System of a Complete Public Health Police* (1786) during his stay in Vienna. Johann Lukas Boer can be considered a pioneer in "natural gentle birth." The theory of both can be summarized as: "The best is that which is natural."[2] In this period, that meant that women should nurse their infants themselves, and that as few instruments as possible should be used in childbirth (Boer was decidedly against the use of forceps – a frequent practice in France and Germany at the time).

Like Rousseau, Johann Peter Frank proselytized the "natural lifestyle": moderation in every respect, be it in eating and drinking, physical activity, or in sexual behavior. Those who do not lead a natural life, he argued, would be punished by particular illnesses: men with a degeneration that amounts to feminization, women with male diseases, for example, with bleeding of the golden vein. Frank was a proponent of "Brownianism" – a dynamic-vitalistic view of medicine that arose in contrast to the traditional humoral pathology. Brownianism was at odds with the worldview of prevailing reactionary forces, and Frank's successful proselytizing in this regard made him the subject of attack. Eventually, the royal physician of Franz I, Joseph Andreas Stifft, was able to drive Frank and Boer into exile; Frank and his son had to leave Vienna in 1804, while Boer was forced into retirement in 1822.

In the following period, the older medical system with its use of bleeding and purgatives came back into practice: "The police-state [*Polizeistaat*] had won the day, the rule of the physician as policeman [*medizinische Polizisten*] had begun," as the Austrian historian, Erna Lesky wrote in her history of the *Viennese Medical School in the 19th Century* (1965).[3] She continued: "Restoration in Stifft's sense meant … not only the exclusion of the new and foreign as suspect,

2. In the last third of the eighteenth century, a kind of reform movement that came from France made itself visible. In contrast to aristocratic women, bourgeois women celebrated the "natural" life with all its implications. This "new" lifestyle, which reached deeply into the life of bourgeois women, was taken up in many disciplines and worked out as the "theory of man and woman" (See Badinter 1981).

3. I understand *Polizei* here in the sense of institutions that maintain political and social order in contrast to Frank's notion of the *medizinische Polizei*, which must be understood in the sense of a "normative guide for living." Also, if Frank's instructions at first appear constraining, they are in many respects "liberating" to the extent that they free society to introduce "new" forms of restraint.

it meant the promotion of all that was indigenous as tried and true" (Lesky 1965: 38).

The new childbirth facilities built under Joseph II had a high rate of infant mortality: around the middle of the nineteenth century, the rate was almost 80 percent as compared to an overall rate of 40 percent when infant deaths from home births are included. In 1847-48, Ignaz Semmelweis discovered the causes of puerperal fever, a bacterial infection suffered by women after childbirth or abortion. But several decades would pass before this discovery would effect the practice of obstetrics and gynecological surgery. Although such well-known Austrian physicians as Skoda and the dermatologist Hebra were convinced of the correctness of Semmelweis's findings from the beginning, there were an important number of opponents in the ranks of Austrian physicians who, for whatever reason, saw Semmelweis's work as an attack on the male-dominated profession. It was, after all, the examining hand of the male physician that Semmelweis named as the most frequent carrier of the infection (Fischer 1909).

How uncertain this "male hand" was with respect to the female body may be gleaned from textbooks describing gynecological examination procedures. To quote from one such text, written by A. Moser in 1843,

> it is very difficult to imagine the barriers to examining the female child-birth organs that are encountered, particularly in a private practice. The beds are almost invariably so soft that the body sinks in under its weight and the pelvis is so positioned that the examination is difficult for the physician, tiring for the patient, and yields no results. If it is possible to introduce the speculum, it is frequently at such an angle that one must bend down very far in order to look through it. The patient at first resists the examination. If the physician insists, she then lies crossways on the bed. In order to avoid further resistance, the physician no longer insists that she position herself properly, but begins with the examination which cannot succeed, and has then certainly lost the patient's trust (Moser 1843: 675).

Thus, the new institutions provided an advantage principally to the practicing physicians and students. Where else could they have mastered their professional insecurities, if not in these hospitals filled with female bodies? Competition from midwives had been successfully eliminated: those who continued to practice did so under medical control. Beginning in 1834 instruction for medical students and midwives was separated (in Vienna).

By the middle of the nineteenth century, gynecology had established itself as a medical discipline firmly in the hands of male practitioners. The number of texts on this subject published in this period is one indication of its success. The female body had become like a map with precisely determined parts, marked-off borders, and identified organs. Psychological diseases and diseases of the nervous system were not described in these texts, nor were the therapies of the past. Gynecologists of this period would not advise a hysterical woman to masturbate or sleep with her husband. On the contrary, they emphatically recommended against such remedies. The question of female sexuality, which previously had not been a taboo subject, did not arise within gynecology. Only in the next era would it return as an inexhaustible secret, a secret that tried to find its voice and whose echoes were not yet understood.

## The Female Body within the Intellectual Context of Pre-1848 Austria: "The Dark Continent"

Although the Enlightenment was followed everywhere in Europe by a long restoration period, reaction in Austria was particularly harsh. Russia, Prussia, and Austria are often mentioned together in the literature as examples of conservative, backward-looking polities, but Austria, characterized as "Europe's China" (Banik-Schweitzer et al. 1980; Hauch 1990), with its system of spies and censorship went much farther than the others. According to Joseph von Sonnenfels, censorship was not restricted to books, plays, and the press, but extended to public speeches, painting, graphic reproduction, indeed to almost anything within the public sphere (Hauch 1990: 19; Brüller and Stekl 1988: 160-92).

Isidor Fischer describes the influences of political reaction on the history of midwifery: as a specialized medical discipline in Vienna, it was introduced only in the first half of the nineteenth century in Austria and Germany (Fischer 1909: 78). The expulsion of artists and intellectuals, a particular aspect of the Austrian reaction during the Biedermeier period, included the prominent physicians and scientists who had been brought to Vienna by Joseph II as part of his policy of reforming the health system. The Metternich system of the Vormärz era placed Austria in a unique situation among European countries: it was intellectually isolated from foreign influences, it had a low level of cultural goods (literary works, newspapers, learning and reference materials, etc.) due to censorship, and, it provided inadequate educational opportunities for the population. Austria, in the Vormärz, was a "historical anachronism" (Pircher 1980: 8).

This anachronism manifested itself in a unique manner within the "world of women." The romantic-liberal ideal of the woman, typified by such figures as George Sand, Madame de Staël, Bettina von

Arnim, and Rahel Varnhagen, was totally missing. Instead, we find such figures as Caroline Pichler (well known for her salon) and Karoline von Woltmann, author of tracts on the feminine and masculine nature that presented the "new idea" of masculinity and femininity (Hauch 1990: 38-45).

While Caroline Pichler's mother, the first maid to Maria Theresa, was still very interested in the "scholarly disciplines," the daughter distanced herself emphatically from such emancipatory views:

> Even the views of my mother about the unjust relationship to men in which we women find ourselves, about the affronts to us in which men are said to have indulged, both in public and domestic life, about the so-called rights of women, did not resonate in my soul, despite the power which, in other respects, her strong spirit and equally strong will exercised over me. I could neither hate nor despise men, still less envy them

and further:

> I felt convinced that inherent sexual characteristics and the structures in the physical, as well as in the moral and public world, had rightly assigned to us the subordinate role; I could not conceal from myself the fact that not only in the arts and sciences, but even in the characteristically female pursuits, such as cooking, sewing, and embroidering, when men took up such things they always left the accomplishments of our sex far behind. In this respect, the lot of our sex, to whom the first painstaking care and education of the young person is entrusted, and to whose hand the sowing of the good and noble seed in the young heart is entrusted – so that it will bear its beneficial fruit in manhood – now seemed all the more honorable and beautiful to me, and I found ... that providence had very benevolently provided for us by the very fact that it had so clearly prescribed for us our duties and thereby guarded us against so many dangerous errors and painful regrets (Pichler 1844, vol. 1: 150-51).

Karoline von Woltmann goes a step further in her judgment on the "sensual drives of women":

> Of themselves delicate, gentle, lively, imbued with imagination, brightened by rhythm, pricked by no thorn of refinement, not focused by an urge of narcissism, spiritualized through sympathy and love, transfigured by the mind, the sensual urges are not even heightened by privation (Woltmann 1826: 30).

According to Woltmann, women have no sensual desires, and their sensual drive is not increased if it is not fulfilled. This assertion is particularly interesting in its historical context. As I will show later, the view of women as asexual and passionless was not widespread in the first half of the nineteenth century. On the contrary, the sexual desires of women were generally viewed as being a part of their nature, even if they were increasingly viewed within an exclusively moral framework. Like Austrian medical pedagogues such as Johann L. Ewald or Raphael Steidele, Karoline von Woltmann begins with the notion of the physical "otherness" of the woman, proceeds to a psychic and a social "otherness," and arrives, finally, at the total "otherness" of the female nature.

Both Caroline Pichler and Karoline von Woltmann knew the writings of women like Mary Wollstonecraft and George Sand, but vehemently rejected these as being unfeminine, that is, masculine. An idea of the antipathy between the Austrian and non-Austrian camps may be gleaned from the reaction of Caroline Pichler's salon to a visit by Madame de Staël. According to Caroline Pichler:

> And so sat our ladies ... crowded around the tea table, each armed with her knitting, each determined, and many ... feeling obliged, to play a silent role ... .

For her part, Madame de Staël described the ladies of this circle to a friend as the "Tricoteuses de la tribune"; word of this got back to Pichler, who was shocked and insulted (Pichler 1844, vol. 2.: 124-26).

The reaction of Caroline Pichler and her salon cannot be ignored as simple bourgeois coffee klatsch. As a literary figure, Pichler is to be ranked with the likes of Madame de Staël and George Sand, and thus was one of the leading female intellectuals of Biedermeier Austrian society. Also, the attitudes inherent in these reactions correspond closely to the medical-pedagogical writings of the Austrian Biedermeier and represent the internalization of "feminine virtues." In the second half of the nineteenth century, when a bourgeois women's movement finally arose in Austria, this internalization by leading women of "feminine virtues" would recur in remarkable forms.[4]

### The Discovery/Occupation of the Female Psychic Inner Space: The Riddle

Signs that something is missing from the gynecological textbooks can already be seen in the writings of Adolf Moser: "For the man, the female psyche is an insoluble conundrum, and the further it is distanced from the natural state, the more refined it is by culture, the more insoluble it appears" (Moser 1843: 42). These fears would reappear later in the writings of Sigmund Freud, for example in the "Taboo of Virginity": "Perhaps this dread is based on the fact that woman is different from man, forever incomprehensible and myste-

---

4. In 1896, Rosa Mayreder, one of the leading representatives of the bourgeois women's movement in Austria, observed: "It is increasingly impossible for me to view men as the enemy of women's causes" (quoted in Anderson 1990: 189).

rious, strange and therefore apparently hostile. The man is afraid of being weakened by the woman, infected with her femininity and often then showing himself incapable" (Freud 1989a: 218ff.).

But we have not yet gotten to Freud and his psychoanalytic theory on the sexual origins of hysteria. Instead, we are in the first half of the nineteenth century, when Moser wrote his instructions for the young, inexperienced physician, and when the German physician Busch formulated his thoughts on *The Sexual Life of the Female* (Busch 1839-44). According to Busch, the male has a "sexual drive," whereas the female has a "sexual capacity." While the male's sexual drive actively desires and demands sexual intercourse, the woman is active only in the sense of making herself receptive: the female "must also be active in bringing about a state in which the man ... as incubus can conjugate with her"(Busch 1839-44: 187, 215). The sexual capacity of the female is manifold: it encompasses "conception, pregnancy, birth, nursing, feeding, and bringing up the child" (Moser 1843: 22). Since the sexual capacity is exclusively under the control of the nervous system, "hysteria must be seen as a general illness affecting the entire organism" (Busch 1839-44: 340): "The sexuality of the female is an important component of hysteria"(Busch 1839-44: 342). This theme would be expanded by Freud: "The change in their main erogenous zone together with the wave of repression at puberty, which, as it were, puts aside infantile masculinity, are the chief determinants of the greater proneness of women to neurosis, especially hysteria. These determinants, therefore, are intimately related to the essence of femininity" (Freud 1989b: 125).

From the middle of the nineteenth century, hysteria was generally considered to be a disease of the nervous system. At the same time, the first male hysterics were described; at issue was the roles played by the genitals and by the sexual drive in causing the illness. The French school, led by Briquet, Charcot, and Janet, considered sexuality to have no significance in the etiology of hysteria. Austrian neurologists and gynecologists were ambivalent until Freud assigned a clear role to sexuality in the development of hysteria. Freud himself repeatedly stated that he owed his understanding of hysteria to three men: Joseph Breuer, Jean-Martin Charcot, the "Napoleon of Neuroses," and Rudolf Chrobak, the head of the Vienna Gynecology Clinic. In varying degrees, these three had brought him to an understanding of the real secret of hysterical women.

There was, however, another Viennese physician who, as early as the 1860s, had pointed to this sexual secret: the neurologist Moritz Benedikt. Breuer and Freud cited him in their first publication on hysteria. Benedikt wrote in his memoirs: "It is age-old knowledge that women are more emotional than men and, for this reason, become hysterical more easily. The shocks to the female nervous system come partly from stresses and stimuli originating in their special organs, and also from the lack of sexual satisfaction, which is so frequent in females, and becomes the main source for the convulsion of the sensitive nervous system" (Benedikt 1906: 133).

The second half of the nineteenth century saw surgeons practicing ovaridectomy and clitoridectomy in Austria as elsewhere. The Viennese gynecologist Gustav Braun, for example, removed the clitoris and vulva of young girls in order to relieve cramps and symptoms that indicated healthy sexual arousal (Shorter 1989: 172). Gynecologists such as Chrobak also recommended removal of the clitoris as the remedy of last resort in cases of chronic masturbation (Chrobak 1900).

It was against this background that Joseph Breuer, a highly respected internist and neurologist, came upon Bertha Pappenheim (alias Anna O.), who later founded the "talking cure" or "chimney sweeping" of psychoanalysis. The literature on this first psychoanalytic case of hysteria is extensive, but the interpretations are highly contradictory. As in later case studies published by psychoanalysts from Freud to Ernest Jones, the descriptions are cursory and fragmentary, and are characterized by bias and distortion (Moi 1981; Rose 1989; Schlesier 1990). According to Freud, Breuer had repeatedly asserted that sexuality played no significant role in the case of Anna O. But Freud himself later claimed that sexuality was the driving factor behind her hysterical fits: her physical symptoms portrayed her inner conflicts.

It was after he returned to Vienna that Freud broke clearly with Charcot's teaching. According to Jacqueline Rose, Freud's differences with his teacher were twofold: "Firstly, he questioned the visible evidence of the disease – the idea that you could tell a hysteric by looking at her body, that is, by reading off the symptoms of nervous disability or susceptibility to trauma. Secondly … he rejected the idea that hysteria was an 'independent' clinical entity, by using what he uncovered of the unconscious and its universal presence in adult life" (Rose 1989: 97). Freud went on to decipher the language of the unconscious, and discovered that:

> hysterical attacks, like hysteria in general, revive a piece of sexual activity in women which existed during their childhood and at that time revealed an essentially masculine character. It can often be observed that girls who have shown a boyish nature and inclinations up to the years before puberty are precisely those who become hysterical from puberty

onwards. In a whole number of cases, the hysterical neurosis merely represents an excessive accentuation of the typical wave of repression which, by doing away with her masculine sexuality, allows the woman to emerge (Freud 1989c: 203).

## *The Intellectual Context of this "Discovery":*
## *"Das sexuelle Problem" (R. Musil)*

Two currents meet in this account: the battle between two schools of masculine thought on female sexuality and the discovery of the male hysteric. One group, exemplified by Krafft-Ebing, Lombroso, and Möbius, held the female to be naturally frigid. The opposing camp maintained that the carnal desire of the female is much greater than that of the male: "The female body is, so to speak, saturated with sexuality" (Eberhard 1924: 248). Charcot's "discovery" of the male hysteric was brought to Vienna by Freud (see also Goldstein 1991). It coincided with the concept of neurasthenia (weakness of the nerves), which was diagnosed in males with increasing frequency in England and the United States after the middle of the nineteenth century. The neurasthenic male complained of increasing weakness, lack of energy, and impotence, which amounted to a "feminization" or a "self-feminization" of the man. According to Jacques Le Rider, the works of Otto Weininger (1910) or Paul Möbius (1900) can be seen as a pitiful struggle against their authors' own weakness and interpreted as an attempt to realize their own identity in the image of the Woman (Fliedl 1989; Le Rider 1985).

Scientific and cultural representations, such as Freud's theory of female sexuality or the paintings of Gustav Klimt, can be seen as dams or walls erected to protect an unsure, fragile, masculine self-image. This crisis manifested itself in Vienna – one of the great cities of its time – in a particularly impressive manner (Eder 1993). Nike Wagner (1987) describes the great tensions of males in this period. Males saw nationalistic, democratic, women's rights, and modern artistic movements as attacks on their psychic inner space and their concrete public sphere. The stronger these movements became, the more rigid became the bourgeois male's reaction (Wagner 1987: 150-51). His integration within bourgeois culture proved repeatedly to be unstable and fragile. Thus Freud's definition of culture was as ambivalent as his definition of sexuality, because the feminine had to be excluded from it. And, exiled from these definitions, the feminine had to return repeatedly within the core of his theory: "Only by acting as women, only if men, like women, fear a loss of love, will they internalize the cultural law in which their masculinity is so fiercely invested" (Rose 1991).

The atmosphere of fin-de-siècle Vienna was pregnant with eroticism – a "coitus culture," according to Otto Weiniger (quoted in Wagner 1987: 153). In spite of, or perhaps because of, this, a new dimension of alienation between the sexes was perceived and experienced as a malaise: "Images of fear arise from the abyss of alienation ... It is the unknown which awakes fear, and the woman was unknown not only herself but above all to the man" (Wagner 1987: 149).

Laura Marholm also describes the great distance between man and woman in her "Book of Women": "It is a peculiar characteristic of our time that – given the strict external division – man and woman have never stood so far apart, never impulsively and from the unconscious have they understood one another as poorly as now"(Marholm 1895: 43).

In his excessive preoccupation with the female nude, the painter Gustav Klimt does not undertake a "reappraisal of the feminine" (Fliedl 1989), but rather an "expropriation of femininity for the man" (Eiblmayr 1988). In this period, "the image of the man increasingly disappears while that of the woman monopolizes art (paintings), although at the cost of its being demonized, mythologized, or fetishized" (Fliedl 1989: 202). In their attentions to the female body or model, artists and scientists neither concerned themselves with the power of Eros, nor tried to come to terms with the femininity they found so "exotic." Rather, they succumbed to their own projections of a masculine femininity (Braun 1987: 24-30).

### *The Masks of Desire*

According to contemporary voices, the sexes were frozen into bizarre poses at the turn of the century: the female sex, hollowed out through art, literature, and science and left only with an ornamental surface; the male sex, exhausted and on the verge of collapse (Wagner 1987: 132ff.). Sigmund Freud concluded that the repression of an originally masculine sexuality lies at the core of female hysteria. Femininity thus becomes a mask hiding that which is within. What this view leads to was shown by Joan Rivière in her remarkable 1929 article, "Womanliness as a Masquerade." As Stephen Heath has summarized Rivière's thoughts: "The masquerade is a representation of femininity but then femininity is representation, the representation of the woman" (Heath 1989: 53).

# Conclusions

I have tried, in this paper, to follow up Ludmilla Jordanova's suggestion "that gender, together with the biomedical sciences of which it was an integral part, expressed and informed cultural processes" (Jordanova 1989: 159). We can see this fusion between gender and medical science in our culture today. Eating disorders, to a very high degree "female diseases," are – not surprisingly – concentrated on the control of the women's bodies. It is the image of the female body that – according to feminist media analysis – guarantees male identity. And it is the image of the female body that represents age, pain, disease, and death. All these resulted from the complexity of shifts during the period I have tried to describe. According to Michèle Le Doeuff, "images" are not, properly speaking, "what I think," but rather, "what I think with," or again, "that by which what I think is able to define itself" (cited in Probyn 1993: 91). This means that images affect all theoretical and cultural discourse, in the broadest sense.

My chapter reports results from a larger, interdisciplinary project entitled "Bourgeois Women's Culture in 19th Century Austria: Fiction, Ideology, Reality." The project was financed by the Austrian Science Foundation (Fonds zur Förderung der wissenschaftlichen Forschung). The project team consisted of Germanists under the direction of Sigrid Schmid-Bortenschlager, historians under the direction of Brigitte Mazohl-Wallnig, and art historians under the direction of Daniela Hammer-Tugendhat.

# References

Anderson, H. 1990. "'Mir wird es immer unmöglicher, die Männer als die Feinde der Frauensache zu betrachten … .' Zur Beteiligung von Männern an den Bestrebungen der österreichischen Frauenbewegung um 1900." In *'Das Weib existiert nicht für sich': Geschlechterbeziehungen in der bürgerlichen Gesellschaft.* Ed. H. Dienst and E. Saurer, 189-201. Vienna.

Angerer, M. et al. 1989. "Von der gewaltigen 'Reinheit' der Bilder: Wandel medialer Körperbilder in Illustrierten zwischen 1955 und 1985." In *Blick-Wechsel: Konstruktionen von Männlichkeit und Weiblichkeit in Kunst und Kunstgeschichte.* Ed. I. Lindner et al., 395-414. Berlin.

Angerer, M. 1990. *Über die Leiden der Tugend: Bildungswünsche und - verhinderungen Vorarlberger Mädchen und Frauen.* Vienna.

Banik-Schweitzer, R. et al. 1980. *Wien im Vormärz.* Vienna.

Bartky, S. 1988. "Foucault, Femininity and the Modernization of Patriarchal Power." In *Feminism & Foucault, Reflections on Resistance.* Ed. I. Diamond and L. Quinby, 61-86. Boston.

Benedikt, M. 1906. *Aus meinem Leben: Erinnerungen und Erörterungen.* Vienna.

Bordo, S. 1988. "Anorexia Nervosa: Psychopathology as the Crystallization of Culture." In *Feminism & Foucault: Reflections on Resistance,* 87-118. Boston.

Braun, C. 1985. *Nicht Ich Ich Nicht: Logik, Lüge, Libido.* Frankfurt am Main.

———. 1987. "Männliche Hysterie. Weibliche Askese: Zum Paradigmenwechsel in den Geschlechterrollen." In *Das Sexuelle, die Frauen und die Kunst.* Ed. K. Rick. Tübingen.

Bruckmüller, E. and Stekl, H. 1988. "Zur Geschichte des Bürgertums in Österreich." In *Bürgertum im 19. Jahrhundert: Deutschland im europäischen Vergleich.* Vol. 1. Ed. J. Kocka and U. Frevert. Munich.

Busch, D.W. 1839-44. *Das Geschlechtsleben des Weibes in physiologischer, pathologischer und therapeutischer Hinsicht.* Leipzig.

Chrobak, R. 1900. *Die Erkrankungen der weiblichen Geschlechtsorgane.* Vienna.

Duden, B. 1987. *Geschichte unter der Haut: Ein Eisenacher Arzt und seine Patientinnen um 1730.* Stuttgart.

Eberhard, E. 1924. *Die erotischen Grundlagen der Frauenemanzipation.* Vienna.

Eder, F. 1993. "'Diese Theorie ist sehr delikat.' Zur Sexualisierung der Wiener Moderne." *In Die Wiener Jahrhundertwende: Einflüsse, Umwelt, Wirkungen.* Ed. J. Nautz and R. Vahrenkamp. Vienna.

Ehrenreich, B. and English, D. 1978. *For Her Own Good. 150 Years of the Expert's Advice to Women.* New York.

Eiblmayr, S. 1988. "Modelle des Weiblichen. Zur 'semiologischen Reduktion' in den Bildern von Helmut Newton." *Kairos* 3/4: 60-66.

"The Failing of Culture." 1991. Paper presented at symposium, "Literatur in März." Vienna.

Fischer, I. 1909. *Geschichte der Geburtshilfe in Wien.* Leipzig.

Fischer-Homberger, E. 1981. "Krankheit Frau." In *Leib und Leben in der Geschichte der Neuzeit.* Ed. A. Imhof, 215-29. Berlin.

*Krankheit Frau. Zur Geschichte der Einbildungen.* 1984. Darmstadt.

Fliedl, G. 1989. *Gustav Klimt.* Cologne.

Foucault, M. 1973. *The Order of Things.* New York.

———. 1975. *The Birth of the Clinic.* New York.

———. 1980. *The History of Sexuality.* Vol. 1. New York.

Frank, J.P. 1786. *System einer vollständigen medicinischen Polizey.* 3d impression. Vienna.

Freud, S. [1918] 1989a. "The Taboo of Virginity." In *Standard Edition.* Vol. 11. Ed. J. Strachey and A. Freud, 193-208. London.

———. [1905] 1989b. "Three Essays on Sexuality." In *Standard Edition.* Vol. 7. Ed. J. Strachey and A. Freud, 135-243. London.

———. [1909] 1989c. "Some General Remarks on Hysterical Attacks." In *Standard Edition.* Vol. 9. Ed. J. Strachey and A. Freud, 229-34. London.

Fryer, J. 1991. "The Body in Pain in Thomas Eakins' Agnew Clinic." In *The Female Body.* Ed. L. Goldstein, 234-54. Ann Arbor.

Geyer-Kordesch, J. and Kuhn, A., eds. 1986. *Frauenkörper-Medizin-Sexualität.* Düsseldorf.

Goldstein, J. 1991. "The Uses of Male Hysteria: Medical and Literary Discourse in Nineteenth-Century France." *Representations* 34:134-65.

Hauch, G. 1990. *Frau Biedermeier auf den Barrikaden: Frauenleben in der Wiener Revolution 1848.* Vienna.

Heath, S. 1989. "Joan Rivière and the Masquerade." In *Formations of Fantasy.* Reprint. Ed. V. Burgin, J. Donald, and C. Kaplan, 45-61. London.

Honegger, C. 1981. "Überlegungen zur Medikalisierung des weiblichen Körpers." In *Leib und Leben in der Geschichte der Neuzeit.* Ed. A. Imhof, 203-14. Berlin.

———. 1991. *Die Ordnung der Geschlechter: Die Wissenschaften vom Menschen und das Weib.* Frankfurt am Main.

Honegger, C. and Heintz, B., eds. 1984. *Listen der Ohnmacht: Zur Sozialgeschichte weiblicher Widerstandsformen.* Frankfurt am Main.

Ideler, K. 1840. *Introduction to E.F. Dubois: Über das Wesen und die gründliche Heilung der Hypochondrie und Hysterie.* Berlin.

Jordanova, L. 1989. *Sexual Visions: Images of Gender in Science and Medicine between the Eighteenth and Twentieth Century.* New York.

Kopetzki, C. 1989. "Zur Entwicklung des Irrenrechts' in Österreich." In *Wunderblock: Eine Geschichte der modernen Seele.* Ed. J. Clair, C. Pichler, W. Pircher, 321-28. Vienna.

Laqueur, T. 1987. "Orgasm, Generation, and the Politics of Reproductive Biology." In *The Making of the Modern Body.* Ed. C. Gallagher and T. Laqueur, 1-41. Berkeley and Los Angeles.

Le Rider, J. 1985. "Modernismus/Feminismus -Modernität/Virilität." In *Ornament und Askese.* Ed. A. Pfabigan, 242-60. Vienna.

Lesky, E. 1965. *Die Wiener Medizinische Schule im 19. Jahrhundert.* Graz.

Lewin, M., ed. 1984. *In the Shadow of the Past: Psychology Portrays the Sexes.* New York.

Marholm (Hansson), L. 1895. *Das Buch der Frauen.* Paris.

Marneffe, D. de 1991. "Looking and Listening: The Construction of Clinical Knowledge in Charcot and Freud." *Signs* 1:71-111.

Martin, E. 1987. *The Woman in the Body.* Milton Keynes.

Mendus, S. and Rendall, J., eds. 1989. *Sexuality & Subordination.* London, New York.

Masson, J. 1986. *A Dark Science: Women, Sexuality and Psychiatry in the Nineteenth Century.* New York.

Möbius, P. [1900] 1977. *Über den physiologischen Schwachsinn des Weibes.* Munich.

Moi, T. 1981. "Representation of Patriarchy: Sexuality and Epistemology in Freud's Dora." *Feminist Review* 9.

Moser, A. 1843. *Lehrbuch der Geschlechtskrankheiten des Weibes, nebst einem Anhang, enthaltend die Regeln für die Untersuchung der weiblichen Geschlechtstheile.* Berlin.

Neuburger, M. 1921. *Die Wiener Medizinische Schule im Vormärz.* Vienna.

Pichler, C. 1844. *Denkwürdigkeiten aus meinem Leben.* 3 vols. Vienna.

Pircher, W. 1980. "Mutmaßungen über den Vormärz." In *Wien im Vormärz.* Ed. R. Banik-Schweitzer et al., 3-8. Vienna.

Probyn, E. 1993. *Sexing the Self. Gendered Positions in Cultural Studies.* London.

Rivière, J. 1929. "Weiblichkeit als Maske." *Internationale Zeitschrift für Psychoanalyse* 2/3: 285-96.

Rose, J. 1989. *Sexuality in the Field of Vision.* London.

____. 1991. *Sexual Difference and the Failing of Culture.* Unpublished Manuscript.

Schiebinger, L. 1987. "Skeletons in the Closet: The First Illustrations of the Female Skeleton in Eighteenth-Century Anatomy." In *The Making of the Modern Body.* Ed. C. Gallagher and T. Laqueur, 42-82. Berkeley and Los Angeles.

Schlesier, R. 1990. *Mythos und Weiblichkeit bei Sigmund Freud.* Frankfurt am Main.

Shorter, E. 1989. "Medizinische Theorien spezifisch weiblicher Nervenkrankheiten im Wandel." In *Medizinische Deutungsmacht im sozialen Wandel.* Ed. A. Labisch and R. Spree, 171-80. Bonn.

Steinbrügge, L. 1987. *Das moralische Geschlecht: Theorien und literarische Entwürfe über die Natur der Frau in der französischen Aufklärung.* Berlin.

Wagner, N. 1987. *Geist und Geschlecht: Karl Kraus und die Erotik der Wiener Moderne.* Frankfurt am Main.

Weininger, O. 1910. *Geschlecht und Charakter: Eine prinzipielle Untersuchung.* 10th impression. Vienna.

Woltmann, K. 1826. *Über Natur, Bestimmung, Tugend und Bildung der Frauen.* Vienna.

*Chapter 10*

◦∕∕≫↩

# REPRESENTATIONS OF THE BEGINNING
## Shaping Gender Identities in
## Written Life Stories of Women and Men

.............................

*Monika Bernold*

## Introduction

M y chapter explores how gender and class identities are presented in life stories. Specifically, I am interested in how dominant notions of gender and class are inscribed in early identity
construction and its subsequent reconstruction. The theme I empha-
size is the *beginning* of life stories, the events and the narrative forms
that open these personal revelations.

The following reflections are based on my consideration of fifty life
stories from the "Dokumentation lebensgeschichtlicher Aufzeichnungen," a Viennese archive founded in 1982 in connection with an
expanded program of adult education, and directed by Michael Mitterauer. The archive grew out of Mitterauer's research work on family history in peasant societies (Hämmerle 1991: 261-78). It contains
seven hundred manuscripts largely collected in response to appeals
in the press and on the radio that solicited autobiographical accounts
from a predominantly rural audience. The majority of the authors
of these "popular autobiographies" come from the lower peasant

classes;[1] most were born between 1900 and 1930 and wrote their life stories sometime in the last twenty years. Approximately 15 percent of the archive's documents were written by authors born in the nineteenth century; only a few manuscripts date back to the eighteenth century. The archive also houses published life stories of rural servant girls and unpublished autobiographies written independently of the media appeals. During the last twenty years the proportion of women as authors of life stories has increased significantly.[2] The narrative forms of the sources, their social and regional origins, and the conditions of their production are extremely disparate in the archive, as well as in my sample.

I use the narratives at the beginning of these autobiographies as a kaleidoscope through which to reflect on some central questions of autobiography, identity, and gender.[3] It should be said at the outset that I am mindful of my position as an interpreter of these documents, and that my gender, class, and feminist theoretical stance all govern my relation to them. The feminist context of the questions addressed to these texts especially influences my reading of them. Such a feminist approach will consider the very evident ways in which existence is marked from the outset by the operation of gender. Yet I intend to interpret the stories of men and women within the context of class as well, for only by observing relations *among* the sexes can relations *between* the sexes be discerned better (Scott 1986: 1063). Finally, as a historian of lower-middle-class origins who interprets life stories of lower-class men and women from an earlier era, my interpretive framework necessarily reflects my own class experience as well as the totality of prescriptive and proscriptive norms generated by the dominant culture specific to my lifetime. While there is no way around this dilemma, creating an awareness of ourselves as less-than-neutral interpreters *and* readers of these texts heightens our sense of both our own historical contingency and that of the texts.

The primary criterion for selecting my sources was the extent to which a particular account comprised a "total life story," that is, one that revealed the explicit intention of the author to claim the story as his or her own definitive life story, as opposed to one that "covers"

1. The term was formulated by Warneken (1985).
2. The significant rise in the number of autobiographies written by women after 1945 is not unique to Austria. Research trips in the context of the project "Autobiographies and Gender-specific Identities" (carried out by my colleagues Christa Hämmerle and Therese Weber) uncovered evidence for that tendency in comparable archives in London, Tübingen, and Nartum.
3. See Israel (1990: 40) on the image of the "Kaleidoscope" as a metaphor for the historian's project in writing the lives of women.

the chronology of the life. The dates of those in my sample span the years from the 1870s to the 1980s. Autobiographies of women and men are equally represented, although, as in the archive, the number of autobiographies written by women increases within this time span. One-fifth of the texts I analyze emerge from bourgeois contexts; the remainder are written by lower-class and lower-middle-class authors, mostly in agrarian settings. Most authors reconstruct their lives from the perspective of an advanced age. Central among the various motivations for writing is its therapeutic value in the face of the crisis and the isolation of old age.

## The Double Beginning: Life/Story

The starting point for the following considerations is the supposition that the sense given to a life, and the purpose given to a story, are nascent in the shape of their beginning. The opening of a story seems to be the proof of its existence. The same applies to life. If the primary characteristic of human existence is its potential for reconstruction in the form of a narrative, the narrative is not then merely a literary convention, but rather *an essential part of experience and consciousness themselves* (Meyer 1989). Such accounts should be understood as authentic rather than "true," since the process of bringing to mind the lived life in a written form is, of course, a selective one. Out of the endless play of experiences, the author is selecting and establishing only certain connections. Moreover, the unlived or desired experiences of a lived life are also inscribed in the autobiographical text.

Taking a look at the double representation of beginning – the beginning of life and the beginning of its reconstruction in a story – offers the possibility of recognizing the degree of fictional mediation of reality within autobiographical texts. Even though the material existence of a person obviously starts with birth, many life stories begin long before this starting point – for example with the birth of grandparents, or the origins of the author's place of birth. A lack of individual memory of one's beginning is often replaced by a kind of collective memory that tells about the relation of the individual to earlier generations in terms of the passing on of status, name, and property.

A traditional and common form of expressing the close relationship of one's own life to genealogical and regional structures is represented in a model of autobiographical writing called "family chronicle." This type of life story is typical of the nineteenth-century autobiographies collected in the archive. One of the oldest documents, written by the clergyman Father Augustin, born as Franz E. in 1870, is entitled: "Family chronicle of the Steinegg village." This son of a peasant woman and a blacksmith embeds the story of his personal life in the history of his family and the village of his birth. The presentation of the personal life begins only on page 36 of a 46-page volume. The chronology of the narrative deals with the topography of the village. In this way the author links the history of the houses in the village with the history of their inhabitants. The specification of birth order delineates the order of succession in this particular region. After a detailed description of the life of his older brother, the narrative of the author's own life story starts: "The second child again was a boy and was given the name Franz as a tribute to the godfather and this Franz is the writer of these lines. Franz was born 3 April 1823 and was, as his mother says, a beautiful child." The individual "self" here is integrated in, and completely subordinated to, a kind of collective family memory. The author expresses the narrative of his own birth grammatically in the third person, and speaks of himself as he would describe any other villager. The "self" of the author, in the sense of speaking of himself as "I," is introduced only at that moment in the narrative when Father Augustin talks about his entrance into the seminary of Zwettl. The decision to become a clergyman, a decision that meant leaving the collective order of the village, and changing his name "Franz" to "Augustin," the name given him by the religious order, acts in the narrative as the transfer point to individualization.

In opposition to the model of the "family chronicle," the opening of the life story with the conventional phrase "I was born in" very often characterizes autobiographies written by people of working-class or lower-peasant backgrounds. For these people, whose existence is primarily dependent on their labor and therefore their body, the story starts with the beginning of physical existence. For example, Maria R., the daughter of a maid in Salzburg, introduces her life story: "In Angerngold near Kitzbühl, in Aurach, I was born on March the first, 1911. My mother thought I would not survive. At three days old, I had a cough like a dog barking in a pot." The reconstruction of this life starts out with the mother's doubts about the author's viability, signifying the daughter's sense of a lack of legitimization for her existence. As in many lower-class life stories, such knowledge is linked to a narrative of physical disease or disability. The weak and suffering body figures as a sign of repetition. In these beginnings there is a consciousness of continuity that is linked not to status and property, but rather to deprivation and deficit. Dismal social and economic circumstances make children a burden. Thus, the ambivalence toward being wanted and not wanted emerges especially in the textual beginning of many lower-class life stories around allusions to the weakness of the body.

Geographical stability is central to the genealogical construction of the self. Yet the living conditions of the lower classes in this era were marked by a high degree of mobility in both urban and rural settings. Unemployment, a high rate of job turnover, and severe housing shortages (especially in Vienna), all characterized the daily life of the majority of the lower classes, even after 1900. The narrative effect of such "rootlessness" is revealed in many working-class life stories. Here the deep need to ground one's own existence responds to the lack of a "pre-history" in which these life stories could be rooted. For example, here is how Charlotte K., born in Vienna, began her autobiography:

> I was born on 14 February 1925, an illegitimate child of Anna D. My mother moved to her sister's place with me. In hospital they advised her to put me up for adoption, because in 1925 an unmarried woman with a child would never find a man. But my mother did not give me away. My father never took care of me and paid very little money.

The "father's house" and its history (so prominent in the clergyman's memoir) is replaced here by the reference to the state-controlled welfare system represented in the institution of the foundling hospital, which started to develop in the early years of the twentieth century. (Pawlowsky and Zechner 1992). Another example is that of Leopold B.:

> B. Leopold is my name and I was born on 12 November 1901 in Vienna, so I am now 86 years old. My mother was a servant in the house of a hotelier and brought me into being in the "foundling hospital" in Vienna, Alserstadt.

Thus, where tradition resonates only as exclusion, the retrospective reference to the self in the sense of a continuity in the family and property is thwarted. There are exceptions to this tendency, mostly provided by authors who wrote their life stories after some experience of upward mobility. These authors (very often men) address their alienation from the norms of life stories by offering legitimation for their account.

"Self-biographies," "autobiographies," and "life stories" (the different terms signal the variety in the forms of written self-reference) are cultural products and therefore part of extant cultural production. By interpreting life stories, we learn about canonical forms of rendering life stories and about the ways in which authors relate themselves to these normative forms.[4] For example, Maria R., the daughter of a Viennese domestic servant, and writing in 1964, begins her life story: "I was born in Vienna, on 26 January 1909. Illegitimate, not wanted, a tiny point in space to live through all the ups and downs each *Menschenkind* [literally, "human child"] is assigned by God." This mode of self-interpretation accords with the "social-atom" phenomenon that Regenia Gagnier described in her analysis of English working-class autobiographies (Gagnier 1990: 103). The model of the singular and unified self is not at all self-evident to Maria R. The narrating self is not conceptualized as the central point *of,* but merely as one little point *in,* the world. The life is not framed by self-determination and singularity, but rather by destiny, and the conviction of being a part of the destiny of the masses (Bergmann 1988: 89ff.).

Individual existence here derives legitimation from Providence and from the religious precept that all are equal in the sight of God. The social experience of inequality is masked by the ideology of equality because, for Maria R., inequality means exclusion from the normality of a legitimate existence. Maria R. did not know her father; she grew up in the country with her grandparents while her mother worked in Vienna. Her childhood experience was not represented in the bourgeois ideology of family; rather, the religious system of meaning into which she inscribes her beginning offers a form of representation through which reconciliation of the contradictions between norm and experience seems possible. As a "human child" she is represented like all other children – it does not matter whether she has a real father or not. Descent has no meaning within the Christian system of representation. For this reason, the ideal of the "spiritual family" constituted through baptism had a special attraction for lower-class women in Austria, a strongly Catholic country with an extremely high rate of illegitimacy (Mitterauer 1990: 73ff.).

Images (like that of the "human child") and myths used to construct self-images in autobiographical texts reveal the distance between social norms and experience. Such images reveal the traces of conflict within the process of identity construction. The difference between images, transformed into self-images, and experience sometimes reinforces change in actual behavior.[5]

---

4. The structures of transforming representations of "high" to popular culture always has to be seen in historical context. Within the reality of the mass media, where paintings of van Gogh are used to advertise tapestries in the streets, the condition of cultural transfer is defined in a new way.
5. For the analysis of symbolic meaning and narrative function of rebellious self-images in women's life stories see Passerini (1989: 191).

In the case of Maria R., the symbolic meaning of the image is different. The emphasis on the religious system of meaning reveals the inscription of gender into her self-construction. This is already seen in the beginning sequence: "a tiny point in space to live through all the ups and downs each 'Menschenkind' is assigned by God." She takes the model of passive suffering (embodied in the Passion of Jesus Christ and construed in literary theory as being analogous with women's experience) and combines this position with enthroning the symbolic order of the father (God).[6] Maria's identification with this image of the child, which is not distinguished by sex or class and therefore suggests equality, nevertheless reproduces the dominant sex-gender system of her era. The symbolic analogy of child and woman here refers to the mode of male dominance and female oppression inherent within the circumambient cultural system of ascribed sexual difference.[7]

Maria R. is also aware of the dominant model governing life history narration. Curiously, this knowledge is confirmed by an afterthought in her own account: Originally the word "Memoirs" was typed on the front page of her life story. This was then crossed out by hand, and below it, written in type again, was: "Life-memories and considerations on the topic, 'My Life'." Obviously Maria R. was deciding between two conventional forms of entitling life stories. The first is situated in the classical bourgeois tradition that links autobiography with fame, while the second appears to be based on the model of essay-writing in school. While Maria R. ultimately resisted the temptation, appropriating bourgeois semantics of individuality is typical for many lower-class autobiographies. In this ambivalent act of adaptation, some of the contradictions produced by the incongruence of ideology and experience become visible. In the very beginning of autobiographical texts, then, we learn about the myriad forms of exclusion and inclusion practiced by the dominant culture, a culture that organizes and values stories in terms of dominance and repression. We also learn about individual forms of affirmation and rebellion in relation to those dominant rules.

6. For the symbolic meaning of the identification of women with the passion and the body of Jesus Christ, see Cavarero (1989: 93).

7. The influence of religious images and narratives (sermon, confession, prayer) on the construction of self-images and the narrative forms of autobiographical writing can only be noticed in that context. For the disciplinary function of prayer-books in the nineteenth century concerning gender and class, see Saurer (1990: 56ff.).

# References of Beginning: Facts and Fictions of Identity

By employing the term "Life Memories" the titles of many texts refer to an essential characteristic of the autobiographical: the process of remembering. Yet the beginning of one's own life lies beyond memory. "Anyone seriously trying to go back to the roots of their own life-consciousness is confronted with the essential limits of self-awareness and remembrance. That means that there is no self-evident knowledge about continuity in relation to the origins of the individual." (Sloterdijk 1978: 123)

Because memory, and therefore experience, have no sway over the beginning of existence, narratives of birth are characterized by a very high level of construction. The uncertainty concerning one's beginning thus demands a "frame of narration which has to be constructed without memory" (Sloterdijk 1978: 123), a frame fleshed out with myths, narrative conventions, anecdotes, and/or fictional memories. How this space beyond memory is constructed illustrates the evolving modes of self-representation under the impetus of historical change.

In the section that follows, I will reflect on two different models of modern self-representation which I term "nationalization of biography" and "individualization of self-reference." It is important to note that I draw upon autobiographical texts whose authors belong to social groups that have a special mediating position within modernization, primarily the peasant- and lower-peasant classes.

In Western culture, the date of one's birth does not become a universally available record of existence until well into the twentieth century. In the nineteenth century, more and more "agencies of biography" (schools, administrative institutions, and so on) began to generate and mediate such knowledge independent of the family. Such information was intimately linked with the administrative machinery of the modernizing state, and embodied in such documentation as birth certificates, censuses, and school records. A knowledge of one's birth date, then, relied on literacy, and coincided with the inclusion of biographical dates within bureaucratic strategies of personal identification mounted by the state.[8] Increasingly, the stereotypical framing device, "I was born on," repeated thousands of times in different contexts, became an essential convention of bourgeois identity.

The autobiographies of my sample reflect how this narrative device of naming the birth date became a universal stereotype in ini-

---

8. For the development of complex systems of identification in the nineteenth century, see Ginzburg (1983: 109ff.).

tiating a life story. In autobiographies written by authors born in the nineteenth century, traces of insecurity about the exact date of one's birth can still be found. This is evident in the account of the shoemaker Hermann F.: "According to the report of my parents and the witness of my documents I was born on 3 December 1876 in Wandsbeck near Hamburg." What we find here is the notion of two concurrent but external guarantees: the oral report of the parents and the written evidence of personal documents.

An interesting example of the intercultural spread of both oral and written sources in establishing birth date can be found in the autobiography of the Russian poet and radical Vladimir Majakovskij. Born in a Caucasian village in 1893, this son of a Russian forest official wrote his autobiography between 1922 and 1928. After reflecting about the genre and the selectivity of human memory, he introduces his life story: "Born on 7 July 1894 (or '93, mother's opinion differs from father's official documents. In any case not before that)" (Hajak 1989: 119). Notice how the knowledge of the mother is implicitly devalued and subordinated to the account of the father's official document. This individual valuation represents an assertion of identity that is linked to documentation and related to the father's knowledge.

Other authors coming out of lower peasant contexts in Upper-Austria, such as Georg L., refer only to the oral form of corroboration: "According to the report of my parents and my elder brothers and sisters I first saw the light of the world on 28 March 1878 at the farm of my parents ...." A sense of the significance of this "oral tradition" in the construction of identity appears often among early documents written within the popular tradition of autobiographical writing. In this context I also note the relevance of gender to the tradition of family story telling: women seem to have played a very important role in the passing on of such stories (Maynes 1990: 106f.).

The social necessity of a documented and exact knowledge of one's date of birth increases with the level of differentiation within society. This correlation becomes most evident in the opening sequence of the autobiography of Johann H., which in structure resembles a police registration form:

> I, Johann H____ saw the light of the world first on 7 November 1879 at Fröllersdorf, district Nikolsburg in Südmähren. The parents, Father: Mathias H____ born on 10.XII 1846 in Guttenfeld. Mother: Maria H____, born on 8.XII 1845 in Fröllersdorf nr.2.

Johann H. was born in the same year as Georg L. and came from a similar social background. Johann H. was the son of a cottager *(Kleinhäusler)* family and, like Georg L., was forced to seek employment in Vienna. The similarities end there, however. Georg L., by marrying into a peasant family, returned to his original life setting and carried on a peasant existence. Johann H., on the other hand, pursued the career of a civil servant in the city. He became a policeman, and later, a criminal investigator. His birth narrative symbolizes the social process of the "nationalization of the individual biography"; that is, Johann H. is both a registrar (in his role as a police officer) and the registered (in his birth), both the subject and the object of this process.

Autobiography is often interpreted by literary theorists as the advent of the bourgeois subject. The concept of "classical" autobiography is based on the idea of a unified self (which appears to be genderless but is in fact ultimately the construction of the male bourgeois subject).[9] Delving into the history of autobiographical writing, however, reveals that beneath this dominant model there are other forms of self-reference that are not so oriented toward the personality, but rather toward everyday life, and toward collective forms of organizing production. Such "individualization of self-reference" marks the process among the middle and lower classes of developing an interpretation of the self that is shaped by the norms of the bourgeois subject. Traces of this process can be found in life stories that document social change: for example, agricultural development in Austria in the 1950s.

The following text was written by a female farmer from Upper Austria who was born relatively late (1937) in comparison to the other authors in my sample. The life course of this woman was very much affected by the initial stages of agricultural rationalization and modernization in Austria. In interpreting the opening sequence of her life story, I reflect on expressions of individualization and pose the question of how female identity relates to the pseudo-neutral conception of the modern self.

Cäcilia L., from Bad Zell, was the daughter of a Mühlviertler farmer. About her "coming into being" she writes in 1984:

> I started my *Erdenreise* (earthly voyage) in summer, on 28 July 1937. People were harvesting the oats. My delivery was faster [that that of her brother]. It was *trabig* (pressing) at that time of the year. Or was I in a greater hurry – was I more curious? -*Ein Paarl* (a pair) – that was important for the parents! My grandmother from Kriechbaum often told me that I was *ein liabs Diandl* (a dear little girl). That I was often told. This grandmother died on 16.7.1939. This relationship ended very quickly.

---

9. For a feminist critique of the idea of the dominant notion of the "subject" in personal narratives, see Smith (1993).

She saw me only a few times. This grandmother lived further away, in the neighboring village.

"I started my earthly voyage in summer ..." Metaphors for life are rich and varied within life histories, yet the image of the voyage is a favorite one. The change in its meaning reflects changing patterns of interpretation of the "self" in relation to the "world." The linking of life and travel is based on the literary bourgeois conception of an ongoing movement toward a fully developed self. The bourgeois novel of individual development is the canonical expression of this concept. But in the image of the earthly voyage, the bourgeois idea of an identity of traveling and living also takes on a religious connotation. By referring to her earthly life and thus, by implication, to the celestial life to come, Cäcilia L. places her self in a religious context of meaning.

Moreover, her narrative of the circumstances surrounding her birth indicates two competing structures of time and consciousness. She begins in a language that represents an agrarian life context: "People were harvesting oats." The event of her own birth is of secondary importance to the necessities of the seasonal and rural work regime. This birth and its conditions are determined by an exterior logic that supersedes individual self-interpretation. Language represents this logic in form of the statement: "It was pressing at that time of the year." Yet the reconstructing, remembering self of Cäcilia L. poses a question against this external logic: "Or was I in a greater hurry – was I more curious?" Thus, within the fictional memory of her birth, Cäcilia L's gesture of "self-determination" replaces "outside determination." The self is constructed here in a vaguely psychological way, expressed in terms of individual attributes or character traits.

For a female subject this act of designating the self as the starting point for interpretation is contradictory, because it is at once included within, and excluded from, the construction of the ungendered, neutral self. In Cäcilia L.'s narrative, this contradiction becomes visible in a very interesting way: the marker she uses to delineate her self is the self of her elder brother Hans (implied in the phrase "*more* curious"). In the broader chronology of subsequent passages, his birth precedes her own: "He was born around Easter-time, on 8 April 1936. He didn't want to come into being, so he had to be taken by forceps – a difficult delivery." Unlike the account of her own birth, that of Cäcilia L.'s brother is not embedded within the logic of exterior conditions. While her interpretation of a difficult delivery as a sign of a reluctance to be born implies elements of a semantics of individuality, it is also a common trope of popular rural culture.

The first time Cäcilia L.'s self speaks, (... or was I in a greater hurry) her brother's self is the standard and the frame of reference for her speaking. Thus, in this sequence, where the female subject tries to express her self but finds this possible only in relationship to the male brother, the gendered nature of identity construction is revealed. Moreover, Cäcilia's use of the interrogative form seems to be a way of diffusing the egregious audacity of constructing her self in the birth story, and in terms more vital than her brother ("faster ... more in a hurry"). In the next sentence, separated only by a hyphen, she explicitly refers to this relationship between identity and sexual difference: "– A couple, that was important for the parents!" This desire of her parents to have both a male and female child is structured by their rural economic setting and by the abstract order of gender in genealogy.

The construction of gendered identities is always defined and mediated within historical contexts. In the case of Cäcilia L., the context is an emerging modern semantics of individuality within the rural economy of necessity. Although she refers to it, Cäcilia L. does not directly comment on the "normative" desire of her parents. What is not expressed is marked by two hyphens only. This silence could be read as Cäcilia's positive identification as a woman in relation to the norm (because she is a woman, she fits the parents' demand for a pair of children), or as a kind of refusal of it (in fulfilling the norm, she is not represented as an individual; only in relation to the parents' demand for a pair is she represented as a woman).

As the narrative proceeds, Cäcilia's rejection of this parental notion becomes clear. A subtle conflict with the given paradigms of gendered identity is detectable throughout her entire narrative of beginning. Her autobiographical references provide evidence of that conflict, expressed mostly in the contradiction between "how I want to be" and "how I should be."

Immediately after Cäcilia L. presents the interpretation given to her existence by her parents, she introduces the grandmother. "My grandmother from Kriechbaum said that I was a dear little girl." In Cäcilia L.'s memory, her grandmother, unlike her parents, refers to her as a woman by employing a uniquely female image. Being designated a woman by another woman (the mother of her mother) represents the first explicit reference to her identity as gendered.

Here we see the bourgeois conception of the neutral "self" shaping the identity construction of lower-class women via a process of contradiction. Identifying oneself as a woman seems to be a balancing act between an elementary tenuousness of female subjectivity and an oversupply of female images within social representation. The opposition of the signifiers "a pair" and "a dear little girl" expresses this tension within the textual self-(re)construction of Cäcilia L.

The closeness and the power of the identification through the grandmother lasts for only one sentence. After this, filters of distance are pushed between the two women. We learn in the following sequence that Cäcilia was told of the grandmother's characterization of her, and that she does not actually remember it. We learn that the grandmother died early in Cäcilia's life, so the relationship was a brief one. We also learn that the grandmother lived at some distance – in the neighboring village. Cäcilia's other grandmother, introduced in the next sentence, is remembered as absent as well. "The other grandmother," she writes, "the mother of my father, died in 1935, and the sister of my father, a "Cäcilia," died four days before, so I became a Cäcilia."

The name is an essential instrument for identifying a person.[10] The specification of the proper name indicates gender. The history of naming in the form of a female genealogy connotes a history of nominal self-assertion – "so I became a Cäcilia" – within the context of the whole life story.

## Conclusion

Interpreting popular autobiographies gives an idea of how varied are the accounts written by men and women who live outside the centers of cultural production. Those accounts differ from, yet interrelate with, the dominant models of telling a life based on the notion of the unified and unique self. The sense of exclusion and the lack of a sense of continuity, which is expressed in so many openings of the narratives I examined, is mediated through the different systems of reference surrounding the individual self. Religion, rural economy, collective memory and oral tradition, and the state and an expanding welfare system are privileged and competing systems of reference within which the men and women who were born into lower rural classes in the beginning of this century write down their life during the last twenty years. These narratives show how gender influences the way individuals structure the self in the beginnings of their written life stories. By interpreting them, we can see how gender is embedded in the language of the beginning, and shaped by the

10. On the meaning of one's name as an institution for guaranteeing identity in the sense of a "constance nominale," see Bourdieu (1990: 78).

specific contexts of class and generation and by the processes of social change. It remains to discover the link between the specific knowledge that we derive from autobiographical writings, and the more generalized information of other historical sources, so that we may learn more about the class and gender-related meanings of modern self-reference.

# References

Bergmann, K. 1988. *Lebensgeschichte als Appell: Zur Theorie Popularer Autobiographik.* Frankfurt am Main.

Bourdieu, P. 1990. "Die biographische Illusion." *BIOS* 3/1: 74-81.

Cavarero, A. 1989. "Ansätze zu einer Theorie der Geschlechterdifferenz." In *Der Mensch ist Zwei: Das Denken der Geschlechter-differenz.* Ed. I. Birkhan, 65-106. Vienna.

Gagnier, R. 1990. "The Literary Standard, Working-Class Autobiography, and Gender." In *Revealing Lives. Autobiography, Biography, and Gender.* Ed. S. G. Bell and M. Yalom, 93-114. New York.

Ginzburg, C. 1983. "Spurensicherung: Der Jäger entziffert die Fährte, Sherlock Holmes nimmt die Lupe, Freud liest Morelli – die Wissenschaft auf der Suche nach sich selbst." In *Spurensicherungen: Über verborgene Geschichte, Kunst und soziales Gedächtnis.* Berlin.

Hämmerle, C. 1991. "'Ich möchte das, was ich schon so oft erzählt habe, schriftlich niederlegen ...' Entstehung und Forschungsaktivitäten der 'Dokumentation lebensgeschichtlicher Aufzeichnungen' in Wien." *BIOS* 4/2:261-78.

Hahn, A. 1988. "Biographie und Lebenslauf." In *Vom Ende des Indiviuums zur Individualität ohne Ende.* Ed. H.G. Brose and B. Hildebrand, 91-106. Opladen.

Hajak, S. 1989. *V.V. Majakovskijs "Ja sam": Untersuchungen zur Struktur einer futuristischen Autobiographie.* Wiesbaden.

Israel, K.A.K. 1990. "Writing Inside the Kaleidoscope: Re- Representing Victorian Women Public Figures." *Gender & History,* 2/1: 40-49

de Lauretis, T. 1987. *Technologies of Gender: Essays on Theory, Film and Fiction.* Bloomington.

Maynes, M.J. 1989. "Gender and Narrative Form in French and German Working-Class Autobiographies." In *Interpreting Women's Lives: Feminist Theory and Personal Narratives.* Ed. The Personal Narrative Group. Bloomington.

Meyer, E. 1989. *Die Autobiographie der Schrift.* Basel.

Mitterauer, M. 1990. *Historisch anthropologische Familienforschung: Fragestellungen und Zugangsweisen.* Vienna.

Passerini, L. 1989. "Myths, Experiences and Emotions." In *Interpreting Women's Lives: Feminist Theory and Personal Narratives.* Ed. The Personal Narrative Group. Bloomington.

Pawlowsky, V. and Zechner, R. 1992. "Das Findelhaus in Wien (1784-1910)." *Projektbericht an den Jubiläumsfonds der Österreichischen National-bank und das Bundesministerium für Wissenschaft und Forschung.* Vienna.

Saurer, E. 1990. "'Bewahrerinnen der Zucht und der Sittlichkeit': Gebet-bücher für Frauen – Frauen in Gebetbüchern." *L'HOMME.* 1/1:37-58.

Scott, J.W. 1986. "Gender: A useful Category of Historical Analysis." *American Historical Review* 3: 1053-75.

Sloterdijk, P. 1978. *Literatur und Lebenserfahrung: Autobiographien der 20er Jahre.* Munich.

Smith, S. 1993. "Who's Talking/Who's Talking Back? The Subject of Personal Narrative." *Signs* 18/12: 392-408.

Steedman, C. 1989. *Landscape for a Good Woman: A Story of Two Lives.* London.

Warneken, B.J. 1985. *Populäre Autobiographik: Empirische Studien zu einer Quellengattung der Alltagsgeschichtsforschung.* Tübingen.

❧

# Chapter 11

# WAR AND GENDER IDENTITY
## The Experience of Austrian Women, 1945-1950

*Irene Bandhauer-Schöffmann* and *Ela Hornung*

..........................

## A Twofold Victimization Myth: Austria's Nazi Past

The life stories of women in the postwar era have often been accepted rather uncritically, including by women's historians. These women, known as "women in the ruins" [*Trümmerfrauen*], were stylized into "heroines" to serve as role models in history. It is symptomatic of these stories that they start from the year 1945, as if there had really been an actual "zero hour," with no antecedents in the Nazi era. Until recently, historical research passed over women's share of responsibility and guilt. This gave rise to an ill-considered image of the "heroines of the reconstruction era." For a long time the only kind of inquiry these women faced was about how they could have failed to make more out of "their" circumstances, how it was they were not able to capitalize on their position at the center of survival strategies, especially considering the relative absence of men. It was only later, in the course of a wide discussion about the graphic notion of women's "complicity," that this glorious image was first tarnished (Thürmer-Rohr 1987: 1989). For a long time, it was customary in women's history to define women's power only in terms of their contribution to postwar reconstruction. When it came to questions of responsibility during the Nazi regime, women were stylized into helpless victims.

In comparison with their German counterparts, very little research has been done on women in Austria after World War II (Mattl 1985; Thurner 1988; Bandhauer-Schöffmann and Hornung 1990, 1991, 1992). Historical myth making, in which women's history has had a share, is not only fueled by the popular notion of the "good fortune of female birth"[1] which excuses women from responsibility and regards them as Nazi victims. The myth is twofold: for the Austrians were, and perhaps still are, convinced that they were the first victims of Nazism. This belief was reinforced for years by the conciliatory historiography produced in the political climate of the Grand Coalition that ruled Austria in the initial post-1945 decades. As Talos et al. (1988) argue in their collection of essays: "The reality bending thesis that Austria had been the first victim of Nazi aggression, central to the Austrian self-assessment after 1945, made it possible to erase the years of NS-rule from Austrian history. As long as only the annexation from outside was considered, these years could be bracketed as German history, and Austria could be seen as having disappeared in 1938 as a victim of German occupation, and as having been resurrected anew in 1945." That this collection first appeared fifty years after the "Anschluss" demonstrates how long Austria's Nazi past had been shut out. Confrontation with this past came very late (Botz 1987, 1989; Pelinka and Weinzierl 1987; Kaindl and Widhalm 1990; Wodak 1990).

Moreover, since Austria was not liberated by widespread anti-fascist resistance, but through the defeat of the German Wehrmacht by foreign forces, national self-consciousness could not develop out of anti-fascism. Instead, the preferred postures were the role of the victim and the denial of all responsibility. The most striking example of this is Austria's refusal to pay reparations to Jewish Nazi victims (Knight 1988; Beckermann 1989). It was only in July 1991 that Chancellor Franz Vranitzky, in a much-noticed official declaration before Parliament, spoke of "a share in the responsibility for the sufferings that, if not Austria as a state, then citizens of this country brought upon other people and nations" (Speech of 8 July 1991).

Needless to say, the confrontation with the Nazi past also followed gender lines. For women, it was doubly easy to back out of the respon-

---

1. This phrase echoes "the good fortune of belated birth," which means that the generations born after 1945 are not responsible for Nazism.

sibility, because their collaboration on the Nazi homefront seemed largely apolitical. Even today, most women are not aware of how household duties were used to serve the state through the work of Nazi girls' and women's organizations such as the BDM *(Bund deutscher Mädel)*, the NSV *(Nationalsozialistische Volkswohlfahrt)*, the DFW *(Deutsches Frauenwerk)*, and the NSF *(Nationalsozialistische Frauenschaft)*. Women's services in the "hinterland," which in fact were as important for the war as those of men at the front, did not seem to demand collective self-analysis after the war. In 1945, men were the losers. They had to admit: "We lost the war"; women more often said: "The war was lost," thus expressing emotional distance, and apparent detachment. Until today, veterans' associations *(Kameradschaftsbünde)* and barrooms provide men with opportunities for socially accepted collective reminiscence, where they can stylize their wartime memories into heroic myths and diminish their fears. Since post-fascist society – unlike Nazism – suppressed knowledge of female support for the war, women have had neither the opportunity for self-glorification nor the occasion to admit their share of the responsibility.

While the end of the war meant a caesura in the lives of all men who had served in the German Wehrmacht, women had no such collective experience. For men, the defeat of the German troops brought with it, as Rosenthal (1987) has shown, a dramatic visible event, the collapse of military structures and the end of their lives as soldiers. As any life-historical caesura, this one also offered a chance for reorientation. For women, there was no such dramatic moment of reorientation.

## Methodology: Life Stories

Until now, the method of oral history has rarely been used to discern continuities in women's life stories. Thus, criticism of the "women in the ruins" myth remained a purely moral issue that was rarely based on empirical research. In the oral-history part of our project – for which we conducted sixty interviews – we always drew on the interviewees' total biographies for interpretation.[2] In open biographical interviews, the interviewees structured their life-story narrations without intervention on the part of the interviewer. In our sample, the women generally included events only through the early 1960s.

2. In addition, we relied on written source material, especially holdings of the *Wiener Stadt- und Landesarchive*, Vienna's municipal archives (hereafter WrStLA).

The interviews were then supplemented by a series of topic-centered follow-up questions.[3]

Our goal was to conduct interviews with women from all social classes; the criterion for inclusion was that they were over 18 in 1945, and had spent most of World War II and the post-1945 period in Vienna. Lehman's (1983: 46) "descriptive class concept" seemed applicable to our research design, since the usual, typical categories of class or social stratification are far more difficult to apply to women – notably to housewives with no job outside the home – than to men. Five percent of women held jobs in the period imme-diately after the war.[4] We placed them into four categories: workers (skilled and unskilled); salaried employees; business owners; and professionals. Women who were housewives after 1945 were classi-fied according to their husbands' occupations. Our intention was to reconstruct as many contrasting experiences as possible.

Of course, we also differentiated among age cohorts, and asked about membership in Nazi youth organizations and the *Reicharbeits-dienst* (RAD). We assumed that indoctrination by the fascist regime had a more lasting effect on young girls than on women who were already adults. Another important descriptive category related to politics and religion; here, we also looked for contrasts and therefore chose women from widely different backgrounds.

The women in our sample were, with few exceptions, not active in political parties and called themselves "unpolitical" in an attempt to keep their distance from Nazism. The interviews were all made after the fiftieth anniversary of the Anschluss in 1988 and the surfacing of the "Waldheim affair." We think that the timing partly accounts for the self-justification apparent in the words of many interviewees who,

---

3. On the whole, we followed the procedure described by Werner Fuchs (1984: 280) who speaks of a "process of 'theoretical saturation'" that develops from the inter-play of first interviews with the questions and notions resulting from them. Inquiry is continued until certain patterns and rules begin to recur. These patterns are specified, modified, or revised in a continuing interchange between the collected qualitative data and the yet undetermined theoretical understanding. This means that theory initially directed our research only in a very general way, and that descriptive categories were developed in the course of study as the empirical data accumulated (Hopf 1979: 17). This qualitative approach does not rely on quantifi-cation, nor does it aim for a sample.

4. Women's share in the total labor force in Austria was:
    1910: 40 percent
    1934: 38 percent
    1951: 39 percent
    1961: 40 percent
During the war it rose to 52 percent.

without being asked, readily offered reasons why they could have "known nothing." In fact, apart from opponents of the Nazi regime and those persecuted by it, most displayed a consistent pattern: recurrent assertions that they "knew nothing" were undercut by unreflected and disconnected, yet detailed, descriptions that gave evidence of such knowledge. All the interviewees told about how the Jewish population of Vienna had been humiliated and robbed of their possessions, and about the pogroms just after the Anschluss and in November 1938. All the women knew of the cruel humiliation rituals, such as the "scrubbings" when Jewish men and women were forced, under the jeers of bystanders, to scrub the sidewalks with brushes.

But Nazism was generally discussed in fragmented ways. Unless they were persecuted by the regime or had more political awareness, the women did not relate their recollections of Nazism to their own personal lives. They often compared the incomparable: the debris-clearing work that the Soviets assigned to former Nazis was equated with the notorious "scrubbing parties" that Jews were subjected to; the "Aryanization" of seventy thousand apartments in Vienna was equated with the evictions of Nazis by the communists after the war. Post-war denazification measures were regarded as inefficient by both victims and opponents of the regime, and as unnecessary by some who refuse even today to admit their necessity. Women who did not take a critical view of Nazism spoke about denazification as a measure affecting the "wrong people," or as "senseless vexations by the Allied forces" that people – either the women interviewed themselves, or others they tell about – had to endure, although it did not in the least change their political attitudes. Nazis who were subjected to denazification (Meissl 1986) were referred to as "persecutees." One example of this is the statement of Inge Schneider[5] who was born into a German-nationalist family in 1921 and was married to a high-level Nazi functionary until 1948: "Well, in '48, I divorced my husband and Doctor K. moved in with me; he was politically persecuted at that time, 'cause he'd been in the SS, and it also was at my place that he was arrested."

## The Last Days of the Third Reich

Eastern Austria was liberated from Nazi rule by the Red Army. On 28 March 1945 Soviet troops crossed the border into Austria; on 5

5. Interviewees' names were changed to protect their anonymity.

April street fighting began in Vienna and went on for nine days (Czeike 1975; Rauchensteiner 1975). The population, consisting mostly of women, waited in cellars for the end of the war. From 1943, when the first Allied air raids were flown against Austria, life in bomb shelters had been an everyday experience for the civilian population of Vienna. Still, the house-to-house fighting in Vienna made things worse for the women, even compared to daily air raids, because now the front had entered their immediate personal lives. The women interviewed told us that they did not dare to go out for days, except disguised as old women, for fear of Soviet soldiers. The racist Nazi propaganda had told them horror stories about the "Russian subhumans" and advised all women to leave Vienna. Nevertheless, many of them had stayed in town, which afterwards turned out to be the right decision, since women were a lot safer in the big city than in the rural wine-growing regions around Vienna, where many women were raped by soldiers intoxicated with victory and alcohol. Helene Schuchter, 41 years old then, lived with her sister in Baden, a well-known wine village near Vienna, at the end of the war:

> And then, one day, there was a lot of shouting and pounding and fussing. Suddenly, the door is thrown open, and in come two Russians. And the landlord. And my sister said, why, sir, how come you let them in here? And he said, well, they wanted to rape *my wife*, and I told them there are younger ones upstairs! Yes, and so they came up of course, those two. And now it was of course a big fuss, back and forth, for they wanted nothing but women. And that's it. And then they pulled out the key and shoved the guy out and locked the door from inside. Okay, now we were locked in. Well, so we began scrambling around with them, saying no and no, and then my sister said, wait, I'll keep them busy, maybe we can get out of this somehow. And so she heated up water and said everything had to be made sterile and so on, and so we were washing and washing, and an hour passed; but those two didn't let up, no matter what. It had to be … . And then I saw one of them taking his coat off and all that, and there was the waist-belt with his revolver. And I sat on that chair, and all of a sudden I had the revolver in my hand and said I don't want to do it. Well, of course, they could have smacked it from my hand or something. And my sister yelled are you crazy! Are you crazy! Our parents are next door, what will they do without us? Don't you think, if you shoot him, we'll get killed, too. Well, so I stood there, trembling, with the revolver. Then one of them took it from my hand and so … . In any case, well, then it happened."

Helene Schuchter was actually lucky, since she got neither pregnant nor infected with a venereal disease. It is a fact, however, that in the first couple of months after the end of the war, it was possible to have an abortion in Viennese hospitals; notices informed women of this officially tolerated, but illegal measure.[6] There are no reliable figures of how many rapes were actually committed by Soviet troops. For many of the women we interviewed, these fears of rape still remain vivid. We were also often told about suicides of Nazi women who feared Soviet reprisals. The most resentful, and therefore strongest, memories of all Allied troops were those pertaining to the Soviets, regardless of which occupation zone the women lived in. When asked about their experiences with "occupation soldiers," the interviewees always spoke about Soviet looting and raping first, and in greatest detail. American, English, and French soldiers are less prominent in the narratives. In women's recollections, it was the Soviet troops who freed Vienna from Nazism, and who represented to them the ten years of Allied occupation.

In the last days of the war, many women lived in so-called emergency communities (*Notgemeinschaften*) with relatives or friends, because their own apartments had been bombed out and organizing day-to-day life was easier together, on a collective basis. Initially there was no gas and no electricity in Vienna, and, in many districts, not even water. Being holed up in air-raid cellars had led to the formation of house communities (*Hausgemeinschaften*), which sought to organize collectively such features of everyday life as cooking and keeping guard.[7] In their narratives, the women gave detailed accounts of these communal efforts. Since these communities did not spring from conscious solidarity, however, they soon broke up, and mutual assistance remained limited to the family and close personal friends.

How can women today relate to those last days of the Third Reich, which they spent mostly in air-raid shelters and in constant fear for their lives? In many cases, simple film images – "That's how I felt, just like Scarlett O'Hara in 'Gone with the Wind'" or "It was like 'Doctor Zhivago'" – offer a way to frame these fearful memories. For example, at the beginning of her first interview, Käthe Bernegger, who had been 24 years old in 1945, was altogether unable to tell about the dramatic events at the end of the war. Hollywood imagery enabled her to glamorize a terrible reality and thus to distance herself from it, a technique that made it possible for her to verbalize a

6. Abortion until the twelfth week of pregnancy was legalized in Austria only in 1975.
7. Written sources about such house communities are scarce. The Vienna municipal archives collected personal reports from private individuals who, in 1956, were called upon by the media to send in personal records relating to the year 1945. See, for example, "Tagebuch der Kriegs-Hausgemeinschaft" in Wien 3, Stammgasse 13, in WrStLA, H.A.-Akten, Kleine Bestände 1945, Berichte von Privatpersonen, 83/2, II. Teil, or the report by Elizabeth Fitzga, in Berichte von Privatpersonen, 83/3.

terrible experience. Several women gave the impression that these experiences had been "locked away"[8] or so repressed that, even today, they are completely unable to speak about the mortal fear they felt back then.

## The End of the War: Liberation or Collapse?

A large majority of the women interviewed saw the military break-down of the NS-regime as a liberation only in the sense of a release from the fear of death and air-raid filled nights. What this could mean for a woman after years of constant fear was described by Friederike Reitmann, who, as a 42-year-old Jew, had lived for years in hiding with a friend as a so-called "submarine" (*U-Boot*). The moment she left her apartment for the first time is still fresh in her memory:

> It was three o'clock in the morning, and they stopped shooting, and all of a sudden the woman who had kept me hidden said: "This must be the Russians," and then I asked her if she could do me a favor and unlock the door for me, I wanted to go down on the street. There was no holding me, I wanted to go out and I did, at three o'clock in the morning. When she said, it's not the Nazis any more, it's the Russians, "The Russians are here,' that was everything to me. The Nazis couldn't do anything, any more.

Friederike Reitmann is one of about six hundred people who survived as "submarines" in Austria, so her story is a very special one (Weinzierl 1985; Ungar-Klein 1990).

Hilde Dollinger, a 50-year-old widow, was on the guilty side at the end of the war. She was a Nazi and a department head at the Local Bureau for Ethnic Questions (*Gauamt für Volkstumfragen*). Talking about the end of the war for her amounts to talking about the collapse of her life plans. When asked how she experienced the end of the war, the first thing she said was: "I can't remember, actually," which illustrates the extent to which she had repressed this biographical episode. The year 1945 meant a decisive break in her personal life, since, through the dissolution of the *Gauamt*, she lost the basis of her existence. She then described the end of the war as follows: "The whole bureau dissolved. Then all the employees, well, we all drove to Zwettl. And there the *Gauamt* released us from our oath of office, and that was it. The head of the bureau (*Gauleiter*) shot him-

---

8. The term "lock away" was used by Mario Erdheim in a lecture given at the international symposium "Kollaboration - Denunziation - Verführung" held at Lindabrunn near Vienna, 12-14 February 1988. In his understanding, this is a kind of repression in the Freudian sense.

self. Was a very nice guy, anyway. Well, and then everybody made off somehow."These two accounts are extreme cases from our sample; most women saw the end of the war more concretely as the end of wartime misery and of fears for survival.

## Hunger and Shortage

Months before the end of the war, the food supply of those Viennese who had neither the money nor the connections to get anything beyond the official food-stamp rations was already insufficient. After the fighting had ended, Vienna was on the verge of famine. The existing scarce provisions were destroyed or given out by the retreating German Wehrmacht, or confiscated by the Soviet Army, or looted by the local population. By looting, women managed to assure their food supply for a short time at least.[9]

In retrospect, the looting, which seems natural as a short-lived negation of legal norms, apparently caused the women moral problems. With Helga Eder, for example, the avoidance of these memories expressed itself in the substitution of the more impersonal "the people" for "we": "And in Altgasse, there was a cookie factory, the Rista, and there we, as we had nothing to eat, well, the people went there, and there still were cartons with cookies which were looted and carried off into the cellars; you had to live on that stuff, practically." Typically, they described themselves as not having taken part, and many interviewees, with the exception of more critical women or women from left-wing circles, blamed the looting on members of the Soviet army alone.

Food supply was secured on a day-to-day basis by looting, by using up the last emergency provisions, and by slaughtering army horses in the streets. The Nazi food-stamp system, which stayed in place almost until the end of the war, had broken down with the rest of the municipal administration. Food distributions by the Red Army averted a famine in Vienna. In mid-May 1945, two pounds of bread per person were given out per week. "There is a growing number of cases," the Vienna market office reported from working-class districts, "where women with children come into the office to ask for food for their children, because they themselves have nothing more

9. The situation report of the market office *Marktamtsabteilung* of 25 May 1945, also noted that the food supply was particularly bad in regions where there was no opportunity for looting. In WrStLA, Nachlaß Körner, Mappe 4.9.

to give them."[10] It was not until June that regular food rationing was re-established. But these were starvation rations: in June 1945, an "ordinary consumer" was entitled to 833 calories per day. A police report described the famine in Vienna: "in the shops, there are signs saying 'out of stock', market stalls are empty, and the women running a household have only one thing to talk about: 'How to scrape up a meal for the family?' On these occasions, weeping women are nothing unusual."[11] In September 1945, the standard ration was raised to 1,550 calories, but, in spring 1946, it had to be cut back again. Long-term food supply from America eventually assured the survival of the Austrian population (Mähr 1989). State-controlled food rationing was gradually lifted only after 1948; on 1 July 1953, food ration cards were eliminated (Sandgruber 1985).

For years, food supply was the vital issue for the Austrian state. As always in times of crisis, the issue of nutrition emerged as a "social question" that transcended its seemingly private context, and as a public problem that affected not only women. The total population was placed in consumer categories that were assigned various caloric rations depending on how heavy their labor was. The underrating of housework, which had actually expanded enormously, is indicated by the fact that housewives and maids only got the card for "ordinary consumers"–the same "starvation diet card" that was given out to unemployed persons and old-age pensioners. Blue and white-collar workers, pregnant women, and nursing mothers got more than this minimum.

In our interviews, the women typically contrasted the comparatively good supply situation under the Nazi regime with postwar famine, with the suggestion that the Nazi state had provided well for its citizens. In most interviews, the reasons and the background for this went unreflected and unmentioned. It was only politically aware women, primarily from the left, who saw the connection between the food supply situation and the exploitation of Nazi-occupied countries.

## Women Secure Survival: The Daily Fight for Food

Official rations were not even enough for bare survival. The extent of attempts to provide additional sources through hoarding, barter-

10. Situation report on the food supply in Vienna from 24 May 1945, in WrStLA, Nachlaß Körner,Mappe 4.9. See also: *Die Verwaltung der Bundeshauptstadt Wien vom 1. April 1945 bis 31. Dezember 1947.* 1949. Vienna.
11. Police report on the morale of the population in the district of Währing, dated 28 August 1945. In WStLA, Nachlaß Körner, 4.21.

ing, and black-marketeering is hard to quantify, because these activities took place in the private sphere or involved payment in kind. Serious estimates for the years 1945/46 suggest that less than one-third of all provisions on the market were obtained through official channels of distribution (*Monatsberichte* 1947: 15ff.). This means that looking at ration cards and calories alone cannot make clear how people in Vienna managed to subsist. Individual strategies for survival have to be considered. We believe that the enormously time-consuming and labor-intensive household work on the part of women assured their and their families' survival, so we refer to it as survival labor (Schubert 1984; Freyer 1984).

Through inventiveness and an enormous expenditure of work, women sought to make up for the pervasive shortages in food and resources. Young girls and women had already been prepared to work with substitute materials and had been introduced to more labor-intensive housekeeping by the Nazi war economy. The BDM and the NS-women's organizations held regular instruction courses; newspapers and magazines were full of suggestions and advice about how to cope with shortages and work with substitute materials (Berger 1989). Older women could also fall back on their experiences from World War I.

For years, housekeeping was based upon improvisation, first because of the ubiquitous shortages immediately after the war, later because economic policy in the reconstruction era gave other sectors priority over consumer-goods industry (Weber 1987). Under conditions of extreme shortage, running a household was not only unusually labor-intensive, but increasingly took place in public places, for example, by waiting in queues for hours, conducting hoarding tours, and dealing in the black market. Housekeeping is an everyday routine that, under normal circumstances, is difficult to discuss. But in its innovative postwar form, it captured a major place in women's recollections of the period and sank deep into their memories. The expansion of women's field of activity turned housework into an "adventure" that became easy to verbalize. Women's narratives show that bartering for food took many forms: from small-time deals in private rooms to professional black-marketeering in public places. The most widespread strategies involved barter deals and adventurous hoarding tours, which were undertaken to acquire foodstuffs from farmers.

Hoarding tours were widely used to augment the official rations. Rucksack-carrying women from Vienna went to farmers to bargain or beg for food. These tours yielded more than in-town barter because they were not confined to the rural outskirts of Vienna. But such tours could not be made in one day, so women joined together in small groups for their own safety. Maria Stingl, who was 44 then, tells about how dangerous and difficult these hoarding tours could be:

> Once we went on the train, and then I had to go on foot with twenty kilos of apricots on my back. If you know Melk, it's such a long way up there from below, and we knew somebody there, and so I got a rucksack with twenty kilos of apricots in it. I almost wanted to throw them away, we had to walk to the next train station, and then we got up the mountain, and I had to sit on the roof of the train car. But there was nothing to hold onto on that car-roof, and they all came along with apricots; and then it started pouring with rain, you know. Well, even today I still don't know how I managed to get up there, I've never been a giant, you know. Never had much strength in my hands. But I climbed on top of that train with twenty kilos on my back, and there we sat one after the other, back to back … There's this bridge, just outside Melk, that has this iron construction, there we had to draw our heads in. I'll never forget this, on top of that train car. And then it started pouring. But we got back into Vienna, with the apricots.

Sitting on the car roofs of crowded trains with their rucksacks full, the exhausted women who got back to Vienna often had to make sure their valuable "prize" was not confiscated. Authorities tried to get this illegal "food scrounging" under control. Remarkably, they made no distinction between women who hoarded out of pure need and people who illegally confiscated foodstuffs or dealt as professionals on the black market: they all came under the rubric "work-shy persons and marauders." Andreas Korp, who in 1945 was undersecretary in the Ministry of Food, spoke of the "degeneration of entirely misunderstood self-help" (Korp 1945: 10). However, even authorities were well aware that expanding the allowed calories through individual effort was necessary if the population was to survive, and so they tolerated it, at least in the first few months.

Amidst general shortages, everything available was bartered for food. Not only private citizens, but also companies offering goods against payment-in-kind, engaged in the barter economy of the post-war period. Bartering was an everyday part of women's survival labor that took place mainly in private, especially in the apartments of friends and relatives. Women who had valuables such as family jewels or sought-after professional services to offer, definitely found themselves in a better situation. For example, Bertha Foggensteiner, then 28, was a doctor for skin and venereal diseases who had services to offer that were in great demand among the local population and Allied troops. This made her office a flourishing barter center. "Of course, I black-marketed, too. Of course. I had, for example, a patient who had nails to offer, all this took place in my office, well, so he had those nails and said what he wanted for them. Stockings or I don't know anymore. In any case, I took the nails and gave them to somebody who I knew needed them. And he in turn brought me something I needed, or he paid for them. I charged a little extra, of course. For I didn't do it out of friendship, and so I made deals, yes."

Maria Nograsek, who was born in 1895, came to Vienna as a housemaid, got married, and eked out a living doing odd jobs, typifies those in the poorest class. She acquired goods for barter through looting:

> We were constantly in search of bread. When a baker opened his shop, one person told the other, you can get something there. Or from the warehouse. There they loaded fat in buckets on their handcarts, as much as they could get. They were close to killing one another! ... I got into a warehouse then to see if I could find a pair of shoes. My husband found a pair that were new. We found onions, too. Well, we were more after foodstuffs. Dried onions, you didn't get those. Potatoes even less. I don't know what else was there. Yes, and the best thing was if you got tobacco, 'cause with tobacco you could go hoarding. With that, I could help myself. Then my husband got a whole round of tobacco, but they came running after us and tore it apart. They were envious, and we had to run with our handcart to save what was left of it. Down in the Prater, that's where the warehouses were. And then, when I went hoarding, I always went to a carter and gave him a little tobacco. So he gave me a ride, also on the way back, or else I had to go on foot. And how much can you carry for hours? That was the only salvation!

In the markets established in public places, trade was carried on with goods in kind as well as with money. In Ressel Park, which housed Vienna's largest black market, food could be purchased with money, cigarettes, and various other goods. The women we interviewed all emphasized that they went to Ressel Park market only in direst need, because prices there were almost unaffordable for them. Even well-to-do women in our sample relied mainly on bartering with friends and acquaintances to secure additional foodstuffs. They avoided Ressel Park because professional black marketeers and frequent police raids made it a dangerous place.

Prices on the black market differed from province to province, reflecting disparities in the supply situation. They were almost always highest in Vienna; in August 1945 food prices on the black market there were 264 times higher than official prices.[12]

This meant that only a very small number of people with high income could afford to raise their standard of living via the black market. Most people barely had enough income to buy the rationed

---

12. The *Monatsberichte des Instituts für Wirtschaftsforschung* reported monthly on black-market prices.

goods. Their savings, which they had put aside during the war due to the shortage of consumer goods, were soon used up. At the end of 1946, the urban population had next to nothing left for bartering.[13]

## Changing Relations in Marriage and Family

Hunger and shortages brought changing social relations inside and outside the family. Within families, women's power increased as their household work became more important. So did the relative value of children who hustled for food on their own, sometimes on the verge of being petty criminals. But social relations changed outside the family, too. The alleged public nuisance represented by the so-called "chocolate girls" produced widespread moralizing (Mattl 1985). Until today, this specifically "feminine way" of self-support has remained a taboo, and our interview partners were ready to talk about contacts with occupation soldiers only under the guarantee of anonymity. It was primarily younger women who were admitted by personal invitation into the dancing clubs of the Allied forces. The image of the generous American distributing nylon stockings, chocolate, and chewing gum is a popular cliché; what is perhaps less known is the attraction that Soviet officers could have for left-leaning women who eagerly accepted offers of a night in the dance hall and (for once) enough to eat. For example, Käthe Bernegger, whose uncle was a communist and had been in a concentration camp, liked to go out with Soviet soldiers, and told us about dining out with Soviet officers:

> And why do you think the girls ran over to the Americans? 'Cause they got things to eat from them. 'Cause the Americans, they had everything. They had it from their shops, all these cans, chocolates, stockings, they had everything. Which our guys did not have. But as I said before, I'm not that type. I'm too spontaneous for that. And when I didn't like something about a Russian, I could really raise hell. Yes! I once was downtown with one guy, on Stephansplatz, everything still bombed down, and there was this Stephanskeller or whatever it was called, there we went, and there were Russians there who invited us. Later it turned out they were two press journalists, but regular officers. They were generous and bought us a dinner, but it was ground-fish balls; I don't know, some sort of fish balls. And I ate them, and because I was raised to be polite, I asked one of them if he wanted a bite. And he said to me: yuck! Well, I lost my temper, took the plate, and threw it halfway across the table. – 'If you don't want to eat

13. See "Die Ernährungsbilanz Österreichs im Wirtschaftsjahr 1946-47." Beilage 4. *Monatsberichte* 1947.

them, I don't want to either!'[laughing] – I was haughty, and his eyes got big, I really was wild! Well, of course, I was just being polite and wanted to offer him a bite, and he said, yuck! he doesn't want any. Well, then I got mad, if he doesn't like them, I'm not gonna eat them either.

Thus, women experienced an expanded scope of action during the war, and this carried over to the postwar period. On the whole, our work confirms the results of Meyer and Schulze (1985; 1986; 1989) who conducted several studies of intrafamilial conflicts with married couples in Berlin. From the moment men were drafted, the women had to learn to provide and make decisions for themselves and their families. It seemed, for a short time, as if the traditional moorings in relations between the sexes had come loose. Unmistakably, the distribution of power and authority within the family had altered. However, most of the women interviewed interpreted this shift toward greater independence as a matter of sheer necessity. In other words, a kind of "necessity-born matriarchy" persisted into the immediate postwar period.

Being separated from one's spouse, often for years, naturally caused feelings of alienation, which were deepened by the quite different experiences of each partner. After a number of years, the married partners met again: men longed for the shelter and safety of home, and an unchanged, young, pretty, loving wife to coddle them after all the physical and mental strains of being on the front and in POW camps. What they expected from their women had risen immeasurably in the intervening time. In turn, the women's expectations, too, had in no way been reduced: strained by their hard life to the point of breakdown, they hoped for relief when their husbands returned from the war. The years of being on their own had not brought only positive experiences, but above all overwork, exhaustion, and physical and mental stress.

With these exaggerated, unrealistic expectations, disappointment was a foregone conclusion. Instead of being a source of help, the men often turned out to be an additional burden when they came home from the war. Moreover, the tension-charged reunions took place in the most unfavorable conditions of famine and housing shortages. Nearly ninety thousand apartments in Vienna had been severely damaged or completely destroyed, which meant that 12 percent of the housing stock was not usable (Riemer 1947: 112).

Another important factor that produced marital problems was the disorientation of repatriated men who could not get along in the everyday life of postwar Austria. The overburdened women saw the returning men as failures; these men could not live up to their wives' memories of them, nor to the prevailing image of males. In contrast, the war had given women the skills to cope with everyday life after the war: they knew where hoarding tours were worthwhile, they had built up relief networks, and they had provided continuously for their families. This "competence to cope" (Meyer and Schulze 1986: 189) was an important element in women's power vis-à-vis men. Many couples found no way to get along and were divorced.[14] Marriages broke up because the partners had become estranged during the long separation or could not reach an agreement on the distribution of power within the family. Also, men coming home from the war had difficulties getting along with their mother-fixated children.

Our analysis of these biographies shows that older women, whose marital experience dated back to the time before the war, stood a better chance of keeping their marriages intact. They were more likely to succeed in identifying with prewar constructions of the couple's life together. In most cases, these older women had already had a family to look out for during the war. If their children had been born before the war, they still knew their fathers as real persons and not just from photographs and idealized stories. This facilitated the reintegration of fathers into the "mothers' families" after the war.

Younger women often were still a part of their families of origin and thus had largely been exempted from sharing the burden of survival labor. This had given them a chance to enjoy some pleasures. If these women had married and started a family during the war, they had little experience of marital life because the men were away. This led to postwar crises in marriage for many couples in the younger age groups. There were also conflicts with children who had never known their fathers. The "shortage of men" not only affected unmarried women from these age groups, but also those married women whose marriages had broken up after the war, or whose husbands had died in it.

## The Short Days of Female Glory

It is a popular view that, immediately after the war, women held a position of power that they lost again with the "normalization" of economic and social conditions. This thesis usually provides the starting point for speculations on why women failed to make the

---

14. The number of divorces increased from 8,226 in 1939 to 14,162 in 1948, an increase of 72 percent. Calculations based on data in official government statistics.

most of "their time" and let themselves be weakened again. The alleged indicators of female power in the immediate postwar era are: first, the demographic preponderance of females; second, their success in securing survival in a war-wrecked society and in laying the foundations for recovery; and third, the break-up of the gender-specific division of labor as women took over men's position in the family and the workplace. It is theoretically correct to define female power in these terms. However, applying these abstract notions of female power to the postwar era without considering the historical context runs the risk of falsely overestimating that power.

It is true that women accounted for far more than half the population immediately after the war because so many men had died in the war or were still in captivity. According to the number of those receiving ration cards – there are no other sources available -every 1,000 males were matched by 1,562 females in Vienna in December 1945; in December 1947 the relationship was 1,333 women for every 1,000 men (*Statistisches Jahrbuch* 1949: 13). But this majority was increasingly perceived to be simply a "surplus" of women, not the statistical rationale for female power. The resulting competition among women for the scarce "good man" became a topic of discussion even at big political conferences (*Frauenzentralkommitée* 1948: 27). Women themselves gave those who were unmarried no chance for a life of fulfillment: "Those many hundreds of thousands of widows will have a joyless existence, with their purpose in life gone," wrote the Socialist Member of Parliament, Gabriele Proft (1945: 11). The predominance of the nuclear family as *the* accepted social standard left single women a marginalized group. For both women and men, the family not only remained the norm after the war; more than ever, it constituted the ideal.

It is also true that women had potential power due to their survival labor, which had assured subsistence during the war and had laid the basis of economic recovery. However, they were not then, and are still not, aware of the enormous power inherent in their labor. Their survival labor remained unpaid and unacknowledged, and when the labor supply situation "normalized" again in the postwar era, household work once again vanished from public places and public discussion.

The reason why women failed to translate such competence into long-term political gain was not sexism. Women themselves downplayed the social importance of their work. Aloisia Weber provides a typical example of how women adopted the male view. Even today, her motto is "From old make new," and she speaks of her work as a "hobby." She describes in detail how laborious it was to provide for her husband and children, only to say: "I did at most a little hoarding with a friend's mother, with marmalade and cigarettes, and those I got from my mother. But he was the big doer! I personally, well, first, I wouldn't have had the money [to control], and second, I had nothing to say, and didn't miss it [a voice in money matters] either."

During the war and the immediate postwar period, women took over men's functions and work. They had to make independent decisions in the family, and thus naturally gained in competence and experience. Earlier, under the Nazi regime, girls and women had become familiar with a different way of life and working conditions in the BDM, and in the RAD and other compulsory services. But what were the actual effects of these new experiences? Did women welcome them, or were they perceived to be simply an additional burden? It seems that women replaced men in the workplace and in the family without posing a fundamental challenge to the division of labor between the sexes. The result for women was not emancipation, but overwork. Women's labor in the postwar period actually overstepped gender-drawn demarcation lines, but was explicitly understood by both men and women as a limited, temporary emergency measure that would have little consequence for fundamental changes in relations between the sexes.

Although women had sole responsibility for all decisions made in the family, they still looked up to male authority. In many families, it was the woman who re-enthroned the man in their role as head of the family and thus reestablished their husband's pride. Men did not immediately resume their roles, but both men and women fell back on the accepted social codes of masculine and feminine behavior. Until the labor market "normalized," and men could once again take over the role of provider, the family was the main stage for acting out the traditional male role. For men to act out this role with the same assertiveness as they had before the war was an impossibility, however, so women benefited in the long run. Women's postwar experiences did not go up in smoke, but continued to make themselves felt, notably through their impact on their children. Women who had led autonomous lives for years would not be forced back completely into old marriage and family patterns; they thus gave the next generation an example of viable female self-reliance.

# References

Bandhauer-Schöffmann, I. and Hornung, E. 1990. "Trümmerfrauen – ein kurzes Heldinnenleben." In *Zur Politik des Weiblichen: Frauenmacht und - ohnmacht.* Ed. A. Graf, 93-120. Vienna.

____. 1991. "Von der Trümmerfrau auf der Erbse: Ernährungssicherung und Überlebensarbeit in der unmittelbaren Nachkriegszeit in Wien." In *L'Homme* 1: 77-105.

____. 1992. "Von Mythen und Trümmern: Oral History-Interviews mit Frauen zum Alltag im Nachkriegs-Wien." In *Wiederaufbau Weiblich: Frauen nach '45 in Österreich und Deutschland. Ein Vergleich.* Ed. I. Bandhauer-Schöffmann and E. Hornung. Vienna.

Beckermann, R. 1989. *Unzugehörig: Österreicher und Juden nach 1945.* Vienna.

Berger, K. 1984. *Zwischen Eintopf und Fließband. Frauenarbeit und Frauenbild im Faschismus. Österreich 1938-1945.* Vienna.

____. 1989. "Die 'innere Front.'" In *Österreicher und der Zweite Weltkrieg.* Ed. Dokumentationsarchiv des Österreichischen Widerstandes und Bundesministerium für Unterricht, Kunst und Sport, 59-81. Vienna.

Botz, G. 1987. "Österreich und die NS-Vergangenheit. Verdrängung, Pflichterfüllung, Geschichtsklitterung." In *Ist der Nationalsozialismus Geschichte? Zu Historisierung und Historikerstreit.* Ed. D. Diner, 141-52. Frankfurt am Main.

____. 1989. "Österreichs verborgene Nazi-Vergangenheit und der Fall Waldheim." *Forum* 430-431: 47-53.

Czeike, F. 1975. "April und Mai 1945 in Wien: Eine Dokumentation." *Wiener Geschichtsblätter* 30/3: 33-48.

Freier, A-E. 1984. "Frauenfragen sind Lebensfragen: Über die naturwüchsige Deckung von Tagespolitik und Frauenpolitik nach dem Zweiten Weltkrieg." In *"Das Schicksal Deutschlands liegt in der Hand seiner Frauen": Frauen in der deutschen Nachkriegsgeschichte.* Eds. A-E. Freier and A. Kuhn, 18-50. Düsseldorf.

Frauenzentralkommitée der Sozialistischen Partei, ed. 1948. *Frauenprobleme nach dem Zweiten Weltkrieg.* Vienna.

Fuchs, W. 1984. *Biographische Forschung: Eine Einführung in Praxis und Methode.* Opladen.

Gravenhorst, L. and Tatschmurat, C. eds. 1990. *Töchter-Fragen: NS-Frauen-Geschichte.* Freiburg im Breisgau.

Hopf, C. 1979. "Soziologie und qualitative Sozialforschung." In *Qualitative Sozialforschung.* Ed. C. Hopf and E. Weingarten, 11-37. Stuttgart.

Kaindl-Widhalm, B. 1990. *Demokraten wider Willen? Autoritäre Tendenzen und Antisemitismus in der 2. Republik.* Vienna.

Knight, R. 1988. *"Ich bin dafür die Sache in die Länge zu ziehen": Die Wortprotokolle der österreichischen Bundesregierung von 1945 bis 1952 über die Entschädigung der Juden.* Frankfurt am Main.

Korp, A. 1945. "Um unser tägliches Brot!" In *Sozialistische Hefte*, Series 3. Vienna.

Kuhn, A. 1989. "Vom schwierigen Umgang der Frauengeschichtsforschung mit dem Nazismus." *Das Argument* 31(5): 733-40.

Lehmann, A. 1983. *Erzählstruktur und Lebenslauf: Autobiographische Untersuchungen.* Frankfurt am Main.

Mähr, W. 1989. *Der Marshallplan in Österreich.* Graz.

Mattl, S. 1985. "Frauen in Österreich nach 1945." In *Unterdrückung und Emanzipation: Festschrift für Erika Weinzierl.* Ed. R.G. Ardelt et al., 101-26. Vienna.

Meissl, S., Mulley, K.D., and Rathkolb, O., eds. 1986. *Verdrängte Schuld, verfehlte Sühne: Entnazifizierung in Österreich 1945-1955.* Vienna.

Meyer, S. and Schulze, E. 1985. *Von Liebe sprach damals keiner: Familienalltag in der Nachkriegszeit.* Munich.

____. 1986. "Krieg im Frieden: Veränderungen des Geschlechterverhältnisses untersucht am Beispiel familiärer Konflikte nach 1945." In *Frauenmacht in der Geschichte: Beiträge des Historikerinnentreffens 1985 zur Frauengeschichtsforschung.* Ed. J. Dalhoff, U. Frey, and I. Schöll, 184-93. Düsseldorf.

____. 1989. "Aspekte des Geschlechterverhältnisses untersucht am Beispiel der Auswirkungen des Zweiten Weltkrieges auf Familien." In *Lebenslauf und Familienentwicklung: Mikroanalysen des Wandels familialer Lebensformen.* Ed. A. Herlth and K.P. Strohmeier, 231-56. Opladen.

*Monatsberichte des Instituts für Wirtschaftsforschung.* 1947. Vienna.

Pelinka, A. and Weinzierl, E., ed. 1987. *Das große Tabu: Österreichs Umgang mit seiner Vergangenheit.* Vienna.

Proft G. 1945. "Dein Weg zu uns: Die Frauenfrage im neuen Österreich." In *Sozialistische Hefte.* Series 4. Vienna.

Rauchensteiner, M. 1975. "Kriegsende und Besatzungszeit in Wien 1945-1955." In *Wiener Geschichtsblätter* 30(2): 197-220.

Riemer, H. 1947. *Wien baut auf: Zwei Jahre Wiederaufbau.* Vienna.

Rosenthal, G. 1987. "'… Wenn alles in Scherben fällt …' Von Leben und Sinnwelt der Kriegsgeneration: Typen biographischer Wandlungen." *Biographie und Gesellschaft* 6. Opladen.

Sandgruber, R. 1985. "Vom Hunger zum Massenkonsum." In *Die "wilden" fünfziger Jahre: Gesellschaft, Formen und Gefühle eines Jahrzehnts in Österreich.* Ed. G. Jagschitz and K.D. Mulley, 112-22. Vienna.

Schmidt, D. 1987. "Die peinlichen Verwandtschaften: Frauenforschung zum Nationalsozialismus." In *Normalität oder Normalisierung? Geschichtswerkstätten und Faschismusanalyse.* Ed. H. Gerstenberger and D. Schmidt, 50-65. Münster.

Schubert, D. 1984. *Frauen in der deutschen Nachkriegszeit. Vol. 1: Frauenarbeit 1945-1949.* Ed. A. Kuhn. Düsseldorf.

*Statistisches Jahrbuch der Stadt Wien 1946-1947.* 1949. Vienna.

Tálos, E., Hanisch, E. and Neugebauer, W., eds. 1988. *NS-Herrschaft in Österreich 1938-1945.* Vienna.

Thürmer-Rohr, C. 1987. *Vagabundinnen: Feministische Essays.* Berlin.

Thürmer-Rohr, C. et al. eds. 1989. *Mittäterschaft und Entdeckungslust.* Berlin.

Thurner, E. 1988. "'Dann haben wir wieder unsere Arbeit gemacht': Frauenarbeit und Frauenleben nach dem Zweiten Weltkrieg." In *Zeitgeschichte* 15(9-10): 403-26.

Ungar-Klein, B. 1990. "Bei Freunden untergetaucht – U-Boot in Wien." In *Der Pogrom 1938: Judenverfolgung in Österreich und Deutschland.* Ed. K. Schmid and R. Streibel, 87-92. Vienna.

Vocelka, K. 1985. *Trümmerjahre Wien 1945-1949.* Vienna.

Weber, F. 1987. "Österreichs Wirtschaft in der Rekonstruktionsperiode nach 1945." *Zeitgeschichte* 14/7: 267-98.

Weinzierl, E. 1985. *Zu wenig Gerechte. Österreicher und Judenverfolgung 1938-1945.* Graz.

Windaus-Walser, K. 1988. "Gnade der weiblichen Geburt? Zum Umgang der Frauenforschung mit Nationalsozialismus und Antisemitismus." *Feministische Studien* 1: 102-15.

Wodak, R. et al. 1990. *"Wir sind alle unschuldige Täter!" Diskurshistorische Studien zum Nachkriegsantisemitismus.* Frankfurt am Main.

# The Contributors

**James C. Albisetti** has held a joint appointment in the history department and honors program at the University of Kentucky since 1979. His publications include *Secondary School Reform in Imperial Germany* (1983) and *Schooling German Girls and Women: Secondary and Higher Education in the Nineteenth Century* (1988).

**Erna Appelt** is an assistant professor in the Institute of Political Science at the University of Innsbruck. Her research focuses on women in politics; most recently she coedited *Feministische Politik* (1994).

**Birgitta Bader-Zaar** is an assistant professor in the Institute of History at the University of Vienna. She has collaborated on research projects dealing with Austrian foreign policy and with the history of women's suffrage. An article, "'Weise Mäßigung' und 'ungetrübter Blick': Die bürgerlichliberale Frauenbewegung im Streben nach politischer Gleichberechtigung," will soon appear in *Bürgerliche Frauenkultur in Österreich im 19. Jahrhundert.*

**Irene Bandhauer-Schöffmann** is an assistant professor in the Institute of Social and Economic History at the University of Linz. Her research interests include Catholic women in the Austrian women's movement during the 1930s, women in postwar Austria, and the business history of Coca-Cola in Austria. Her recent publications include articles on "Coca-Cola im Kracherlland" and "Von der Erbswurst zum Hawaiischnitzel: Die Hungerkrise im Wien der Nachkriegszeit in ihren geschlechtsspezifischen Auswirkungen."

**Monika Bernold** is a lecturer in the Institute of History at the University of Vienna. She is coeditor of *Familie: Arbeitsplatz oder Ort des Glücks?* and has published articles on popular culture and the use of popular autobiographies in historical research.

**Gudrun Biffl** is a research fellow at the Austrian Institute of Economics in Vienna, and consultant to the OECD on migration issues. She has published books on labor policy; *Theorie und Empirie des Arbeitsmarktes am Beispiel Österreich* was published by Springer Verlag in 1994.

**Gertraud Diem-Wille** is an assistant professor at the Institute for Interdisciplinary Research and Further Education. Her research interests include the emotional aspects of learning, and gender and power. Her book on *Karrierefrauen und Karrieremänner* will soon be published by Westdeutscher Verlag.

**Eve Nyaradi Dvorak** is a Ph.D. candidate in history at the University of Minnesota. She is writing a dissertation on prostitution in late nineteenth century Austria.

**David F. Good** is a professor of history and formerly Director of the Center for Austrian Studies at the University of Minnesota, and Honorary Professor of Economic History at the University of Vienna. He is the author of *The Economic Rise of the Habsburg Empire* (1984) and editor of *Economic Transformations in East Central Europe: Legacies from the Past and Policies for the Future* (1994).

**Margarete Grandner** is an assistant professor of History at the University of Vienna, and author of *Kooperative Gewerkschaftspolitik in der Kriegswirtschaft: Die freien Gewerkschaften Österreichs im ersten Weltkrieg* (1992).

**Ela Hornung** lectures at the Universities of Salzburg, Innsbruck, and Vienna. She has collaborated on several major projects dealing with women in post-1919 Austria. Her publications include *Wiederaufbau – Weiblich* (1992), which she coedited.

**Pieter M. Judson** is an associate professor at Swarthmore College. His work focuses on the rise of liberal political culture in Central Europe from 1848 to 1918, particularly as it relates to questions of national identity and social mobilization. He is the author of the forthcoming *Exclusive Revolutionaries: Liberal Politics, Social Experience and National Identity in the Austrian Empire, 1848-1914.*

**Karin Jušek**, born in Austria, lives in the Netherlands and is an associate professor at the University of Groningen. Her research centers on the relationship between gender and culture. Her *Auf der Suche nach der Verlorene: Die Prostitutionsdebatten im Wien der Jahrhundertwende* was published in 1994.

**Mary Jo Maynes** is a professor of history at the University of Minnesota. Her recent works include *Interpreting Women's Lives: Feminist Theory and Personal Narratives* (1989) and *Taking the Hard Road: Life Course in French and German Worker's Autobiographies in the Era of Industrialization* (1995). Her current research focuses on the history of girlhood in Europe.

**Gerda Neyer** is a lecturer in political science and history at the University of Vienna and a research fellow in the Institute for Demography of the Austrian Academy of Science. Her research focuses on issues of migration, maternity leave, and family policy. She has recently coedited two volumes: *Feministische Politikwissenschaft* (1994) and *Auswanderungen aus Österreich* (1995).

# WOMEN OF PRAGUE
## Ethnic Diversity and Social Change from the Eighteenth Century to the Present

**Wilma A. Iggers,** *Professor Emerita, Canisius College, Buffalo, NY*

*"Wilma Iggers offers English-reading audiences fascinating new perspectives ... in a sensitive introduction to the city's modern experience and translated selections from the writings of twelve women ... This volume is particularly welcome since the work of most of these writers has not been readily available in English before."*
**Gary B. Cohen, The University of Oklahoma**

*"A book which brings together hitherto unpublished manuscripts and informed commentary, this is an invaluable resource for the field of Women's Studies as well as for anyone interested in the culture and history of Prague."*
**Helen Epstein**

For many centuries Prague has exerted a particular fascination because of its beauty and the richness of its culture and history. Its famous group of German and Czech writers of the earlier part of this century has deeply influenced Western culture. However, except for Milena Jesenska, Kafka's friend, virtually no attention has been given to women from the Czech lands. This book offers a first attempt to paint a fuller picture. From the four main ethnic groups in Prague (Czech and German Gentiles, Czech and German Jews), the book introduces twelve women spanning the period from the late Eighteenth Century to the present. The vivid and often moving portraits, which emerge from the varied material used by the author, offer new social, cultural and familial elements to the history of this region hitherto unknown or overlooked. An extensive historical introduction is followed by individual chapters in which each woman is presented in her own words and/or in the words of someone close to her.

**Wilma Abeles Iggers,** born and raised in Czechoslovakia, is currently Professor Emerita at Canisius College, Buffalo, New York. Her publications include a book on Karl Kraus (1967) and on Bohemian Jews (1993).

Available · 400 pages · bibliog. · ca. 90 half-tones
ISBN 1-57181-008-0 · hardback · **$59.95/£44.00**
ISBN 1-57181-009-9 · paperback · **$25.00/£17.50**

165 Taber Avenue • Providence, Rhode Island 02906
Phone: 401-861-9330 • Fax: 401-521-0046 • E-mail: BerghahnBk@aol.com
For MasterCard and Visa orders, please dial 1-800-540-8663.

# SEXUAL POLITICS AND THE EUROPEAN UNION
## The New Feminist Challenge

Edited by **R. Amy Elman,** *Assistant Professor of Political Science, Associate Co-Director of the Center for European Studies, Kalamazoo College, Michigan*

*Comprehensive examination of EU policy implications for the most burning issues concerning women and therefore indispensable reading for scholars and activists alike.*

Just as feminist scholars have begun to develop an analysis of "the state" and women in Europe have gained access to its political, legal and bureaucratic arenas, increased attention and reliance on European institutions have begun to take precedence over the more parochial concerns of the nation state. With the creation of the European super-state, feminist scholars will have to enhance their understanding of the European Union while activists will increasingly focus their efforts upon its institutions. This is the first book to transcend the emphasis on economics, the conventional basis for EU public-policy discussions, thus providing a basis upon which one can begin to assess the politics of European integration from a feminist perspective.

*Contents:* R. A. Elman, Introduction: The EU from Feminist Perspectives – C. Hoskyns, The EU and the Women within: an Overview of Women's Rights Policy – E. Collins, EU Sexual Harassment Policy – A. G. Mazur, The Interplay: the Formation of Sexual Harassment Legislation in France and EU Policy Initiatives – S. Baer, Pornography and Sexual Harassment in the EU – C. Itzin, Pornography, Harm and Human Rights: The UK in European Context – D. Leidholdt, Sexual Trafficking of Women in Europe: a Human Rights Crisis for the European Union – U. Winkler, Reproductive Technologies in Germany: an Issue for the European Union – A. Smyth, "And Nobody was any the Wiser": Irish Abortion Rights and the EU – J. Hanmer, The Common Market of Violence – C. Delphy, The European Union and the Future of Feminism.

Available · 192 pages · bibliog., index
ISBN 1-57181-062-5 · hardback · ca. **$29.95/£22.00**
ISBN 1-57181-046-3 · paperback · ca. **$12.95/£10.50**

165 Taber Avenue • Providence, Rhode Island 02906
Phone: 401-861-9330 • Fax: 401-521-0046 • E-mail: BerghahnBk@aol.com
For MasterCard and Visa orders, please dial 1-800-540-8663.

# TURKISH CULTURE IN GERMAN SOCIETY TODAY

Edited by **David Horrocks** and **Eva Kolinsky,** *Department of Modern Languages, Keele University*

*Provides valuable information on the social and cultural life of the Turkish minority in Germany.*

For many decades Germany has had a sizeable Turkish minority that lives in an uneasy co-existence with the surrounding German community and as such has attracted considerable interest abroad where this tends to be seen as a measure of German tolerance. However, little is known about the actual situation of the Turks. This volume provides valuable information, presented in a most original manner, which combines literary and cultural studies with social and political analysis. It focuses on the Turkish-born writer Emine Sevgi Özdamar, who writes in German and whose work, particularly her highly acclaimed novel *Das Leben ist eine Karawanserei*, is examined critically and situated in the context of German "migrant literature." An interview with the author and a sample of her work are followed by a sociological survey of the general situation of minorities in Germany today; their views and experiences, official government policy towards, and popular perceptions of them. The volume furthermore includes a study of a particular Turkish community, that of Frankfurt am Main, which is supported by a collection of documents and statistical data. General surveys and detailed analyses thus combine to provide a multi-faceted picture in which the life and cultural activity of the Turks in Germany is set against the background of other minorities in the country.

Available · 240 pages ca. 20 tables and diagrams, 1 photograph, bibliog., index
ISBN 1-57181-899-5 · hardback · ca. **$29.95/£22.00**   ISBN 1-57181-047-1 · paperback · ca. **$12.50/£9.95**

# POSTWAR WOMEN'S WRITING IN GERMAN

Edited by **Chris Weedon,** *Centre for Critical and Cultural Theory, University of Wales College of Cardiff*

*A comprehensive introduction to contemporary German-speaking women writers.*

Women in the Federal Republic, the former German Democratic Republic, Switzerland and Austria have initiated a remarkable literary movement, particularly since 1968, that is also attracting growing attention elsewhere. Informed by critical feminist and literary theory, this broad-ranging collection, the first one of its kind, examines the history of these writings in the context of the social and political developments in the respective countries. It combines survey chapters with detailed studies of prominent German authors whose work is often available in English.

Forthcoming · ca. 288 pages bibliog., index
ISBN 1-57181-902-9 · hardback · **$49.95/£35.00**   ISBN 1-57181-048-X · paperback · **$17.50/£14.95**

165 Taber Avenue • Providence, Rhode Island 02906
Phone: 401-861-9330 • Fax: 401-521-0046 • E-mail: BerghahnBk@aol.com
For MasterCard and Visa orders, please dial 1-800-540-8663.